CAR BOOT

COLLECTABLES

CAR BOOT

COLLECTABLES

A collector's
guide to everyday antiques
from the British Isles

TIMES EDITIONS

This edition published by Silverdale Books
An imprint of Bookmart Ltd
Registered Number 2372865
Trading as Bookmart Limited
Desford Road
Enderby
Leicester LE9 5AD

Produced by Times Editions
An imprint of Times Media Private Limited
A member of the Times Publishing Group
Times Centre, 1 New Industrial Road
Singapore 536196
Tel: (65) 2139288 Fax: (65) 2854871
E-mail: te@tpl.com.sg
Online Bookstore: http://www.timesone.com.sg/te

First printed in 1997
Reprinted 1998, 1999, 2000, 2001, 2002

Printed in Malaysia

ISBN 981 232 390 2

Contents

INTRODUCTION

If you enjoy collecting but love a bargain, you are probably often frustrated by the price of antiques. If this is so, why not try hunting in alternative markets? Beautiful objects do not have to be over 100 years old – the text book defintion of an antique – to be highly desirable and very collectable. After all, modern products, too, can be collected.

You might be excited and delighted at spotting the toys of your childhood or the kitchenware used by your mother. This can be the beginning of an exciting and potentially profitable hobby as a collector of 20th century artefacts. *Car Boot Collectables* makes sense of this market.

Car boot sales began as a way of selling old or unwanted household goods but they have now become the perfect source for these collectables. This informal way of selling makes the hunt for collectables both exciting and exasperating. The bargain hunter in you may enjoy the search through piles of second-hand goods, but the choice can be bewildering. Uncertainty about the value or integrity of the bargains on display may cause the collector to give up. But *Car Boot Collectables* is a picture-packed reference book that will be an invaluable aid to finding the best at any car boot sale.

Informative without giving dry lists or categories, the book gives a sense of the rich industrial history behind household items, and of the domestic hopes of by-gone lives expressed through clothes, toys, games and accessories. But the information is also extremely practical. It ranges over ordinary, but now rare, household china of Victorian or Edwardian days, across the chic Art Deco fashion accessories of the 1930s, right up to contemporary comics and telephone cards. Hundreds of illustrations help identify the best examples, and show design details that the discerning collector appreciates. There is a price guide indicating the investment value of these collectables.

Car Boot Collectables tackles the uncharted territory of the car boot sale. This handy reference book guides you through the maze of goods on offer, showing you what to look for when forming your collection and how to spot the valuable and the rare.

Happy hunting!

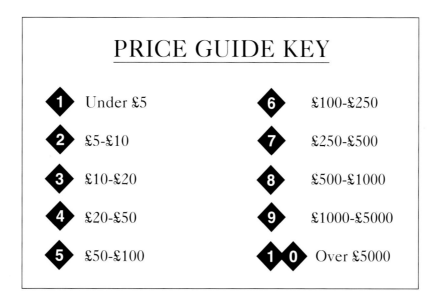

PRICE GUIDE KEY

1	Under £5	**6**	£100-£250
2	£5-£10	**7**	£250-£500
3	£10-£20	**8**	£500-£1000
4	£20-£50	**9**	£1000-£5000
5	£50-£100	**1 0**	Over £5000

CAR BOOT SALES

*If you like a bargain, then a car boot sale is the place for you.
Nowhere else will you find such an exciting mix of items for
sale at such affordable prices*

Rex Features/Ray Duns

Car boot sales can be quite small affairs, held in school grounds and organized to raise funds for school or charitable projects. The larger boot sales, held in a field or in a large car park, are often professionally organized and will have more amenities for both buyer and seller, such as hot food stalls, ice cream vans and portaloos.

BEATING THE RUSH

You have to be quick off the mark at a boot sale. The advertisement in the local press or specialist handbook may state ten o'clock as the opening time, but the keen collector will be waiting for the first car to arrive from about eight in the morning. You'll have to learn to push and shove, too, for enthusiasts will crowd around an arriving vehicle and will be peering through the windows before the driver has had time to switch off the engine. And, as soon as the car boot is opened, scores of pairs of hands will be diving into the various boxes.

However, don't be put off by all this scrambling. Bargains are not necessarily snapped up in the first ten minutes – many can be missed, giving you a chance to look them over.

Try to examine the goods on every stall, even if at first glance there seems

The treasures are there for sharp eyes to spot. This 1950s fantasy cruet set is worth about £40.

nothing there for you. The people who book a pitch at a boot sale are often amateurs, clearing out their loft, or dealing with the house contents of a deceased relative, so they'll see nothing wrong with throwing a heap of jewellery into an old tin box and putting it next to a pile of old jigsaws. The jewellery could be Victorian, could be valuable, and you could be the one to spot it.

Learn something about hallmarks. Marks on silver plate are often confused with those on silver and indeed, during the Victorian era, these were copied with a deliberate intent to deceive. So, EPNS (electroplated nickel silver) could, by being stamped in ornate Gothic letters accompanied by the maker's initials, be made to resemble a silver hallmark at first glance.

WHAT TO LOOK FOR

If items in china and glass catch your eye, check them carefully for cracks or chips. Damage will always devalue a piece. Old books should be sound and not dog-eared, watercolour pictures clean and not marred by small rusty spots.

Jewellery can be cleaned and repaired, although the re-threading of beads can be expensive, but watches and clocks can cost more than they're worth to put right.

Some items look authentically antique but are very likely to be reproduction. Examples of these are: 'oil' paintings in gilded frames; round ceramic plaques with cherubs or lovers; automaton singing birds in a cage; 'Victorian' doll's prams; carved wooden tobacco pipes with male and female figures and glass eye baths in

Boxes of old books deserve a second look – this delightful Teddy Tail's Annual *is worth around £10.*

various different shapes and colours. If you are at all in doubt, say no.

If you want to sell at a boot fair, the procedure is quite simple. You can either pre-book with the advertised organizer, which will sometimes save a little on the fee, or just turn up on the day. This is perhaps more advisable in winter, as there's no protection from the weather and, if it snows, everyone will simply pack up and go home.

Rex Features

Ray Duns

The cost of a pitch varies, but should not be more than a few pounds.

All you need is a wallpapering table or some card tables on which to put your goods, and a lightweight garden chair to sit on. If these are a problem, then lay everything out on an old blanket and sit in the car.

Keep what money you take tucked away safely. A 'bum bag' is ideal, or a small shoulder bag. It helps everyone if items are priced – but write in biro as felt-tip pen will run in the rain.

Electrical goods are a danger area whether buying or selling. Legislation now insists that all electrical goods should be tested before sale so, if possible, avoid this grey area.

LUSTREWARE

Proving that all that glitters is not gold, the metallic gleam of lustreware pottery has delighted china collectors since early in the 19th century

Lustre is a finish applied to pottery that gives it a metallic sheen. Ranging in use from all-over application to fine details, lustreware has been popular since the beginning of the 19th century. Metallic lustres were used in medieval Europe, but by the 1800s, lustreware was an exclusively English ceramic.

The earliest datable examples – from 1805 – are by Wedgwood, but the first patent for lustre was granted in 1810 to Peter Walburton of New Hall. The first 'recipe' for the process comes from a potter called Thomas Lakin in 1824. In this formula, a little powdered gold was dissolved in a mixture of hydrochloric and nitric acids known as aqua regia. This solution was combined with an oily amalgam of balsam of sulphur and turpentine and then brushed on to the piece of china. This oily medium vaporized in the firing, leaving a thin metallic film on the pottery.

LUSTRE FINISHES

The quality and quantity of gold used affected the final colour of the lustre, as did the colour of the pottery to which it was applied. A convincing gold effect was achieved with two or more coats of lustre over a reddish-brown glazed body. Pink tones were created with a small amount of tin in the mixture, painted over a white ground. Silver lustre was made by using platinum, though it is always called 'silver' because of the final effect. Because of platinum's higher value, silver lustreware is rarer and more sought after than gold.

The use of lustre decoration on china varies. Some pottery is completely lustred, whereas on other pieces it is used to pick out patterns and as relief decoration. There is a wide range of lustreware available for the collector (below) and prices range from £30 for a small plate to £100 for an all-over silver lustre sugar bowl.

GOLD AND SILVER

During the 19th century, many potteries produced all-over lustreware, sometimes gold, but more commonly silver. Many silver lustre pieces were direct copies of traditional silver designs, such as tea sets and candlesticks, and were sold as cheaper alternatives to the all-metal versions. In fact, almost anything that could be made in silver was, at some time, reproduced in silver lustreware. But by the 1840s and the invention of electroplating, cheap silver plate became available and the manufacture of silver lustreware declined.

Gold and silver lustre continued to be used for decorative detail throughout the Victorian era, particularly on jugs and mugs. Silver resist lustre was frequently used to decorate sporting jugs showing hunting and shooting scenes. Resist lustreware was most commonly used on a cream or white glazed earthenware but sometimes blue, canary yellow or rose backgrounds can be found, though examples of these are rare and more valuable. Copper lustre, which is found on a hard red-brown clay body, was scarce until 1823, but from then on it was often used as broad, banded patterns on both mugs and jugs.

6 A SILVER LUSTRE COFFEE POT *made in the Staffordshire potteries. The design of this piece closely resembles the traditional style of a silver coffee pot; all-over silver lustreware was known as 'poor man's silver'.*

COPPER LUSTRE 4 *has been used on this Staffordshire goblet. It dates from the 1820s when copper lustre was first introduced. A floral pattern is painted around the goblet and over the lustre.*

A MUG FROM 1860 4 *decorated with a broad band of gold lustre that is almost yellow in colour. A darker, more coppery, gold lustre stripe runs around the top and bottom of the mug and along the handle.*

A STAFFORDSHIRE JUG ◀ 6
from c1850. Decorated mainly with
copper lustre, the orange bands have a
resist pattern on them. The quality of the
decoration is reflected in the relatively
high price for this damaged piece.

6 ▶ **A SILVER LUSTRE TEAPOT**
decorated in a delicate
resist pattern that was used
from 1810 onwards. White or
cream glaze was most
commonly used as the base
colour until the 1830s.

AN ORIENTAL DESIGN ◀ 4
decorates this small
cup and saucer. This is
a fine example of how
lustre was used to pick
out details; the silver
highlights the pattern
and finishes off the rim
of both cup and saucer.

4 ▶ **A MOULDED RELIEF**
of hand-painted
flowers decorates the
blue band on the
centre of this copper
lustre mug. The deep
bronze colour of the
piece was achieved
by adding more
copper to the
lustre mixture.

3 ⋯ **A SMALL BOWL** ▲
decorated both
inside and out with a
rich, shining copper
lustre. A broad
mustard-yellow and
narrow blue band run
around the centre, on
the outside of the bowl.

Duncan Smith

IN THE PINK

Pink lustre is also sometimes known as purple lustre because the colour was originally made from a gold and tin powdered compound called purple of cassius. Early Wedgwood used a pink lustre in a marbled pattern known as 'Moonlight'. At first, this pattern decorated anything that could be modelled in the shape of a nautilus shell, such as cups and vases, but it was later used by other manufacturers on all manner of ware.

   Pink lustreware is most commonly associated with Sunderland, where many potteries used it for the commemorative ware and gifts for sailors that were their stock in trade. The most common items made were jugs, mugs and wall plaques featuring black transfer-printed designs and mottos or amusing doggerel. A 'splashed' effect lustre was often used as a border decoration on these wall plaques. Many other curios were produced using the same decorative effect, including watch stands, rolling pins, novelty jugs and carpet bowls. 'Splashed' lustreware was also made in nearby Newcastle-upon-Tyne, by many Staffordshire potteries, in Liverpool, Bristol and in Swansea, where daubs of lustre, for instance, were frequently used to decorate their cow-creamers.

A TRANSFER PRINT
7 *of Queen Victoria and Prince Albert features on this commemorative jug. The body of the jug is bright blue with a white handle and spout, and is decorated with pink and gold lustre.*

A SMALL DISH
4 *with a pink lustre border, produced in around 1880. The transfer print on the bottom of the dish is an amusing picture of a lady playing with her pet monkey on a sofa.*

'SPLASHED' LUSTREWARE 6
in pink and purple was chiefly made by Sunderland potteries and is among the most valued of lustreware finishes. An undamaged piece in all-over splashed lustre can fetch a high price today.

PINK LUSTRE 4
is used to
decorate this
Staffordshire jug
made in 1815. The
border at the top
and the handle are
both decorated with
a mottled effect in
the lustre.

A RESIST PATTERN 5
jug in pink lustre.
The shade of pink
achieved depends on
the ratio of gold to
tin, one part to four
producing a light
purple and one to
five producing a
paler rose shade.

In thee O Lord do I put my trust; let me never be Confounded. Psa. XXXI. Ver. I.

PREPARE
TO MEET THY
GOD

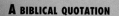

5 **A DELICATE MILK JUG**
made by a Staffordshire
pottery in c1810. The borders
at top and bottom are in pink
lustre, as is the wavy line that
winds through the finely
painted pattern of roses.

A BIBLICAL QUOTATION 5
with a rather stern warning
adorns this plaque with a
splashed lustre border. Pieces
with mottoes such as these
were intended to hang on the
walls of cottage parlours.

A DELICATE TEACUP 4
dating from around
1820. The pink lustre
border around the top has
a slight coppery hue. The
bowl of the cup is
decorated with a
hand-painted
rural scene,
picked out with
the same lustre.

A HAND-PAINTED DESIGN
4 of cottages runs around
the centre of this large
pink lustre mug from the
Staffordshire potteries.

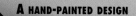

Duncan Smith

15

COLLECTOR'S NOTES

Dating lustreware can be a problem for the collector. Early pieces by makers such as Wedgwood, Spode or Enoch Wood were sometimes marked, so can be dated. However, the vast majority was left unmarked. Unfortunately, some of the best clues to the age of lustreware are only evident when a piece is damaged. For instance, wear or chipping might reveal a purplish glaze under gold lustre. This shows the use of purple of cassius, a mixture of gold and tin oxides used only in early lustreware. Silver lustreware is equally hard to date, though pieces that imitate actual silver can be dated roughly to before the introduction of electroplating in the 1840s. More generally, silver lustre can only be approximately dated by the

COMPARE & CONTRAST

Lustre decoration has long been popular for commemorative china. The pink lustre cup and saucer on the right were made c1896 to commemorate the opening of London's Tower Bridge. The cup and saucer on the left have a subtle lustre sheen and were produced by Maling & Sons, Ltd to mark the present Queen's coronation in 1953.

Duncan Smith

CLOSE UP on DECORATION

In resist ware, a pattern was covered with glycerine that would 'resist' the lustre coating. The glycerine evaporated during firing, leaving the pattern free of lustre.

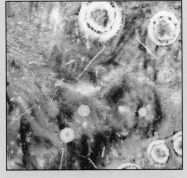

The splashed, or mottled, lustre effect was achieved by making bubbles of oil in the lustre which exploded during firing to leave a mottled appearance.

In a reverse of the resist process, the silver lustre seen here was stencilled on to the surface. This pattern has then been further decorated with hand-painting.

Duncan Smith

Pink lustreware was often used for hand-decorated china. Look closely at designs for the broad irregular strokes that characterize hand-painting.

ageing of the finish – the surface of early pieces will have blackened over the years with exposure to the light.

There is a tendency to attribute any piece of unmarked 'splashed' lustreware to Sunderland because such pieces fetch a higher price. Sunderland lustre was largely made by Dixon, Austin & Co of Sunderland but other manufacturers to look out for are Dawson & Co, Southwick Pottery (Scott) and Moore & Co at Wear. Staffordshire potteries, such as Cork and Edge, Thomas Till & Sons and Beech & Hancock, also made 'Sunderland' lustre.

CHOICES AND CONSIDERATIONS

Before beginning to collect lustreware it is a good idea to decide on which type you want to concentrate. Silver resist ware is very rare and, therefore, has the greatest investment value but there is plenty of choice at the other end of the scale. You might like to focus on one particular colour or application of lustre, such as pink 'splashed' ware. Alternatively, you could concentrate on lustreware jugs or wall-plaques. Look out for rare prints or verses on plaques; some were used thousands of times whereas others have survived only on a few pieces.

When buying lustreware, first judge the item as a piece of pottery before considering the lustre. As with all china, good condition is vital – a good plain jug with a little lustre banding may well be a better buy than a chipped piece with all-over lustre. As lustre was often very thinly painted on to the body of the china, it is prone to wear and some examples may be rubbed. It is best to avoid such pieces. False makers' marks are rare but make sure marks have not been removed to make the lustreware seem earlier than it is.

VICTORIAN TILES

Brilliantly coloured and patterned Victorian tiles are relatively inexpensive to collect and can be made up into attractive displays to adorn your home

The Victorians revived the art of tile-making which had almost died out in Britain in the early 19th century. In fact, tiles became so popular that their use was extended from floors to walls, fireplaces and washstands. Their glazed surfaces were easily cleaned, so tiles were often incorporated into the designs of bathrooms and kitchens. Shops, too, especially butchers, grocers and dairies, tiled their walls with spectacular moulded tiles and transfer-printed friezes.

Victorian tiles were available in a huge variety of patterns and, because they were securely fixed to surfaces, many have survived.

TOP MAKERS

Perhaps the most prolific manufacturer of the age was Minton of Stoke-on-Trent. The company published its first simple catalogue in 1842 which showed a range of 96 designs. By 1870, however, the range had grown to many hundreds from which builders and home owners could choose. Other makers to look out for include: the Campbell Tile Company; Pilkington; Craven Dunhill; Doulton; and Wedgwood. Another large manufacturer was Maw and Company which, by the turn of the century, had grown to overtake Minton as the largest producer of tiles in Britain.

In terms of design, the Victorians were great borrowers and nowhere is this more evident than in the field of tiles. A huge range of historical styles were used: Greco-Roman; Gothic; medieval; Persian; and many more. In the 1880s, the fashion for things Japanese was reflected. The ideals of William Morris's Arts and Crafts movement also influenced tile makers. William de Morgan, particularly, produced some stunning, richly coloured tiles. The art nouveau style, with its flowing designs of plants, birds and stylized flowers, was also taken up with gusto at the turn of the century.

TILE MANUFACTURE

The decorative patterns were almost always produced by one of three methods: the encaustic process; transfer-printing; or moulding.

The encaustic process involved inlaying dif-

Elizabeth Whiting Associates

ferent colours of clay – with the aid of dies or moulds – onto the surface of the tile, which was then fired. By the nature of the process, these tiles were usually simple in design and, as they were sturdy, were often used for floors.

Nearly all the major manufacturers made transfer-printed tiles and the flexibility of this process lent itself to numerous colours and designs. Moulded tiles are usually a single colour – that of the glaze. The quality of the designs was very variable and many were rather coarse and naturalistic. Maw, however, produced good moulded tiles in the 1880s.

The collective effect of a fine range of glossy decorative tiles can transform a dim hallway. This style of interior design was very popular in suburban interiors at the turn of the century.

FLORAL DESIGNS

TWO BROWN TILES. ❷❸

At left are autumn fruit and flowers. Below are four botanical vignettes in underglaze brown on a beige ground.

Floral patterns were among the most popular of designs and offer the widest range of choice for the collector. Many plain, mass-produced transfer-printed tiles can be bought for very little indeed, but with added hand colour the same design will be dearer. Even quite rare tiles are not hugely expensive, unless they are by William Morris or his friend, William de Morgan. A single hand-made moulded and painted tile from either commands a high price, while a complete panel of the same is worth as much as a fine painting. Prices are per tile from the left.

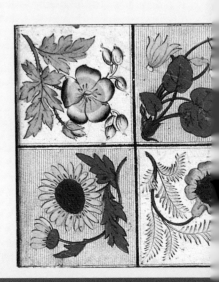

THREE STYLIZED DESIGNS. ❷❸❹

Above is a c1885 floral tile, transfer-printed in pinks and yellows on a cream ground, set in quarters. Above right is an art nouveau tile of c1905 of three acorns in moulded relief within stylized curving leaves. On the right are wild roses surrounded by a stylized border design, the corners forming a repeat pattern; it dates from c1890.

Rosemary Weller

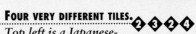

FOUR VERY DIFFERENT TILES. ❷❸❷❹

Top left is a Japanese-inspired design of a fish, crane and flowers in circular reserves on a floral and cracked ice ground, c1880. Top right is a tube-lined tile in green with orange marigolds, c1900. Bottom left is a blue and white transfer-printed tile with flowers set randomly. Bottom right is a detailed illustration of lily-of-the-valley.

STYLIZED ❷
autumn fruits and leaves transfer-printed in brown against a dark blue ground.

THREE DIFFERENT FLOWER DESIGNS. ❸❹❸

At left is a quartered tile showing four types of flowers in rich colours, c1885. In the centre is a moulded tile in low relief with a symmetrical art nouveau pansy, c1905. At right is a spray of convolvulus in a circular reserve, surrounded by a geometric cone design, c1880.

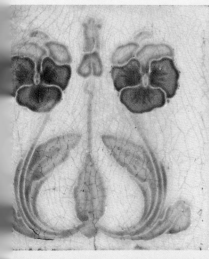

TWO EYECATCHING DESIGNS. ❹❹

At the top is an art nouveau tile with leaves around a stylized image moulded in relief. Below it is a botanical print of foxgloves set within an octagonal frame.

GEOMETRIC DESIGNS

Geometric designs ran a close second to floral designs in popularity. In this they reflected the many borrowed styles of the Victorian age. The years up to and after 1850 were the decades of Gothic Revival in architecture and many inlaid floor tiles were produced based on Gothic motifs, such as a stylized fleur-de-lys. Classical patterns, many from Roman or Greek examples, were copied too, especially the well known 'key' pattern. This was often used as a border to define blocks of symmetrical or plain tiles. Many symmetrical designs were transfer-printed on plain tiles to ensure the regularity of pattern and were mass-produced to cover large areas. These tiles are quite easy to find and not expensive. Prices are per tile from the left.

A QUARTET ◆◆◆◆
of very different geometric designs. At the top is a bathroom tile in a simple pattern of pink and white. In the centre is a striking pattern of circles and diamond motifs that would have been used over large areas. Bottom left is a sunflower at the centre of a geometrical design enlivened by flowers and leaves. Below is a tile with a running pattern of fleur-de-lys and a border of crosses.

TWO ORNATE TILES. ◆◆
At far left is a central flower in a circular reserve surrounded by scrolling foliage, c1880. At near left the tile has a rococo scroll border encompassing finely drawn flowers set on a white ground. The central motif is composed of further scrolls. It is c1890.

3 ▶ **DIVIDED IN QUARTERS,** ▶
this transfer-printed blue and white tile is decorated with a design of highly stylized leaves. It dates from around 1890.

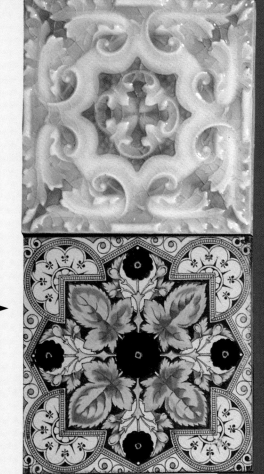

3 3 ▶ **STYLIZED LEAVES** ▶
feature in both tiles. At the top is a tile in moulded low relief, with leaves in muted colours. On the right is a design in autumnal colours in geometric divisions.

SIX DIFFERING DESIGNS.
Top left is a three-coloured encaustic tile for large areas. Below it is a pink and white one with repeating corners. On its right is a printed repeating pattern. At bottom left is a brown and white version of a design opposite. Bottom centre is a repeating pattern and below is a moulded tile.

Rosemary Weller

MINTON'S CHINA WORKS

Minton's China Works in Stoke-on-Trent was the style leader of Victorian tile design from the 1840s onwards. By the 1870s, their beautiful coloured catalogues showed hundreds of tile designs. The company won gold medals around the world for its artistic designs.

A red and white octagonal design, based around a many-petalled flower surrounded by scrolled foliage.

A blue and white floral design (above) and (right) the underside of a tile with a catalogue pattern number.

Rosemary Weller

COLLECTOR'S NOTES

Tiles are a pleasure to collect. They are easy to display, or can be used functionally, and need no attention beyond a wipe with a damp cloth. The only problem may lie in deciding what to collect, as there are so many types and designs. If you were to collect randomly, but without duplicating designs, you could easily amass several thousand tiles and yet still not form a comprehensive collection.

TYPES OF TILE

The tile on the left is an encaustic tile – the geometric pattern is formed using three simple colours. The tile below left is a transfer-printed design with a blue floral design. The tile below has a raised moulded pattern of marigolds with stylized leaves formed by slip squeezed from a tube.

Ray Duns

Collectors adopt themes, yet even this can lead to a huge collection.

Floral themes are popular, as such tiles are very common and therefore inexpensive, but, again, you may find that you want to narrow down the idea. One way is to choose, for example, a floral theme, but represented only by inlaid tiles. Another is to choose a theme based on transfer-printed nursery-rhyme characters, though this would be more expensive and restricted than choosing almost any floral theme. Given possibilities as wide as your imagination, the best starting point may be to identify the type and design of tile you like most, and take it from there. You can always change your mind and take another tack later.

ON THE TILES

Trying to track the history of your tiles is part of the fascination of collecting. Manufacturers usually stamped their names boldly on the backs of tiles. Dating tiles, though, can be more difficult as some of the more popular designs remained in production for 60 years or more. Some, like the Minton tile above, will have a registration number which establishes the year of manufacture, but many do not (reference books on ceramics have lists of registration numbers). The majority of wall tiles you may come across will usually have been made after 1880, while inlaid tiles may go back four decades earlier. The best way to pinpoint precise details about designs and patterns is to look for the catalogues published by the big manufacturers; these are still held in some of the major public libraries.

FAIRINGS

*Inexpensive china ornaments, bought or won at
Victorian country fairs, are now collected
as authentic pieces of folk art*

Duncan Smith

*By turns charming,
ribald, folksy and
witty, fairings were
made as
unpretentious
ornaments for
country cottages
and were originally
sold for a few
pennies. They are
always colourful,
and the best of
them show real skill
in the original
moulding.*

At one time, the annual fair was the biggest event in every country district. The whole neighbourhood took a holiday and went along. Most were essentially commercial affairs, dedicated to purchasing livestock and domestic essentials. During the 19th century, though, they gradually changed to something like the fun-fairs we know today.

The second half of the century was the heyday of cheap china ornaments known to collectors as fairings. Some were given as prizes, but most were sold for a few pence to adorn cottage mantelpieces. Much of their charm lies in their very British humour, bright, cheerful and often a little crude.

They shared a cast of characters with music-hall skits and Edwardian saucy post-cards. Buxom matrons, hapless youths, innocent and not-so-innocent maidens, out-raged fathers, henpecked or erring husbands, nervous newly-weds, old lechers and swaying drunkards were all grist to the comic mill.

Most fairings were made in Germany. Conta & Boehme, the first manufacturers, were the best. Their fairings were made of solid soft paste porcelain, while their competitors made hollow models, which tended to be less well finished and painted. German dominance meant that the trade in fairings ended at the start of World War 1.

BOXES AND HOLDERS

Some items that come under the heading of fairings had practical uses. Trinket boxes, watch stands, spill holders and match holders were all made by Conta & Boehme and their competitors. Some trinket boxes had lids which copied popular fairings, though without the captions. Match-holders, made for phosphorus matches, incorporated a rough surface for striking as well as a holder disguised as a tree stump, capstan, broken column or something similar.

Not all fairings were funny. Some portrayed famous figures, while others featured scenes from the Crimean War. In the Edwardian period, when the fairs were in decline, the manufacturers sought more respectable markets, such as shops. Fairings traded ribaldry for sentiment, and featured angelic children or cats, dogs and farm animals striving to be lovable.

4 THIS MATCH HOLDER OF ABOUT 1880 *is unusual for the date both in its subject matter and its decoration; apart from the boy's golden hair, it is all floral patterns in underglaze blue.*

4 THIS UNUSUAL SPILL HOLDER *depicting a Welsh tea party dates from the 1890s. Though it is Victorian in style, its subject is Edwardian in its lack of salacious humour.*

5 'COME AT ONCE' *is a rare match holder showing a man entreating his sweetheart to elope as her father approaches, unseen, with a large stick in his hand.*

5 'OYSTERS, SIR?' *is a fairly common match holder of the 1860s which alludes gently to the shellfish's reputation as an aphrodisiac.*

THIS MATCH-HOLDER ◀ ◆
is probably Edwardian. The legends 'Scratch my back' and 'Me too' show that both the sow and the piglet act as strikers.

THIS PERKY PIG, ◆
with its trotters in a shallow dish, is Edwardian in origin and was probably intended as a pin tray.

WINSOME PIGS ◀ ◆
also decorate this Edwardian fairing. The lack of a striking surface suggests this may not be a match holder.

◆ ▶ **THIS SPILL HOLDER**
in the shape of three hollow branches is crudely modelled and painted compared with similar Victorian pieces.

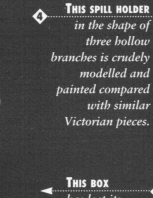

THIS BOX ◀ ◆
has lost its lid, which greatly reduces its value. What remains is a well-modelled, but badly rubbed hearth.

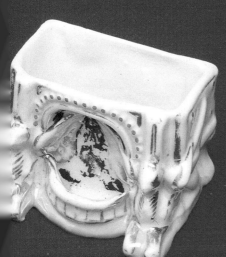

FIGURES OF FUN

Fairing figure groups were always small, with bases no more than 13cm/5in long. Some were made in two sizes.

Most fairings had captions. Puns were a particular favourite; a woman rifling her sleeping husband's pockets is titled 'Robbing the mail', amd a pair of drunks in the stocks, 'Babes in the wood'. Slapstick was also popular. 'The last in bed to put out the light' has a couple crashing heads as they leap beneath the covers. Much of the humour was based on marriage and courtship, such as 'Twelve months after marriage', which features a gloomy husband nursing the baby while his wife sleeps on, and had a risqué tone, such as 'Two different views', where a young woman sits between two standing men. One of them is looking through a telescope and the other peering over her shoulder and down her dress.

'TO LET' ▸ 7
is a very rare fairing of a young woman in widow's weeds. The caption subverts the poignant image, suggesting she is a femme fatale.

◂ **'GOING TO THE BALL'** 6
dates from 1870. Its innocent depiction of a mother dressing her young daughter for a dance is rather out of character for the time.

FIRST MADE BY CONTA & BOEHME IN 1860, ◂ 5
'The last in the bed to put out the light' was later copied by many other makers.

THIS GERMAN FAIRING ▸ 5
is a copy of a Conta & Boehme original. The original version, one of the earliest fairings, is now very rare.

Duncan Smith

'ANIMATED SPIRITS' 6 features two comic staples, the buxom wench and the lusty cleric. It was made from 1863 to 1875.

THIS RARE PIECE, 6 captioned 'If you please, Sir', shows a barmaid asking a champagne drinker's help in removing his popped cork from her cleavage.

'IF YOUTH KNEW' 6 is an unnumbered Conta & Boehme piece, presumably made as one of a pair with 'If age could'.

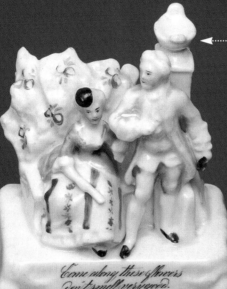

THE COARSE HUMOUR 6 of this fairing only becomes apparent when it is turned around to reveal a small boy squatting behind the shrubbery.

'THE POWER OF LOVE' 5 shows a wife catching her erring husband in the act of stealing a kiss from the maid that has 'knocked his hat off'.

'JUST AS IT SHOULD BE' 6 is a rare fairing of about 1880 showing a young girl fawning over her mother who is reflectively – and not a little incongruously – smoking a large pipe.

COLLECTOR'S NOTES

The really collectable fairings are those made by Conta & Boehme, with amusing mottoes in black or red copperplate script. It is important that the script is still readable. Early Conta & Boehme pieces are unmarked, but after the late 1870s they adopted the mark of a crooked arm holding a dagger. Earlier pieces tend to be better, as the pieces lost definition with wear and tear on the moulds.

REAL ? FAKE

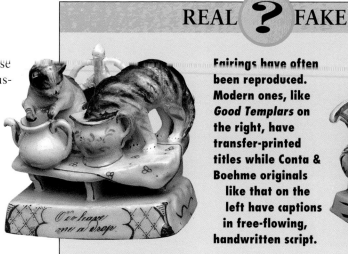

Fairings have often been reproduced. Modern ones, like *Good Templars* on the right, have transfer-printed titles while Conta & Boehme originals like that on the left have captions in free-flowing, handwritten script.

DESIGN IN FOCUS

A VISIT TO THE DENTIST

This Conta & Boehme fairing is one of a pair; the other, captioned 'Out! By Jingo' shows all three men on the floor with their legs in the air. The model is numbered 3335, dating it to c1880. The bright colours, vigorous modelling and copperplate script are all typical of Conta & Boehme work, as is the rather rubbed gilding.

❶ THE FIGURES ARE ALL DRESSED IN CONTEMPORARY BRITISH FASHIONS

❷ COPPERPLATE CAPTION IN BLACK

❸ VIGOROUS MODELLING OF COMIC CARICATURE FIGURES

❹ GILDED DECORATION THAT TENDS TO RUB OFF WITH AGE

Conta & Boehme began to number their pieces about the same time as they marked them. Numbers run from 2850 to 2899 and from 3300 to 3385. At first, the numbers were scratched into the base; later they were embossed. Any pieces that are unmarked, have a heavy Germanic or Roman script and are stamped 'Made in Germany' on the base are not Conta & Boehme fairings.

REAL OR REPRO?

The value of a fairing depends largely on its rarity. Many were made, but these were cheap and cheerful ornaments, not meant to be treasured, so many of them were thrown away or broken. They have also been widely reproduced. The best way to tell an authentic piece is to check for wear, especially on the gilding. The glaze on old pieces may be irregularly crazed. Uniform crazing is the sign of a modern glaze.

Small repairs do not necessarily reduce value. Most of the charm of fairings is in their folksy appeal, and do-it-yourself mending may enhance this.

When buying, make sure that the number, mark (if any), style and subject all point to the same factory. If they do not, then the piece is a reproduction.

A base with a continuous ridge, top and bottom, is from the first half of the 1860s. Numbers may help you date a piece, and so will fashions. Crinolines suggest the 1860s, while bustles came in after 1870. A bicycle indicates that a piece is from after 1867. Some fairings have themes based on popular music or prints, and these may be dated easily and exactly.

Fairings may come in pairs, typically before and after scenes. These companion pieces are worth a lot more if you manage to get both pieces of the set.

COMMEMORATIVE CHINA

Created as tributes to the great people and events of the past, commemorative china is not only attractive but also highly collectable today

Rosemary Weller

During the 19th century, commemoratives enjoyed great popularity and notable people, events and places were celebrated on all manner of ware from biscuit tins to beer bottles. China commemoratives, bought as souvenirs or gifts, occupied pride of place on many a Victorian mantelpiece.

ROYALTY REMEMBERED

Royalty and royal events are probably the most popular subjects covered in china commemoratives. Coronations, births, jubilees and deaths are all remembered in this way and can form the base of an interesting and valuable collection.

Political events and personalities were often featured in the 19th century. China pieces appeared as souvenirs of battles, wars and other empire-building events. Cups and plates bore the portraits of politicians and reformers and were vehicles for satire and propaganda. Certain subjects proved so popular that they continued to be made for several years, long after the actual event.

Also remembered in china were the great industrial triumphs of the Victorian age, such as openings of railways, bridges, mines and factories. The Great Exhibition of 1851, when 'the industry of all nations' was displayed at the Crystal Palace in London's Hyde Park, produced a great wealth of commemoratives.

PERSONAL POTTERY

Particularly interesting are those pieces of pottery made to celebrate personal rather than historical events. Pieces can be found recording births, christenings, comings of age, marriages and wedding anniversaries.

Commemorative china is as attractive as it is plentiful and a pleasing collection can soon be amassed. The practice of recording momentous events on china dates from 15th-century Italy, but it was during the 19th century that a real craze for commemoratives began in Britain, and collectors will find many Victorian pieces on the market today.

29

ROYAL COMMEMORATIVES

British potteries have produced countless souvenirs to commemorate royal events – far more than anywhere else in Europe. This is an indication of the high profile the monarchy plays in British national life. A few pottery items were made to mark the coronations of both George III and George IV, but it was the succession of Queen Victoria to the throne in 1837 that marked the beginnings of a royal souvenir industry. From that time on, every major occurrence in the life of the royal family was celebrated in ceramics and Queen Victoria's descendants continue to be commemorated in china today. Complete tea and dinner services can be found but individual plates and mugs are more common. China figurines and other ornamental royal commemoratives were also highly popular.

6 **STAFFORDSHIRE FIGURE** *commemorating the coronation of Edward VII. These figures are not always accurate portraits of their sitters.*

KING EDWARD VII

7 **COMMEMORATIVES OF THE CORONATION** *of Queen Victoria in 1838 can command high prices. This octagonal plate decorated with the Queen's portrait bears the dates of both her proclamation (1837) and her crowning (1838).*

A MUG *made to mark Victoria's Golden Jubilee in 1887. It is decorated in an effect know as 'clobbered': enamel colours are applied to the china to make it look richer and, therefore, pricier.*

A BLUE AND WHITE *plate, unusual in commemorating Queen Victoria's proclamation rather than her coronation. It also mentions her date of birth.*

MADE IN 1897, THIS MUG *marks Victoria's Diamond Jubilee after 60 years on the British throne.*

DEALER'S TIPS

- Look out for pieces commemorating Queen Victoria's coronation since they are fairly rare. Later Jubilee commemoratives are more plentiful and will be far cheaper.
- Some china made for the June coronation of Edward VII has the wrong date on it, as he was rushed into hospital with appendicitis. The rare items are those bearing the new (August) date.
- Though the coronation of Edward VIII never took place, commemorative ware is plentiful and not particularly valuable. Those pieces over-printed with the date of his abdication, or which give details of it, are rare and collectable.

THE PORTRAIT ROUNDEL 6
on this ewer bears a picture of Edward, Prince of Wales, the future King Edward VII. The decoration has been picked out in lustre. Lustred decoration was achieved by applying metal oxides in the required pattern to a piece during the final stages of firing.

AT A SPECIAL DINNER GIVEN BY THE MAYOR OF WORCESTER 5
to celebrate Queen Victoria's Golden Jubilee in 1887, gentlemen were given blue plates like this one, and ladies received red versions of the same.

THE MARRIAGE 7
of Queen Victoria and Prince Albert is commemorated in this fine lustreware jug. A uniquely English form of decoration, lustre was popular for commemoratives.

DOULTON 7
made this unusual saltglaze vase when the Prince of Wales visited their factory in 1885. Saltglaze is a hard glaze made by adding common salt to the hot surface of the clay.

QUEEN VICTORIA 6
died in 1901 and this charming, tiny porcelain cup, saucer and plate were made to commemorate the event.

JUBILEE YEAR
WALTER HOLLAND
DEI GRATIA
VICTORIA
REG.t IMP. 1837-1887
MAYOR of WORCESTER

Rosemary Weller

POLITICAL POTTERY

Political movements and events were common subjects for 19th-century commemoratives. Popularity died down after 1900, though a few items relating to the suffragette movement and World War 1 were made.

Politicians, military heroes and other notables were all immortalized in china and people like Gladstone and the Duke of Wellington are commonly found. Wars were among the great patriotic events of the 19th century commemorated in china, and both victories and defeats were recorded with equal fervour.

7 LORD NELSON *featured on many Victorian jugs and plates. This piece is valuable since it was actually made at the time of the Admiral's death in 1805.*

7 J GREAVES' TEA *and a strike for the nine-hour bill in 1871 are both promoted on this plate.*

5 DECORATED WITH PRIMROSES, *his favourite flower, this plate, c1887, honours Benjamin Disraeli.*

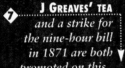

6 THE HIGHLIGHTS *of Sir Robert Peel's political life are shown on this Staffordshire plate, produced at the time of his death in 1850 at the age of 62.*

6 MAJOR POLITICIANS, *such as Gladstone, were popular figures for commemorative china like this mug.*

THE CRIMEAN WAR 7 (1854-56) was frequently commemorated in china. The Charge of the Light Brigade, shown on this jug, was one military engagement that often featured.

In 1857, the Borough of Stockport in Manchester had a set of dinner-ware made up to this pattern for S H Cheetham Esq to mark 20 years of service. Pieces that commemorate more personal events like this can form an interesting collection.

STANLEY'S FAMOUS DISCOVERY 6 of Dr Livingstone in 1871 - and other British exploits in Africa - are recalled on this plate.

THE BOER WAR 5 and other colonial struggles were frequently depicted in patriotic designs, such as the one adorning this plate.

THIS STAFFORDSHIRE PLATE 6 shows Crimean War soldiers receiving their post before the siege of Sebastopol in 1854.

THE GREAT REFORM BILL, PASSED IN 1832, 6 is remembered on this mug showing its architects, Lord John Russell and Earl Grey.

Rosemary Weller

COLLECTOR'S NOTES

Because they were produced in such large quantities, you can find many commemoratives in junk shops and antiques fairs. They can be relatively inexpensive, making them ideal subjects for a first collection. However, some pieces can fetch high prices, as commemoratives are currently in vogue and there are several specialist dealers around.

STYLES AND MATERIALS

Commemoratives take on a wide variety of forms, including jugs, tankards, plaques, vases, ornaments and figurines, but it is mugs that are most commonly collected. And, because it has been fashionable for the last 200 years, commemorative china has been made by many different manufacturers all over the country in a wide range of styles and materials. You can find pieces in such diverse ceramic forms as porcelain, slipware, pearlware, creamware, Parian ware or earthenware. You might find some early pieces decorated with hand painting but, most commonly, transfer printing was used.

PRICE FACTORS

As a rule, the factory that made the commemorative item is of less importance to the collector than the quality of the piece or the actual event commemorated, but pieces by

TOMORROW'S TREASURES

Royal commemoratives are still made today and certain pieces are worth buying with future investment in mind. For instance, limited edition items are generally worth more than mass-produced pieces. Quality is not always as important as rarity when judging the value of a particular piece. For instance, a thick pottery mug made to commemorate the divorce of Princess Margaret is regarded as a very valuable piece, despite its poor quality, because it is so unusual.

Today priced at (in anticlockwise order) £18, £32 and £50, the pieces shown here commemorate two royal weddings and the Queen's Silver Jubilee.

Lyndon Parker

REAL ? FAKE

Beware of the reproduction mugs and beakers that have appeared on the market. Look at the base – on a reproduction piece it will be clean, white and shiny and show no signs of wear. The overall glaze of reproduction ware is also quite shiny.

The royal souvenir industry was not controlled by the Palace and some appalling portraits of Queen Victoria appeared. Pieces like the two mugs shown below were known as 'uglies'.

the better-known manufacturers will be more expensive because they tend to be of higher quality. Many factors influence price: porcelain will command higher prices than pottery, limited editions will be more valuable and pieces portraying unusual events are highly sought after. And the nearer the date of manufacture of the object is to the date of the event commemorated, the more collectable the piece. For instance, items showing Nelson were made throughout the 19th century – long after his naval victories – and contemporary examples are fairly rare. So it is important to remember that you cannot necessarily use the event or person shown on commemorative china to date a piece accurately.

COLLECTION THEMES

When building up a collection you might like to concentrate on one or two themes – such as railways, military, sporting or royal pieces – rather than buying at random. You might also like to collect objects made in different materials – such as papier mâché or tin – but all commemorating the same subject, such as the Great Exhibition of 1851.

Rosemary Weller

COW CREAMERS

Though originally intended as useful wares, colourful cow creamers were one of the most delightful, even humorous, creations of the 18th-century ceramics industry, and are collected today purely as ornamental pieces

Rosemary Weller

Tea drinking was a fashionable habit for a while before anyone thought of adding a little milk or cream to their cuppa, but by the mid-18th century, virtually everyone was doing it. The British ceramics industry responded by quickly adding all manner of milk jugs and creamers to its growing repertoire of household pottery. By far the most endearing was the cow creamer.

Shaped like a dairy cow, with a looped-over tail providing a handle and an open, lowing mouth serving as a spout, they may have started life as a novelty item, or a joke, but soon caught the popular imagination. The hollow belly of the cow held the milk or cream – about a quarter of a pint – and it was refilled through a lidded hole in its back.

DUTCH OR ENGLISH?

Though they seem quintessentially English, right at home in a country cottage kitchen, cow creamers may have originated in Holland. Two emigré Dutch silversmiths, Johann Schuppe and David Willaume the Younger, made finely modelled, free-standing silver cow

creamers around 1750. The hinged lids were modelled in the shape of a pad of flowers, with a bee as a knob. Enterprising potters may have copied them. However, to confuse the issue, an earthenware creamer in Stoke's City Museum has been dated to 1740.

Wherever they came from, cow creamers were soon being made in potteries all over Britain. Some featured a milkmaid, inevitably wildly out of scale, others had daisies applied to the base. The modelling of the cow ranged from naive to fairly realistic, but the painting was usually surreal, to say the least; some had transfer-printed rural scenes on their sides.

The heyday of cow creamers lasted just 100 years. Difficult to clean, they caused several outbreaks of salmonella poisoning, but it took the new respect for hygiene brought about by the cholera scares of the 1850s to finally retire them from the table to the quieter pastures of the mantelshelf or kitchen dresser.

Though Edwardian potters revived the manufacture of cow creamers as decorative pieces with some success, these aren't as collectable as their working predecessors.

You don't have to like cows, or even cream, to enjoy cow creamers. Their great attraction lies in their variety of expression and their naive decorations. Some of them are richly comic, and some surreally proportioned, but all but the most crudely made have undeniable character and charm that makes them one of the most popular types of 18th- and 19th-century ceramics with today's collectors.

THE STOCK MARKET

Cow creamers are hardly ever marked, and can rarely be attributed to a specific potter. In the 1760s, Thomas Whieldon experimented with coloured clays under clear glazes and came up with agate ware, which had a tortoiseshell effect. Another pioneer, William Pratt of Lane Delph, produced cows with a distinctive palette of colours under a bright glassy glaze; anything in the Pratt or Whieldon style is very collectable.

Otherwise, the price of a cow creamer depends on a variety of factors including its age, the quality and gaiety of the decoration and the charm of the piece. Anything that adds an individual note, such as a crumpled horn, a cheery expression, a suckling calf, a milkmaid or – joke upon joke – a rare bull creamer, will add value. Other details to look out for are kicking straps around the cow's hind legs, a daisy in the turf at her feet, a bell around her neck or a moulded knob on her back. Edwardian cow creamers, which often lack the naive charm of early examples, are relatively inexpensive.

A LOW, AWKWARDLY-PLACED TAIL *suggests that this creamer was never really intended for serious use, and the decoration of blobs of gilding over a shiny black body isn't particularly attractive. The straight horns are an unusual feature.*

MADE AROUND 1800, *this Staffordshire creamer has been haphazardly decorated with an iron-red and black clover-leaf pattern applied with a sponge. The hasty paint job – especially on the feet – is typical of cow creamers, and part of their appeal.*

Rosemary Weller

36

◆ ❻ RANDOM DABS OF RUST AND LILAC LUSTRE *identify this as a Sunderland cow creamer. Other colour variations include pink or lilac combined with blue or green.*

THE RUST-BROWN AND WHITE COAT ❻ ◆ *of the Herefordshire breed attracted some rare stabs at the more naturalistic decoration of cow creamers. This example from around 1870 has also been modelled with the breed's characteristic squat, stout build.*

◆ THIS COW CREAMER ❼ *is from Sunderland and was probably made around 1800. Its decoration is very similar to the later Sunderland model above, but it has an oblong, not rounded, base, suggesting its greater age. Value is also added by the unusually realistic face and the cow's rather fetching expression.*

ORIGINAL JACKFIELD ❻ ◆ *cows were made in Shropshire in the third quarter of the 18th century. The glossy black finish and gilded horns typical of the factory were often copied, as in this rather crude 19th-century creamer from Staffordshire.*

COLLECTOR'S NOTES

Cow creamers have been widely collected for a while now, and you're unlikely to find them at car boot sales. Auctions, country house sales and antiques dealers and fairs are your most likely sources.

A bit of research helps a lot in this field. A visit to the City Museum in Stoke-on-Trent, where huge herds crowd the shelves, is well worthwhile. Choose a breed that appeals to you to collect. Staffordshire creamers were made in salt-glazed stoneware, creamware, glossy black 'Jackfield ware', pearlware and bone china. Some lustre glazes were used, but the commonest finish was tan dappled with green, black, yellow, blue or orange. The bases are usually green.

Early Welsh pieces were in splashed lustre ware, but later ones had transfer-printed rural scenes on the side. Yorkshire creamers had oblong, waisted bases with chamfered corners, and colourful lustre-ware creamers were usually made in Sunderland.

Creamers have been widely copied, so be careful when buying, especially 'Jackfield' cows with golden horns and hooves, prime candidates for Edwardian reproduction. One way to tell early pieces is to run your finger round the outside. Those made before 1830 tend to be rough to the touch. Remember, too, that old lustre ware looks mottled pink in a soft light, but shows up gold in the sunshine.

Beware heavy gilding on horns or hooves; it may well have been put on to conceal a repair. A missing or replacement stopper will cut the value dramatically, so make sure the stopper fits well and is a perfect match in glaze and body. Crude modelling is a feature of early cows, and can only add to their charm, but damaged or missing horns will devalue them.

DESIGN IN FOCUS — A FLAT-BACK COW CREAMER

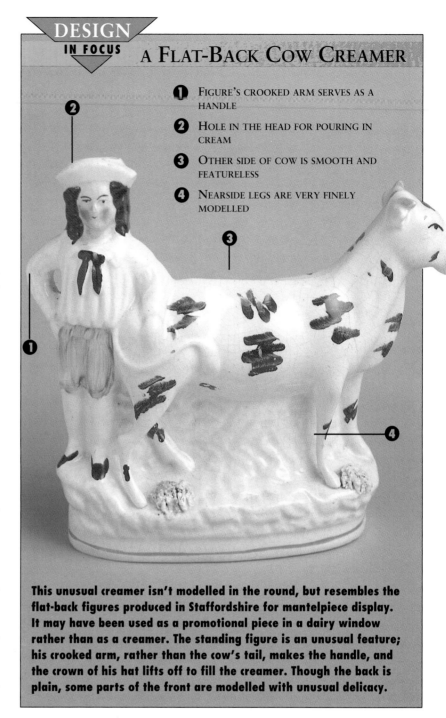

1. FIGURE'S CROOKED ARM SERVES AS A HANDLE
2. HOLE IN THE HEAD FOR POURING IN CREAM
3. OTHER SIDE OF COW IS SMOOTH AND FEATURELESS
4. NEARSIDE LEGS ARE VERY FINELY MODELLED

This unusual creamer isn't modelled in the round, but resembles the flat-back figures produced in Staffordshire for mantelpiece display. It may have been used as a promotional piece in a dairy window rather than as a creamer. The standing figure is an unusual feature; his crooked arm, rather than the cow's tail, makes the handle, and the crown of his hat lifts off to fill the creamer. Though the back is plain, some parts of the front are modelled with unusual delicacy.

CLOSE UP on COW PARTS

Naturalistic colours lend this cow an unusual sense of realism.

Small filling holes meant the inside of a creamer was very difficult to clean.

The lowing expression gave a more satisfactory shape for pouring.

Rosemary Weller

CREAM JUGS

Serving tea has long been a cherished part of British culture, and the excuse to show off some fancy china has spawned some highly collectable jugs

Taking milk in tea did not become customary until the latter part of the 18th century. Before this, milk was used to make butter and cheese but was generally drunk only by children or invalids. With milk and cream suddenly finding a place on the tables of the gentry, the British ceramics industry set about producing jugs for serving it.

At first they took a back seat to the silversmiths. Since milk was brought to the table hot, silver was thought preferable. The first silver jugs were tall and gilt-lined, with a wide lip. They stood either on a broad foot or on three small legs. As the vogue for hot milk declined later in the century, cream jugs, similar in shape to sauceboats, were introduced.

As tea-drinking spread through the classes, porcelain factories and potteries produced their own versions of cream jugs, almost always selling them as part of a tea service. The jugs usually copied silver styles, though the broad foot was adopted instead of the all-too-breakable three legs.

Some jugs had less generous lips. The sparrow-beak jug, tall and shapely with a sharp-angled lip, was a popular style in pottery but rarely seen in silver. Various shapes and styles went in and out of fashion through the 19th century, though the underlying trend in cream jugs was away from tall, slender jugs towards shorter, squatter styles. By the Edwardian period, most decorative styles of the previous two centuries were available in several versions, from the cheap, unmarked, transfer-printed pottery jug to specially commissioned, hand-painted Minton porcelain.

There is an enormous variety of cream jugs available to the collector, in all shapes, sizes, colours and materials. Milk or cream could be served in anything from a simple, cheap pottery jug to a specially commissioned hand-painted Minton porcelain one, depending on the budget available or the popularity of the guest!

Rosemary Weller

JUGS GALORE

Cream jugs in perfect condition can span a wide price range. Simple jugs with printed decoration will be the cheapest. Distinctive styling, good-quality modelling, attractive hand-painting and/or a signature all add value. Wedgwood, Crown Derby and Royal Worcester command higher prices than other factories, while art nouveau pieces by continental factories such as Limoges or Royal Copenhagen can be very expensive. Majolica ware, Mason's Ironstone and other distinctive wares also attract a premium price.

Rosemary Weller

4 THE VICTORIANS *often drew on earlier styles. This white porcelain jug with spreading foot dates from around 1880, but is reminiscent of the 18th-century baluster shape.*

5 METALLIC LUSTRE GLAZES *were used on earthenware and bone china from the early 19th century onwards. This mid-Victorian Staffordshire jug has a copper lustre band.*

6 THIS UNUSUAL CREAM JUG *looks like a cauliflower. Minton produced a huge range of quality majolica ware between 1851-62, which was much imitated.*

4 THE LOW, BOAT SHAPE *was typical of early 19th-century jugs. This Wedgwood jug, dated 1810, is a good example of the 'fish roe' pattern. The damaged handle reduces the value.*

SMALL FEET, ◆ characteristic of many Victorian jugs, were derived from 18th-century silver jugs. This high-handled, broad-spouted jug dates from 1840.

MASON'S IRONSTONE ⑤ octagonal jugs were made in a graduated range of sizes, of which this is the smallest. There is a strong Japanese influence.

UNMARKED EXAMPLES, ◆ like this unusual abstract-patterned cream jug with mauve transfer-printing, are difficult to date. This one is probably mid-Victorian.

THE SAUCE-BOAT SHAPE ◆ was popular at the beginning of the Victorian period, while oriental patterns went in and out of fashion throughout the 19th century.

CL**O**SE UP *on* DECORATION

The two most common ways of decorating china are hand-painting it then firing it with a vitreous coating to make it smooth and waterproof, or using a coloured overglaze or enamel, usually on top of an initial white tin-glaze.

The jug above has some splendidly intricate decoration, but a clumsy rivet repair has lowered the value.

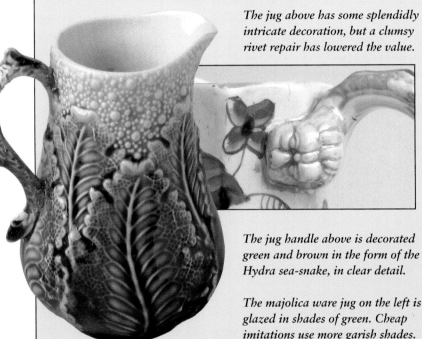

The jug handle above is decorated green and brown in the form of the Hydra sea-snake, in clear detail.

The majolica ware jug on the left is glazed in shades of green. Cheap imitations use more garish shades.

COLLECTOR'S NOTES

The sheer quantity of jugs available from late Victorian and Edwardian times makes it possible to assemble a fair collection, representing a wide range of styles and factories, relatively cheaply.

Although the great majority of cream jugs were sold as parts of sets or services, most of these will have been split up by now, and jugs can be found in flea markets, second-hand shops and boot sales, as well as in the more conventional antiques shops and fairs which you will have to visit to find earlier jugs.

The best Victorian jugs, made in bone china or porcelain, were hand-painted, usually with flowers or fruit. Japanese, Chinese and English styles of decoration all went in and out of fashion in the 19th century.

SIGNS OF THE TIMES

All good wares from the Victorian period should be clearly marked with the date, factory and sometimes the retailer of the piece. Some hand-painted pieces may also have the decorator's signature. Factories to look out for include Royal Worcester, Crown Derby, Minton, Copeland and Royal Doulton.

Most jugs will have had some wear and tear. Look for small cracks and chips, especially around the rim, on the base and on the handle. Make sure that the handle has not been broken and repaired. Generally, the cost of professional restoration will be greater than the value of the jug, although it may be worth having a particularly rare or desirable piece brought back to its full glory.

REAL **?** FAKE

Silver lustre glazes could look very like real silver (right). The jug on the left is earthenware, fired with a platinum-oxide glaze. On closer inspection you will notice that there are slight surface imperfections, and of course if you were to pick them both up you would notice a tell-tale difference in weight. All-over silver lustre, or 'poor man's silver', was made in considerable quantity up until 1840, particularly in Sunderland.

Rosemary Weller

WILLOW PATTERN CHINA

Of all the chinoiserie designs that were produced in Britain in the middle years of the 18th century, none has had the same success and enduring appeal as Willow Pattern

Once upon a time, a young Chinese girl was betrothed by her mandarin father to a rich but elderly merchant. The girl, though, had lost her heart to the young man who worked as her father's secretary; so, on the day appointed for her wedding, the young lovers eloped.

They fled across a bridge, pursued by the girl's father, and escaped in a boat to the young man's island home. They were soon caught, and threatened with death for their crimes, but the gods took pity on them; the lovers were transformed into turtle-doves, and flew away together.

This story – the details vary in the telling – is often presented as an ancient Chinese legend, but was invented around 1800 by the Regency equivalent of an advertising copywriter to explain the basic elements of an extremely successful design for decorating pottery, the Willow Pattern.

Traditional Willow Pattern has a pagoda or tea house centre right, a bridge with two or three running figures on it on the left, a boat above the bridge, and, beyond that, the youth's 'island home'. Two doves fly above and in the foreground are two trees, one known as either a cherry, apple or orange, and a willow. A densely-patterned blue border surrounds the scene.

Ray Duns

MADE IN ENGLAND

Though many of the motifs were copied from Chinese painted porcelain, the Willow Pattern was essentially an English creation. Caughley works are credited with first using it in transfer-print form in 1780. The Spode factory produced a definitive version around 1810.

At first, Willow Pattern was almost always seen on useful wares such as tea and dinner services, but later was applied to just about everything, from candleholders to cutlery handles and cow creamers. Potters elsewhere in Europe produced their own version of Willow Pattern, and in the 20th century, factories in the USA and Japan also copied it.

The great majority of wares were transfer-printed in blue, though prints in other colours, a few pieces painted in underglaze blue and polychrome versions of the pattern were also produced. None had the same commercial appeal as the basic blue and white.

Willow Pattern remained the most popular ceramic decoration, ahead of the Italian Pattern and Asiatic Pheasant, well into the 20th century. It's still made today, and has also appeared on plastics, textiles, enamelled metal pots and pans, and glassware.

The Willow Pattern has been, and still is, the most popular design ever used to decorate tableware but it has also been used on other kinds of china, such as vases, chamber pots and candlesticks. You may find slight variations in the Pattern on earlier pieces, particularly in the border design, although most 20th-century pieces follow the familiar style.

TABLE WILLOW

Porcelain, bone china, ironstone and stoneware Willow Pattern pieces will all cost a little more than similar ones in plain earthenware. Marked pieces tend to fetch more than unmarked ones, and those from collectable factories will fetch most of all. The great prize would be an 18th-century Chinese hand-painted porcelain piece containing some of the Willow Pattern elements, but these are very rare.

In the general category of useful ware, good prices are paid for fairly large, well-modelled serving pieces such as meat platters and soup tureens, or unusual items such as cake stands, cheese dishes, moustache cups, baby bottles or ewer and basin sets, while tea-cups, saucers and plates are generally inexpensive.

THIS STONEWARE *teaplate, like much Willow Pattern ware, carries no maker's mark but dates from around the 1820s when a deep blue was the fashionable colour on such wares.*

A PICKLE DISH *from the 1830s, on which the central pattern is a simplified version of the standard pattern. It dispenses with the doves and boatman, for instance. Unusual items like this are sought after.*

THIS LATE VICTORIAN *ironstone platter is similar to thousands produced at the end of the last century as attractive and affordable tableware. Because they were originally produced in such quantities, pieces like this can still be found at very reasonable prices.*

Ray Duns

44

A LARGE MEAT PLATTER ⑤
with the traditional Willow Pattern centre and border. It is almost identical in shape and style to the platter opposite, except that it dates from around 1830 and is therefore older and more valuable.

AN UNMARKED ⑤
sauce ladle from the 1830s. The bowl of the ladle shows part of the Pattern, with a traditional border, part of which is repeated on the handle.

ONE OF A PAIR OF ASHWORTH PLATES ④
dating from the 1890s. The centre pattern here, called Canton, imitates early hand-painted Chinese patterns and was used on much Ashworth Willow stoneware from the 1860s. The price is for the pair.

PRETTY WILLOW

Some decorative pieces, by virtue of their small size, were printed with just part of the pattern, which was often adapted to fit pieces that lacked the circular outline of a plate.

As is also true of useful wares, transfer-printing in colours other than blue, especially early examples, tends to command a slight premium, and the same applies to hand-painted multicoloured wares, though these are largely a speciality of US potteries and not often seen in Britain.

Anything that is not transfer-printed or is otherwise unusual tends to be highly prized. An example of this rule are the stoneware jugs produced by Doulton, with a variation of the border pattern impressed around the neck and the pattern itself in blue relief against a brown ground around the body of the jug. Variations on the traditional pattern are numerous and not unusual.

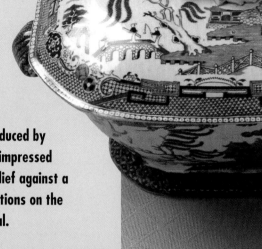

AN 1825 STONEWARE TUREEN ❻
with the traditional pattern and border. An undamaged piece like this, complete with lid, commands a fairly high price, although value would be increased if its missing ladle were included.

❹ **A STAFFORDSHIRE** ►
tureen base dating from the 1890s. Although it lacks its lid, it is attractive enough – thanks to part of the Willow Pattern in the bowl – to be used, and sold, as a vegetable dish.

Ray Duns

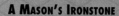

A MASON'S IRONSTONE 6 *cylindrical vase dating from the 1870s. Willow Pattern vases from this period are fairly unusual and, as a result, relatively expensive.*

A TILE FROM THE 1920s, 4 *encased in a wicker frame, with a traditional Willow Pattern plate as its central motif. It was probably used as a stand for a tea or coffee pot.*

A VICTORIAN SUGAR BOWL 3 *with lid. The transfer print on the lid has been rather inexpertly cropped off in a square which looks a little odd on the curved surface and it is a fairly run-of-the-mill piece, although not unpleasing.*

THIS DESSERT DISH 5 *with a pretty fluted border and rim is dated around 1815. It has the traditional Willow Pattern centre and border but its relatively early date and unusual shape add to its value.*

COLLECTOR'S NOTES

Willow Pattern wares from last century and this survive in huge numbers, and aren't at all expensive, unless they bear the mark of a rare or important maker or are in porcelain. They can turn up almost anywhere, including car boot and jumble sales, flea markets, junk shops, antiques fairs and markets, house sales – where you may find a complete service – and, in the case of rarer items such as cow creamers, in auctions and specialist dealers.

The pattern is widely collected, particularly in the United States, where there are several flourishing collectors' clubs. People tend to specialize in collecting a particular period or a particular type; just porcelain or bone china, say, or only serving dishes or tea sets. Some want only colours other than blue, and others concentrate on just one variant of the pattern.

VARIATIONS ON A THEME

In the 19th century, more and more potteries bowed to public taste and produced versions of the pattern. Some of these were more or less straight lifts from Spode, but there was great scope for variation, in the number of birds and people shown, in the shape, size and position of the trees, pagoda and boat, and in the decorative border, which often incorporated non-oriental motifs. American collectors have identified nine border types and eleven broad categories of centre pattern, but even within these categories, variations of detail are possible. Because of these variations, it can be quite a challenge to build up a complete service of Willow Pattern ware.

The exact details of the pattern can suggest the provenance of a plate, but not always; some factories used several versions of it. Variations aren't always helpful in dating a piece. Age is best judged by marks, if any, and the type of body and glaze used. Registered

This 18th-century Cantonese dish features some of the elements – tea house, temple, boat and trees – used in the Willow Pattern.

DESIGN IN FOCUS
VARIANT WILLOW PATTERN

As well as the traditional Willow Pattern, there are many variations to be found on both old and 20th-century china (see the Canton pattern, page 1673). This tureen of around 1900 has a tea house and a pagoda to which the bridge, with two figures on it, is linked. There is a small boat in the foreground and two doves at the top of the picture but there is no fence and no willow tree. Floral motifs appear in the foreground and border. The lid repeats some of these.

❶ TEA HOUSE AND TEMPLE

❷ TRADITIONAL DOVES, BRIDGE AND BOAT

❸ FLORAL MOTIFS

❹ FLORAL BORDER

❺ ELEMENTS OF CENTRE PATTERN REPEATED ON LID

Ray Duns

design marks may also be a help.

Whatever you choose to collect, buy only wares in excellent to perfect condition, with no chips, cracks or missing pieces, particularly lids. Earthenware is particularly prone to damage, and also to crackling of the glaze and staining. The quality of the transfer printing varies, too. Look for good, clear prints with no obvious seams, and avoid any that are faint, muddy or smudged. A rich, deep colour and high glaze are desirable qualities.

POT LIDS

Some Victorian goods were sold in small ceramic pots with attractive printed lids. Many were thrown away, but those that survive are avidly collected today

The Victorian age saw the flowering of mass production and the appearance of the first branded goods. Competition was stiff, and rival firms clamoured for the attention of the shopper with wall posters, newspaper advertisements and ever more eye-catching packaging. Even relatively mundane goods were considered worthy of elaborate attention. Products such as hair oil and fish paste, for instance, were sold in little, round china pots with beautiful, decorative lids.

These pots were themselves mass produced, and used for a wide range of products. Usually the pot was discarded when the contents were used up, but sometimes they were saved in much the same way as we save jam jars and biscuit tins, as handy containers for storing other things.

Other cheap china products, such as cups and plates, tended to get broken, chipped or cracked from use. The pots, though, often survived relatively unscathed because they were kept full of pins in a cupboard or graced the mantelpiece as part of the decorative clutter that the Victorians enjoyed so much.

Chris Barker

TRUE COLOURS

At first, the pots were produced in black and white. The lids had a printed, decorative border and the maker's name emblazoned in black lettering. Any instructions for use and other information was in smaller, less elaborate type. These early examples often held health and beauty products.

By 1845, a way to mass produce coloured designs on pottery had been developed. In colour transfer printing, the colour was mixed with oil, then worked into the engraved printing plate. Tissue paper was spread over the engraving and rolled until the paint adhered to the paper. The tissue was then placed onto the unglazed pottery and rubbed hard until the colour was transferred. A full colour picture was built up using successive layers of yellow, blue and red, with a black outline added last. The final stage was to dip the ware in a liquid glaze and fire it at a low temperature to bring out and fix the colours.

The manufacturers of pots seized on the new invention; pot lids became increasingly colourful and elaborate, and many more products were sold in them. Relatively few firms produced the bulk of this ware, which means that the designs are well-documented. It is usually fairly easy to follow a particular design back to its manufacturer and the year of production, something which greatly adds to the enjoyment of the collector.

There were three principal factories. F & R Pratt, the major manufacturer, set up in 1820, while J Ridgway and Co began in 1830 and, after several changes of name, became Cauldon Ltd in 1905. In 1920, Pratt and Cauldon merged and are now part of the Wedgwood Group. The third factory, Mayer, began in 1843. Original designs by all three companies continued to be reproduced as decorative ware through the 20th century.

The Victorian manufacturers of toiletries and food products who marketed them in distinctive transfer-printed pots thought of them as disposable, in much the same way as plastic packages are seen today. However, a collector is likely to value the pot shown here more highly than the gilded, transfer-printed shaving mug that is standing beside it.

A DECORATIVE BORDER
*and fanciful coat of arms add
decorative value to this pot of
anchovy paste, but hide the fact
that there is no maker's name.*

TASTY PASTES

The first decorative pots held potted shrimps from Pegwell Bay and fish paste. Both of these products were strictly local delicacies until they were marketed nationwide in their ceramic pots. Ever since, various fish, meat and vegetable spreads have been packaged in this way. Some up-market treats such as caviar and Gentlemen's Relish are still sold in similar ceramic pots, albeit ones with monochrome lids. Old pot lids reflect the British people's changing eating habits. Anchovy paste was a great favourite with the Victorians, though its strong, salty taste is not widely enjoyed today, while slices of thin-cut bread spread with bloater paste or potted meats, once a tea-time staple, have all but disappeared from the nation's tables.

THE SHEPHERD BOY
*was a popular subject made by the
Cauldon factory around 1860.
Later issues had a white border.*

THE ROYAL COAT OF ARMS
*on this blue-printed lid suggests the
Queen's approval but was, in fact,
an early advertising gimmick.*

GREAT YARMOUTH,
the major Victorian fishing port,
was mainly known for herring, but
was also celebrated for fish pastes.

GILSON & SON'S CREAM OF PRAWNS,
an up-market version of potted
shrimp, was sold from one of
London's premier shopping streets.

THIS ANCHOVY PASTE LID
is a later version of the one top left.
The faint image and lack of border
are signs that a worn printing plate
was cunningly adapted and re-used.

AN ATTRACTIVE SEPIA PRINT
distinguishes this Victorian lid from
Fortnum & Mason in Piccadilly,
who still sell goods in ceramic pots.

Ray Duns

TOILETRY POTS

Victorian gentlemen used a great deal of highly scented hair oil to keep their hair in good condition and, in some cases, to attempt to restore it. Bears were a popular subject for the lid of their pomade pots, as bear grease was the basic ingredient of the most popular preparations. All the leading manufacturers produced bear subjects. Typical of them is The Bear Pit, originally produced by the Pratt factory in 1850, but reissued many times, with some slight variations. Some had an added dome over the ostrich cage and others came with a fancy border. Pomade was not, however, the only toiletry product to be sold in decorative pots. Tooth pastes and an assortment of creams, lotions and ointments were also packaged in this way.

FLAVOURED TOOTHPASTES ▲
4 *were as popular with Victorians as they are today. The portrait of the Queen dates this to the 1850s.*

THE BEAR PIT ▲
6 *came in several versions. In later ones, the dome on the cage on the left was replaced by some trees.*

ATKINSON'S BEAR GREASE, ▲
5 *sold from a Bond Street address, was not a cheap pomade; 2/6d (12½p) was a tidy sum in the 1850s.*

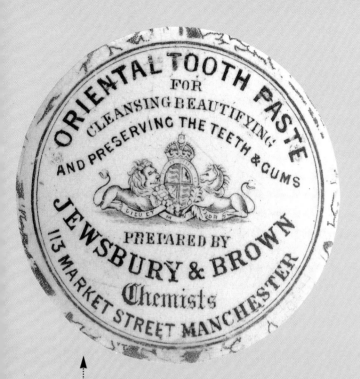

A MARBLED BORDER
and another fake royal coat of arms
decorate this lid. It isn't clear what
made the contents 'Oriental'. ◆4

ROSE-SCENTED COLD CREAM
was a standard product. This
heavily crazed pot was sold by the
Army & Navy Co-operative. ◆4

RUSSIAN BEAR'S GREASE
dominated the market; brown bears
were plentiful there. It had to be
scented to mask the rank smell. ◆5

THE LEGEND ON THIS LID
shows that pomade was sold as a
hair restorer as well as a dressing.
The Greek key border is unusual. ◆5

Roy Duns

53

COLLECTOR'S NOTES

Pot lids have been collected for some time, so it is unlikely that you will be lucky enough to spot them in car boot sales, junk shops and flea markets, though some enthusiasts do turn up interesting finds by excavating Victorian rubbish tips. Special auctions are held for collectors, and pot lids sometimes appear in general auctions. They are often sold in lots, which means you may have to buy several to get the one you particularly want.

There are so many types to choose from that most collectors concentrate on specific subjects; dogs, animals, birds, flowers, wars, exhibitions and portraits are just a few of the possibilities. Two of the most collectable subjects are bears and the Pegwell Bay series.

As a general rule, lids made before 1875 are more valued than those made after, and full colour prints are more valuable than those printed in one tone of ink. Lids which have extra gilt finishes, or come with decorated bases, usually cost more. Many manufacturers reissued their designs at regular intervals, sometimes with slight variations, which themselves make a specialized area of collecting.

Look out for lids that have the name of the goods' manufacturer in the design, either as part of the border or in the picture. Keep a special watch for the name 'Tatnell & Son' on Pegwell Bay subjects.

PEGWELL BAY

Pegwell Bay pots originally held potted shrimps. The future Queen Victoria sampled this delicacy on a visit to Ramsgate when she was a girl, and must have enjoyed them, as she issued a Royal Warrant to Tatnell & Son of Pegwell Bay when she came to the throne.

This led to a huge boom in sales, and all the major manufacturers made lids showing shrimpers, shells, fishing scenes or local landmarks. Even though these may display views of Ramsgate, Margate or Walmer Castle, they are still known as Pegwell Bay subjects. Many lids show the Belle Vue Tavern in Pegwell Bay itself.

Pegwell Bay subjects are found on very early lids, produced before 1860. These pots

COMPARE & CONTRAST

Because pot lids were mass produced by just a handful of firms, they all basically had the same dimensions; all the difference is in the decoration. Prints could be either multi-coloured or single-coloured. Some had a clear or an ornamental border, and on others the design was carried right to the edge.

The Russian bear is subdued by the British lion on a lid from the Crimean War period (1853-5).

The Shrimpers, one of Pratt's most popular lids, was first used in 1850, and was often reissued.

Monochrome prints usually had a border, even if it was only a black circle around the design.

Chris Barker

Most printed pot lids were round, but ovals, oblongs and squares like this one can also be found.

have flat tops, a black border and small crazing on the glaze. Lids produced between 1860 and 1875 are similar, but tend to be convex in shape and may lack a border. 'Late' pots, made between 1875 and 1900, can be recognized by their larger crazing and less brilliant colours.

LATER LIDS

Lids made after 1900 were intended for decorative use only, and were reissues of earlier designs. They are usually flat, with no crazing, and have holes in the top rim so they can be hung on a wall. They may be marked as reproductions on the underside.

It is possible to buy lids complete with the original pot, which are sometimes decorated themselves, but these are more expensive. As with all pottery, it is important to check the condition. Chips, cracks or repairs will lower the value, while any damage to the picture, unless it is a very rare example, may well make a lid worthless.

SEASIDE POTTERY

Sold in their thousands as a keepsake of a day by the sea, small pieces of seaside pottery are now collected both for their charm and as mementos of a bygone age

Ray Duns

The development of the railways in the mid-19th century opened up the British Isles to trippers and holiday-makers. Citizens of the Victorian industrial towns took to the new travel possibilities with enthusiasm, packing special excursion trains and turning sleepy seaside towns into bustling resorts.

Even a day out was a special event; people sought out keepsakes of their trips. Small pottery items suited the Victorian taste for busy, even cluttered, interiors, with every available surface crammed with ornaments, and were produced in great numbers. Every resort had its own vases, teapots and cruets.

Some of these items were hand-painted, with simple inscriptions. The red-bodied wares with a creamy glaze known as Torquay pottery were typical. Most pieces, though, were mass-produced in Europe, mainly in Germany, and imported by British wholesalers, who decorated them with transfer prints of local landmarks or printed crests before selling them on to the resorts.

The crested ware of W H Goss was of better than average quality. The models were produced in Britain and transfer-printed with the outline of the town crests which gave the pottery its name. This was then coloured in by hand-enamellers and the piece was re-fired.

In the 1920s, holiday habits began to change, and the once great demand for seaside souvenir pottery began to drop off.

Cheap and cheerful souvenir pottery is as much a part of the Great British Holiday as boarding houses, sand castles, saucy postcards and walks along the prom.

KEEPSAKE POTTERY

Seaside souvenirs had been available since the late 18th century when the first seaside resorts were established – Lowestoft, for example, was catering for the needs of holiday-makers at that time. However, the heyday of seaside pottery was in the 25 years leading up to World War 1, when railway excursion travel was at its peak. The Victorians and Edwardian collected seaside ware in both traditional and novelty designs. Novelties, in the shape of boats, shells or lighthouses, are the most collectable.

AN EDWARDIAN JUG *has been decorated with a mixture of coloured slip (on the rocks) and paint, and has a printed name.*

A CHINA EGG-CUP *has been given a soft, apricot glaze and a legend in gilt gothic lettering.*

THIS PEPPER POT *was originally part of a cruet. In the Torquay style, it was made for sale in neighbouring Paignton around 1900.*

TOWN CRESTS *were a popular decoration. This opalescent pin-tray, made in Germany, sold in Great Yarmouth.*

A HIGH GLAZE *and rich colours are used in this slop bowl, made by one of the Torquay potteries in the Edwardian period.*

THIS JAUNTY BOAT *is a condiment set made just before World War 1. The price reflects the damage to the gilding.*

Duncan Smith

5 THIS COFFEE POT is immediately recognizable as Torquay ware by its typical and distinctive colours, despite the legend 'Ramsgate'.

A TRANSFER-PRINTED PLATE 2 like this reveals its recent date by the subject matter rather than any difference in the printing process.

3 THIS TORQUAY JUG carries the popular 'Rooster' design and was made in the 1920s for sale in the Devon resort of Teignmouth.

AN EDWARDIAN CHINA JUG 4 has here been given a gilt rim and an attractive transfer-printed view of the Coliseum in Rhyl.

S UNUSUAL SOUVENIR s made by Russians rking at a hospice in ange over Sands in the ke District during orld War 1.

THE COLISEUM, RHYL.

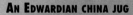

4 THIS CHINA SHAVING MUG was made in Germany, and was given its blue glaze, gilt rim and print in Britain.

A GERMAN CHINA SHOE 3 smothered with gilding, dates from around 1910 and was 'A Present from Margate'.

TORQUAY

THE SLIP DECORATION 3 of this pintray shows that it was made, as well as sold, in Torquay.

57

COMPARE & CONTRAST

The late Victorian watch stand with recessed cherub design (left) was mass-produced for several resorts. The Brighton egg cup (below) is a modern piece while the Torquay ware Whitstable jug (right) is Edwardian.

COLLECTOR'S NOTES

The sailing ship design was particularly common on Torquay ware. It is featured on this sugar bowl, dated between 1900-20, along with the Ryde place name and a motto.

There are all sorts of ways of building up a collection of souvenir pottery. You could concentrate on snapping up anything from a favourite resort, or collect particular items like souvenir pill boxes, candle-holders or watch stands from a variety of places.

Alternatively, you might like to collect particular makers, such as Goss, or types like the popular and distinctive Torquay pottery. Several factories in south Devon produced it from the local dark red clays, whose rich colour contrasted beautifully with the pottery's characteristic slipware glaze.

Slip is a mixture of clay and water produced in a variety of consistencies from a thin, milky mixture to quite a thick, creamy paste. Torquay pottery was then dipped or painted in a thin slip to produce a cream-coloured glaze. Thicker slips using different coloured clays were used to outline and fill in decorative designs.

Torquay pottery was by no means confined to Devon; the factories' wares were sold all over the place, and may well bear legends such as 'A present from Brighton' or simply 'Lowestoft'. Other pieces carried no place name, simply a motto.

WHERE TO BUY IT

Seaside pottery can be found in junk shops, flea markets and car boot, garage and jumble sales. Most of it can be bought relatively cheaply, although some Goss models can be pricey because Goss has always attracted enthusiasts; there was a craze for collecting it in Edwardian times. Several manufacturers, such as Willow Art, Carlton, Grafton and Shelley, copied Goss ware, while Arkinstall & Sons made crested wares under the trade names Arcadian, Swan and Clifton. All these makers clearly marked their products on the base, so there should be no confusion.

CARE AND REPAIR

Because examples of seaside pottery are generally so easy to find, chipped, cracked or otherwise damaged pieces are virtually worthless. Look out particularly for hairline cracks. Some objects may have been broken and repaired, but this should be obvious. Repaired rare pieces will fetch only about half as much as those in mint condition.

GOSS WARE

The small porcelain crested models made by W H Goss were enormously popular around the turn of the century, and are now avidly sought by collectors

John Hollingshead

William Henry Goss was born in 1833. By the age of 25 he was chief designer at the Spode works in Stoke-in-Trent. At this point he struck out on his own, producing ornamental wares in terracotta and Parian, a type of unglazed, fine-grained porcelain. He also discovered a method of setting gemstones in porcelain to create a range of costume jewellery.

In the mid-1880s, Goss's son, Adolphus, joined the firm. While no potter, Adolphus Goss had a genius for marketing, and saw an opportunity to expand the family business. His father had been producing specially commissioned commemorative pottery bearing heraldic emblems for various schools, colleges and hospitals. Adolphus saw that such wares would make excellent souvenirs for the ever-growing legions of people who had been liberated by increased wages, leisure time and the railway network to explore their native land on day trips and other holidays.

Over the next 20 years, the tireless Adolphus criss-crossed the country, building up a network of more than 1,000 local agents, each responsible for promoting their local coats of arms, which could be placed on any one of upwards of 600 small, mass-produced named models. The first of these were copied from museum pieces, but the later ones reproduced animals, lighthouses, fossils, fonts, statuary and crosses, among other things.

Each piece was hollow and moulded in porcelain. They were fired for up to a week in a high-temperature kiln, cleaned and sanded, then the Goss trademark was applied before glazing and refiring. The black outline of the required coat of arms was transfer-printed onto the piece and hand-coloured and gilded before being fired for the last time in small enamelling kilns.

COUNTRY COTTAGES

Although the heraldic crested wares made up the bulk of the company's sales, Goss also made a handsome and popular series of hand-painted buildings known as Goss Cottages, as well as domestic wares. Perhaps the most distinctive of these was the Bag-ware tea service, in which each piece was made to look like a draw-string bag tied with blue ribbon. Crests also appear on domestic ware.

Crested ware was never as popular after World War 1 as it was before, and the Goss family sold out to a competitor, Arcadian China, in 1929. Standards increasingly fell, and the models lost much of their crispness and definition. The factory closed in 1944.

Though they were often derided as poor man's porcelain, the models, busts and crested ware produced by W H Goss & Co graced millions of mantelpieces in the late Victorian and Edwardian periods, and were seriously collected in the first 30 years of the century. More recently the factory's products have been rediscovered as relatively inexpensive and inexhaustible collectables that give a real flavour of the innocent pleasures of a time within living memory but still very remote from the hurly-burly of modern life.

NAMED MODELS

More than 7,000 different heraldic devices have been recorded on Goss ware, many of them intended solely for the export market. At the local agent's request, just about any device could be applied to any named model, no matter how inappropriate. The agent for Blackpool was especially zealous, and the town's arms can be found on almost anything, even the great pyramid of Gizeh. A named model with the coat of arms of the town that inspired the piece – the Maldon incendiary bomb with the Maldon crest, for example – usually fetches a higher price than the same model featuring any other design.

The most collectable range of named models as a whole is probably the animals, though some of the more obscure crosses and fonts can fetch very high prices.

THIS WARWICK BEAR AND STAFF *has no heraldic crest and was presumably sold as an ornament rather than a souvenir.*

THIS SEAT *bears the Blackpool crest. The thin gilt stripe marks it as a 'gaudy gold' version.*

THE HASLEMERE ARMS *decorate this model of an ancient covered jar, which must have its lid if it is to be of any value.*

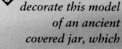

THE HEXHAM TOWN CREST *makes this version of the seat slightly more valuable than the one from Blackpool shown above.*

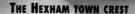

Ray Duns

THIS URN FROM READING MUSEUM 3
*is known as the 'Reading Jug'.
Though it has the 'correct' arms, it is
not a particularly popular piece,
hence the relatively low price.*

3 **THE WELSH TOWN OF BETTWS-Y-COED**
*seems a strange place to find a
replica of the Las Palmas
Earthenware Jug of the
Canary Islands, but it was a
very popular model.*

4 **THE HEREFORD KETTLE**
*is modelled on a
terracota one in the
town's museum, and
bears the arms of
Tintern Abbey, a
tourist trap even in
Edwardian times.*

2 **IPSWICH**
*houses the
original of this ancient
ewer, here decorated with
the arms of Lucerne in
Switzerland.*

A WELSH MILK CAN 4
*is a suitable
bearer for the coat
of arms of the
town of Denbigh.*

THIS SHOE 5
*is modelled on one worn by the
fisherwomen of Boulogne, but here
turns up bearing the arms of
Whitstable in north-east Kent.*

THE GOSS AGENTS IN CEYLON 5
*were very active, and a wide
range of products bear the
national emblem. This one is an
old bottle found in Canterbury.*

COTTAGES, CUPS AND BUSTS

The Goss cottage range was started in 1893. Some of them were produced as nightlights, as well as models. Some were glazed, some not. Each of the models was hand-painted and should have a paintress's mark on the base, in one of the colours she used on the piece.

The hollow Parian busts that were the firm's main line before the heraldic ware was developed are less sought after today. Parian, an unglazed, soft-paste porcelain with trace mineral elements that gave it a silky sheen, was introduced by Copeland & Garrett and Minton in the 1840s and was greatly valued for producing statuary and busts because of its resemblance to fine carved stone. W H Goss was a master of it, and made various small technical adjustments to the manufacturing process.

The firm also manufactured various porcelain and Parian tablewares, but these are rarely the subject of great collector interest.

4 ▸ SOME PARIAN BUSTS *produced by Goss are quite small. This one of William Shakespeare is about 12.7cm/5in tall and is a companion to the one of Anne `Hathaway shown to its right.*

THE POET JOHN MILTON, 6 *as befits his stature, is the subject of a finely-modelled, full-size Parian bust.*

ANNE HATHAWAY, *Shakespeare's wife, may seem like an unusual subject for a bust, but it was probably made for sale to tourists in Stratford-upon-Avon.*

5

WILLIAM SHAKESPEARE'S HOUSE 6
in Stratford-upon-Avon, one of the commonest
Goss cottages, clearly shows the detailed work
that went into their painting: notice the delicate
diamond-pane leading in the windows.

ANNE HATHAWAY'S COTTAGE, 5
like others in the series, was painted
according to a colour scheme faithfully
adapted from the real thing.

4 **THIS MUG**
is one of a range with the
letters of the alphabet
worked in blue forget-me-nots.

SHAKESPEARE'S HOUSE 5
was produced in two
sizes. This smaller
version was as closely
modelled and
authentically painted as
the larger one.

5 **ROBBIE BURNS' BIRTHPLACE IN AYRSHIRE**
is, perhaps, more accurately described as a
cottage than others in the Goss range.

Ray Duns

COLLECTOR'S NOTES

The wide range of models and prices available make Goss ware very appealing to today's collectors. There is plenty of scope for making specialized collections. Some people collect models bearing the crests of a particular town or group of towns, while others concentrate on collecting as many variations as possible of a certain type of model, such as animals, lighthouses, crosses and so on.

Although the high prices fetched by some

Ray Duns

W H Goss also produced commemorative ware. This coronation mug dates from 1937, towards the end of the factory's life.

Goss ware is changing the situation, it isn't the sort of thing you are likely to find being sold by a specialist dealer in ceramics. It's often offered at auction, though, and you should be able to find some at an antiques fair. Market stalls and bric-a-brac shops are also a good bet, while jumble sales, boot fairs and the dustier corners of an elderly relative's china cabinet may provide good hunting.

BRIGHT AND BEAUTIFULLY MADE

Much of the appeal of Goss ware is in the jewel-bright enamel used to decorate it. It's best to avoid pieces where this, or the gilding, has been rubbed and worn, or where transfer prints have peeled or faded. Goss models were a byword for their crisp modelling. Ones that have blurred, indistinct outlines may be fakes or have been produced late in the company's life, when standards had slipped and worn moulds were not so often replaced.

Look carefully for chips or cracks. These will make the less expensive pieces more or less worthless and, if repairable, will halve the price of rare pieces. Repairs can be made

DESIGN
IN FOCUS   HERALDIC CHINA

The named models were usually based on museum pieces, works of art or local landmarks. The Welsh leek is none of these, but proved a popular souvenir all over the principality. Rare in being partially painted, for the sake of authenticity, this leek shows the sharp, well-moulded edges typical of Goss. The transfer-printed outline of Crickhowell's arms has been handpainted in strong, vivd colours.

❶   CRISP, CLEAN MODELLING

❷   UNUSUAL PAINTED DECORATION

❸   TRANSFER-PRINTED OUTLINE

❹   BRIGHT COLOURS IN THE COAT OF ARMS

almost invisibly, but they will still detract somewhat from a piece's value.

From 1883 onwards, all Goss pieces were marked with a bird of prey, punningly known as the Gosshawk, with W H GOSS printed beneath. Very early pieces have an impressed mark, and those made after 1931 had the word ENGLAND added.

Forged pieces of Goss ware are rarely encountered, although you may find pieces of crested china made by other manufacturers, such as Shelley, Swan or Willow Art, with faked marks. These marks may look distorted, and the colour and texture of the piece beneath the mark is often different from the rest. The majority of them have not been fired on, and will come off if you scratch them with a fingernail.

All Goss models have a full description of the subject on the base and are marked with a hawk and the factory name.

SALT & PEPPER SHAKERS

You can bring some fun to mealtimes and start an intriguing collection by specializing in novelty cruet sets. You can even join a club of like-minded enthusiasts

Victorian mealtimes were formal affairs with immaculate cloths, gleaming silver, and glittering glassware. Salt, pepper and other condiment containers were usually made of glass and set in silver or silver-plated holders that were known as cruets. As the century drew to a close, manners and mealtimes became more relaxed and the stately cruet gave way to the less formal alternative of salt and pepper shakers, with or without the addition of a lidded mustard pot.

Perhaps the first unusual ones were German imports and, although these are nowadays classed as novelties, they were finely made in porcelain. They often took the shape of a central figure of a boy or girl, with a basket on each side containing the salt and pepper.

Some sets were made as souvenirs for the traveller and can be found with the transfer-printed message 'A souvenir from...'. A common shape was that of binoculars, the removeable cylindrical shakers being set in the eyepieces. Shakers were often decorated with coloured transfers of scenic views, such as 'Holyhead, South Stack'. Others were in the shape of small boats, gondolas or lighthouses.

FRUIT AND VEG

Containers in the shape of fruit and vegetables have always been popular as tableware and this extends to shakers. You can find shakers in the shape of cauliflowers, tomatoes, apples, pineapples, strawberries, grapes and bananas. Oddly enough, fruit (which needs no salt) seems to outnumber vegetables.

Flowers were not ignored either. Charming shakers were, for example, made to resemble pansies or roses. Other food-related shakers are shaped like loaves, wedges of cheese and, appropriately enough, eggs in egg cups.

Transport was a popular subject, with cars and ships dominating. Souvenir sets decorated with a town crest are sought after. Planes and steam engines are rarer, as are wartime shakers featuring submarines or zeppelins. Covered wagons and stagecoaches also appeared, while donkeys and carts were made in large numbers. Shakers with domestic appeal include those in the form of cottages, beehives, sheaves of corn and haystacks.

Figural shakers were imported in large numbers from Japan and Germany, as well as being made in Britain. The people depicted range from jolly monks and cheerful dwarves to coy children or colourful American Indians.

Nudes have always been popular and these are usually found reclining provocatively. Saucy shakers were also made and usually featured a couple in a naughty posture. Some shakers were modelled as complete figures, others merely as heads.

The animal kingdom was not forgotten either. Ducks, hens, owls, pheasants and penguins, dogs, cats, squirrels, elephants and pigs were all made in large numbers.

Miniature shakers were made as novelty items or for use on a breakfast tray, as they are too small to hold much salt and pepper.

Novelty salt and pepper shakers are amusing and are therefore great fun to collect. Much of their pleasure lies in sharing them with others – guests will remark on them at the meal table, and a shelf or cabinet display will also prove a lively conversation piece.

Ray Duns

TWO CLOWNS' HEADS 5 *on a stand which has a central finger grip. This German-made salt and pepper set was produced during the period 1910 to 1920.*

FIGURES

Prices can vary from a nominal amount to three figures, depending on the age, rarity and design, thus giving the collector plenty of choice.

As there is such variety, you can afford to be fussy and reject those with damage, although if the price is right and the shakers are rare or different, it can still be worth buying them. Look out for cracks and chips, especially on handles, spoons and projecting pieces such as hands.

The Japanese produced shakers with a lustred finish and this can wear badly with use and have a rubbed appearance; avoid these. Base stoppers are frequently missing as the cork crumbles with age, but this is not necessarily a drawback unless the shakers are to be used, in which case plastic stoppers can be bought as replacements.

4 *MRS GAMP* *and Sam Weller are two well-known fictional characters immortalized by the novelist Charles Dickens. These salt and pepper shakers were made by the Goebel factory during the period 1948 to 1953.*

A JAPANESE SET 5 *from the 1920s, featuring a maid carrying two eggs on a tray – the salt and pepper. Beside her, acting as the mustard pot, is the hen that laid the eggs. The set was also made without the mustard pot.*

A DUTCH COUPLE 4 *in traditional costume. They were made in Germany in the 1920s. Their hands fit together but are not actually joined.*

Ray Duns

SALT AND PEPPER POTS

modelled as airmen, although they have strangely feminine or child-like faces. They originated in Germany in the 1930s and were part of a series.

TWO CHEEKY-FACED BELLHOPS,

each carrying a message and a bunch of flowers. These salt and pepper shakers were manufactured at the Goebel factory between 1923 and 1935.

THE TOBY FAMILY

are an English-made Carlton Ware set. They may be found in their original presentation box.

A SAILOR AND HIS GIRLFRIEND.

This is a German-made salt and pepper set from the 1930s. She sports a light blue beret and he carries three red roses. Each carries a similar bag. There are many similar sets.

A DELIGHTFUL SET

that is an instantly recognizable caricature of Stan Laurel and Oliver Hardy. This comic duo was produced by the English Beswick factory in 1934. They sit neatly on a stand decorated with their bow ties.

TRANSPORT & NOVELTIES

AEROPLANE SETS,
including modern fighter jets, are quickly snapped up by collectors. This prop plane, made in the years 1916-1939, is embellished with a transfer of 'Welsh Ladies'.

THIS CERAMIC VINTAGE CAR
is a German-made condiment set, dating from the 1920s. The pepper shaker forms the bonnet, the mustard pot is in the centre and the open salt is in the boot.

OCEAN LINERS
are easily turned into condiment sets. Here the funnels are the salt and pepper shakers and the mustard pot is in the centre. Many were sold as souvenirs.

Victorian cruets were often three-piece sets with an open salt container, a pepper shaker and a mustard pot. The covered mustard sometimes came with its own spoon but this is often missing now.

Ensure that the lid to the mustard pot is present; mustard pots always have lids. Make sure, too, that the lid matches the pot and is not a replacement. The shakers should also match and obviously be a pair and not a marriage of similar containers. Check that the stand (if present) is right for the set and not a later addition. The shakers should sit comfortably in any depressions and not move around too much.

German, Czechoslovakian and Japanese manufacturers rarely marked their cruets and shakers, although one can occasionally find the words 'Japan' or 'Foreign' on the base. Makers such as Carlton, Beswick and Royal Winton will have their name printed or stamped on the base. However, if the shaker is small and was intended to be complete with a stand, it is the stand that will be marked, not the shaker.

THIS GREEN CERAMIC FISH
is a German-made condiment set dating from the 1920s or 1930s. It is a souvenir piece overprinted, appropriately enough, with the message 'A Present from Bognor'.

THESE TWO BIRDS,
based on parakeets or lovebirds, are salt and pepper shakers. The German manufacturers made a series of 12 bird designs in a variety of colours in the 1920s.

PANNIERS ◄ 4
were an easy way of holding salt and pepper shakers. Here they are slung across the back of a cow, with a mustard pot in the centre. This piece was made in Germany in the 1920s.

4 ► **A PANSY CONDIMENT SET**
produced in the 1920s. It has an open salt on the left with the mustard pot in the centre. This set was one of a series of six flower sets produced by the German manufacturers. Their poppy set proved popular.

4 **MADE IN GERMANY AND SOLD ALL OVER EUROPE,**
this elephant often had a picture of a resort on one side. It was made between the wars.

MADE BY THE ROYAL BAYREUTH POTTERY 6
in Germany these unusual 'Devil on Cards' shakers date from the 1920s.

WALT DISNEY 6
shakers are popular. These German-made Mickey Mouse shakers from the 1920s are very rare.

5 **THE THREE WISE MONKEYS**
lend themselves to a three-piece condiment set and appear in many different designs. These are German from the 1920s.

Ray Duns

69

COLLECTOR'S NOTES

Salt and pepper shakers are easily found at antiques fairs, car boot sales and at local auctions. Some dealers specialize in them and a whole stall of shakers can look quite stunning.

It is perhaps the ceramic salt and pepper shakers made from the 1930s onwards that are the most colourful, imaginative and most easily found today. Some sets consist of a salt and pepper shaker with or without a stand, other sets include a lidded mustard pot. There is such variety it is hard to know where to start. Some collectors aim at a theme, perhaps transport or figural, while others collect those made by a particular factory such as Carlton, Royal Winton (Grimwades) or Beswick.

THE FACTORIES

The Japanese produced shakers in huge quantities and the best known are those by Marutomo. These are extremely colourful and can be found fairly easily and reasonably cheaply. Less readily available and more expensive are those made by Noritake.

The Goebel factory produced a series of cheerful monks – the Cardinal condiment set – and shakers can be found in both brown and red habits, the latter being more collectable.

Beswick made figures, including a Sairey Gamp pepper and a Mr Micawber salt shaker, and Laurel and Hardy as a pair. Royal Winton produced several versions of cottages, and also made water mills, beehive and pixie sets. Flowers were featured in sets such as Primula and Gera (based on the geranium) while they also produced 'chintz' patterned shakers in a huge variety of designs. Carlton ware shakers include those based on leaf forms, flowers and vivid red

CONTA & BOEHME SHAKER

This girl with twin baskets on her back – one is the salt shaker, one the pepper – was made in porcelain by the German firm of Conta & Boehme during the period 1895 to 1907. They also made a similar set featuring a blond-haired boy standing between two baskets. These are rare and valuable although the company, based in Thuringia, exported widely in the 19th century. The outbreak of World War 1 destroyed its export sales.

Ray Duns

This valuable three-piece cottage set was made by the German firm Sitzendorf in 1920. The top of the mustard handle is a head sticking out of the dormer window. The outbuildings are the salt and pepper.

tomatoes. They also produced bird sets, the best known being a pair of pheasants. Look out, too, for their three-piece Toby Family cruet set, based on Toby jug characters.

Some shakers are not readily identifiable as a pair and if you buy one as a single, it can be difficult to work out what its companion should be. For example, a scrum-capped head would accompany a rugby ball, a pair of fish go with a fishing creel and so on.

ON THE NOD

'Nodding' cruets have been popular from the turn of the century. The majority of these have a hollow, oblong base set with two large holes intended to take the salt and pepper containers. The shakers were usually figural and sat loosely in the holes, supported on two lugs which allowed them to rock gently when the base was moved.

Among animal shakers, frogs, dogs and fish are extremely collectable, while figural shakers such as nudes and 'naughties', clowns, pixies, elves, gnomes and dwarves are also sought after. Nursery rhyme and Disney characters are worth searching for; look out for Humpty Dumpty and Mickey Mouse figures. Cottages are also popular.

NOVELTY TEAPOTS

Some speak of country living and all things English; some satirize, some are sentimental and some surreal; all novelty teapots, though, add an extra fillip to one of Britain's best-loved social rituals

The British love affair with tea has produced an enormous variety of interesting collectables, but none as ingenious and imaginative as the novelty teapots that have been made since the 18th century. Some have been potted in unusual shapes, others just painted and decorated, but all have been fashioned to resemble something other than a humble teapot.

Staffordshire potteries produced them in the shapes of houses, camels, squirrels and monkeys in the 1730s, when tea-drinking was still a very expensive pastime and customers were prepared to pay for conversation pieces.

In 1759, Josiah Wedgwood and his partner, Thomas Whieldon, produced globular teapots realistically potted and painted as cabbages, cauliflowers, melons and pineapples. They proved so successful that other factories copied them, without achieving the same fine results.

By the 19th century, novelty teapots were well-established pieces. Some of the best were made from moulded and richly-glazed majolica, especially by the Minton factory, while the Irish firm, Belleek, made shell-shaped teapots in delicate porcelain with a pearly lustre.

TWENTIETH-CENTURY POTS

Novelty teapots have been made throughout the 20th century, particularly in the years between the world wars, when there was a fad for them. Advertising figures like the Michelin man and the Guinness toucan have provided subjects, while fashions in design, such as art deco, and art movements, especially surrealism, have inspired potters to ever-wilder flights of fancy, many of them one-off or very limited edition collectors' items.

Several traditional subjects remained popular. Beswick, Price's, Sadler's, Lingard Webster and Grimwade's all made teapots in the form of idyllic thatched and/or half-timbered cottages, most with roses round the door, while cats, dogs, cockerels and elephants were among the animal themes. Beswick produced a panda teapot in 1939, while Minton reintroduced their majolica monkey, first produced in the 1870s, in 1932.

Transport was an important new theme. James Sadler produced a racing car, while Sudlow's and Beswick made aeroplanes. Coaches, motorcycles and even tanks were made to take tea.

Figure subjects include Sadler's Daintee Ladye, with the main body of the pot hiding beneath her crinolines, and Beswick's popular series based on Dickens's characters.

Animals, people and buildings are among the most popular traditional themes explored by the makers of novelty teapots. Some, like the half-timbered inn below, are also perfectly practical for brewing and pouring tea. Other pieces – the kneeling camel is a good example – are less so, losing heat quickly and pouring irregularly.

Roy Duns

ELEVEN FOR TEA

There is an enormous range of prices for 20th-century novelty teapots, ranging from single figures to many thousands. The 11 examples pictured here give some idea both of prices and the variety of subjects that are likely to be encountered.

The hunger for Clarice Cliff's work, even those pieces designed some time after her heyday in the 1930s, makes her Teepee Teapot the most expensive shown here, but one-off creations by leading lights in the design world cost much more; the Christopher Dresser pot on page 1224 is valued at around £50,000. At the other end of the price range are the various country cottages and pieces mass-produced in the last 30 years or so. Among the mid-priced pots, most of them originating in the inter-war years, ones with a transport theme tend to attract a premium price, while portrait pots lag behind.

VARIATIONS OF THE COUNTRY COTTAGE DESIGN ❸
were made by many firms. This one is 50 years old, but very similar versions are being produced today.

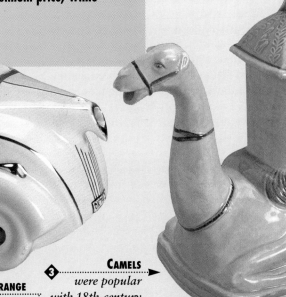

THE RACING CARS ❺
of the 1930s were the model for this James Sadler teapot, complete with chrome trim and helmeted driver. The model bears the punnish licence plate OKT42.

THE INTARSIO RANGE ❼
produced by the Foley Pottery at the turn of the century caricatured prominent political figures of the day.

CAMELS ❸
were popular with 18th-century potters. This one, burdened with a strange 'howdah' and out-of-scale passenger where its hump should be, is modern.

JAMES SADLER'S AEROPLANE, ❻
with wings for a lid and an opening for pouring where the propeller should be, is typical of the 1930s in its subject matter and streamlined style.

CLARICE CLIFF 8
designed the Teepee
Teapot around 1950 for
the Canadian market. It is
marked 'Greetings from
Canada' on the base.

BESWICK POTTERY 4
made four teapots based
on characters by Dickens.
Sairy Gamp, released in
1939, was the first.

BUSES AND COACHES 6
don't have the
glamour of aeroplanes or
racing cars, but they do
have their fans. Beswick
made a coach in 1938,
but this one, by
Sudlow's, is earlier.

A HALF-TIMBERED INN 4
is a welcome variation
on the country cottage.
The colourful detail of
the mullioned windows,
tiles, ivy and inn sign
suggest Ye Olde Swan is
modelled on a real pub.

4 **A SEASIDE POSTCARD**
captioned 'Has any-
one seen my little
Willy?' inspired this
teapot. The rotund
bather brandishes a
copy of Picture Post as
a spout, suggesting
this 1930s teapot may
have been made as a
promotional item.

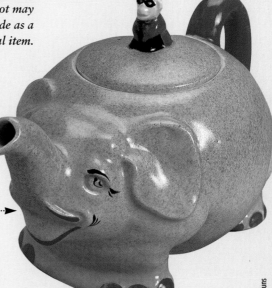

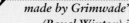

5 **THIS ENGAGING ELEPHANT**
made by Grimwade's
(Royal Winton) is
obviously a circus
animal, ridden by a tiny
costumed monkey who
makes the knob on the lid.

Ray Duns

COLLECTOR'S NOTES

Teapots are fun to collect and novelty ones even more so, whether you try to make a specialized collection or simply go for the ones that particularly amuse or interest you.

Early teapots by famous makers such as Minton, Wedgwood and Worcester are difficult to find and expensive to buy. They tend to turn up only at high-class antiques fairs or at fine art auctions. Teapots from the 20th century, and particularly the 1930s, are much more readily available and can be found not only at antiques fairs and at auctions but also in general second-hand shops and occasionally in flea markets and boot sales.

Most 20th-century pots are marked with a maker's backstamp, but not all. Sadler's Daintee Ladye and Motor Car were not always marked, for instance, and in the case of the Daintee Ladye, where several similar pots have been made by other companies, this can cause confusion. The car, however, is identifiable by its licence plate, OKT42.

CHECKING FOR CHIPS AND CRACKS

Examine any teapot carefully before you buy it. The spout, lid and inner rim are all prone to damage. Ensure there are no chips, cracks, or signs of restoration. Make sure, too, that the handle isn't cracked and that it hasn't been repaired or restored.

Fine glazing cracks can and do occur to the interior of any teapot, especially if it has been well used. The interior is often also heavily stained. Soaking for a few hours in a weak solution of household bleach should remove staining and clear up the crazing, but don't leave the bleach in too long or the smell will linger.

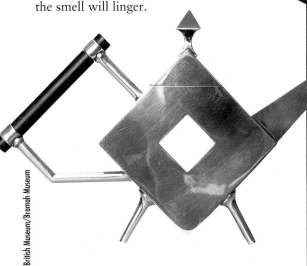

Although it looks very modern, this teapot, a one-off creation by the designer Christopher Dresser, was made in the late 19th century.

British Museum/Bramah Museum

CLASSIC TEAPOTS

By Courtesy of the Trustees of the Wedgwood Museum

Royal Doulton (Minton)

The realistically moulded and coloured vegetables, like the cauliflower (above), produced by Wedgwood and Whieldon in the late 18th century, are now very collectable.

Minton's majolica monkey teapot (above) was one of the most successful novelties of the 19th century, so much so that it was relaunched to catch the 1930s fad.

By courtesy of the Dyson Perrins Museum Trust

Made by Worcester in 1881, the Aesthetic Teapot (above) satirizes the art movement led by Oscar Wilde. The other side shows a young woman. The octagonal house (right) in white saltglaze is typical of the time it was made, around 1740.

Bramah Museum/Andrew McIntosh Patrick

ART DECO TABLEWARE

Decorative ceramics from the 1920s and 30s bring a welcome burst of colour and zest into the modern dining room, just as they did when they were first introduced

Ronald McKechnie

Pottery designs by Clarice Cliff and Susie Cooper have become synonymous with the art deco period. The work of both designers is still easy to find, but well out of most people's price range.

Art deco had no single founder – it had a variety of influences including cubism and African art. Vibrant and energetic, it proved so popular that it was soon applied to almost everything – from architecture and furniture to textiles and jewellery.

In the 1920s, the introduction of art deco tableware came as a breath of fresh air. After the drabness of the war years nothing could be more welcome in the country's dining rooms than the brightly coloured designs of the latest plates, cups and bowls.

The new tableware designs were instantly popular, being both novel and inexpensive, and people jumped at the chance of an affordable way to keep up with the latest fashions.

ANGULAR LINES

The most noticeable characteristic of the art deco style was the geometric patterns, used in both painted designs and shapes, many of which were based on angular lines. Many British craft potters felt that clay didn't really lend itself to these angular shapes and they shunned the new style, refusing to go to the extremes of the Continental potteries. But other manufacturers exploited the art deco style to the hilt. Many designs were aimed at the younger generation, who found these cheap and cheerful pieces ideal.

It was Clarice Cliff who first saw the possibilities of applying art deco designs to everyday tableware. Her products were a world away from the staid, traditional dinner services that were popular in previous decades.

While working at Wilkinson's Newport pottery, Clarice Cliff produced an innovative range of tableware decorated with diamond shapes and semicircles painted in bold shades of blue, orange, yellow and black.

A BURST OF COLOUR

Despite the initial worries of retailers, these new lines were eagerly snapped up. Encouraged by this success, Clarice Cliff produced range after range of new patterns, using stylized flowers, landscapes, houses and windmills, all in the bold and vibrant colours that became her trademark.

At about the same time, Susie Cooper was also devising radical new floral and geometric patterns at AE Gray & Co. Both potters made use of the improved production methods, although they still used hand-painting.

Thanks to their popularity, the output of Wilkinson's and Gray's was soon dramatically boosted. Other factories followed suit and by the mid-1930s, major department stores such as Harrods and Heal's were selling art deco ware produced by established firms like Wedgwood, Worcester and Royal Doulton.

CLARICE CLIFF

Clarice Cliff did most of her training at A J Wilkinson's Royal Staffordshire Pottery, which she joined in 1916. Her obvious talent was soon rewarded, and she acquired her own studio at the company's Newport Pottery in 1927.

Within a year, the Newport Pottery was turned over entirely to producing her 'Bizarre' range. Her early designs consisted of geometric patterns outlined in black and painted in bright colours. Later, she went on to floral designs, which proved equally popular. An all-time favourite was the 'Crocus' pattern, with its several colourways.

She was also renowned for her use of distinctive and unconventional shapes, including 'Conical', 'Stamford' (a D-shape with flat sides), and 'Bonjour' (circular with flat sides). All these shapes were decorated with the popular 'Crocus' pattern at one time or another. Later patterns included 'Rhodanthe', in different shades of orange and brown, 'Viscaria' and 'Aurea'.

Clarice Cliff constantly experimented with glazes and firing techniques. She also created such an abundance of designs that by the end of her career there were over 2000 patterns and more than 500 shapes.

7 **DINNER PLATE**
made in 1930 as part of the 'Fantasque' range.

6 **CONICAL SUGAR SHAKER**
c1930, decorated with the popular 'Crocus' pattern.

6 **CIGARETTE AND MATCH HOLDER**
from the 'Bizarre' range, made in 1933.

7 **BISCUIT PLATE**
decorated with the 'Melon' pattern. It was made in 1930 as part of the 'Fantasque' range.

SPILL VASE ◄ ········· ◆6
c1929, decorated
with the 'Umbrellas
and Rain' design.

RARE NOVELTY TEAPOT 7 ········· ►
titled 'Bones
and Butcher';
it is part of the
'Bizarre' range.

SUGAR BOWL ◄ ········· ◆6
from 1935, with a bold geometric
design in the 'Bonjour' shape.

TOAST RACK ◄ ········· ◆5
decorated with the
best-selling 'Crocus'
pattern, from 1936.

TEAPOT IN 'BONJOUR' ········· 7
shape, which
matches the
teacup below.

TEACUP 6 ········· ►
produced in 1927 as
part of a matching
set, comprising two
cups, a teapot
and sugar bowl.

Ranald McKechnie

77

SUSIE COOPER

It was Susie Cooper's daring use of bright colours and geometric and banded patterns which first brought her recognition. In 1922 she went to work at A E Gray, a Burslem company specializing in pottery decoration. The Susie Cooper name soon appeared on her designs as well as the Gray's mark.

By 1930 she had set up her own business, buying in 'white ware' and decorating it, just as she'd done at Gray's. The following year she started designing as well as decorating her own pieces, contracting Wood & Sons (also in Burslem) to produce them.

Among her most successful shapes were 'Kestrel' and 'Curlew'. Particularly elegant and simple, they were as modern in concept as her patterns. Most designs consisted of stylized flowers, spiral motifs, simple banding and *sgraffito* (where the design was cut into the glaze).

In the 1930s she experimented with lithographic transfers. As well as creating new shapes and patterns for this method, she also adapted her old ones. New shapes such as 'Falcon', 'Rex' and 'Spiral' were decorated with lithographic transfers of patterns such as 'Acorn' and 'Nosegay'.

◆ 6 LARGE SERVING PLATTER *(top) from the 1930s, decorated with a simple ship design.*

◆ 5 HORS D'OEUVRES DISH *finely decorated with subtle leaf patterns in green and beige.*

SMALL TEAPOT ◆ ❹
with a
lithographed
tulip design using
the popular shades of
green and pink.

TEAPOT ▲ ❹
in the 'Kestrel'
shape, which was
popular for decades.

DINNER PLATE ❸
with a particu-
larly light and
delicate design.

HAND-PAINTED VASE ⑥
decorated with an
unusual abstract design
based on leaves.

COFFEE SET ❼
made in fine
pottery at the
Crown works.
It came with
a matching
dinner service.

VEGETABLE DISH ❹
from the 'Kestrel'
range. The
banded pattern
around the lid
has been hand-
painted.

Ronald McKechnie

79

COLLECTOR'S NOTES

Although most British art deco tableware was made for the mass market and was relatively cheap, it has become highly collectable and is probably now too valuable for daily use.

The most expensive pieces are Clarice Cliff's hand-painted designs. Some of her more affordable ranges are the tea and dinner services with patterns such as 'Crocus' and 'Rhodanthe'. Among the rarest are patterns that were unsuccessfully launched and quickly withdrawn, such as 'Delicia' and 'Goldstone'.

A complete set of Clarice Cliff may be prohibitively expensive; a cheaper alternative is to acquire a tea or coffee service. You can easily

REAL ? FAKE

Look out for fakes, especially when buying expensive Clarice Cliff designs. The jam pot on the right is a rare example of the 'Target' pattern, while the jug on the left is a crude reproduction.

Ray Duns

CLOSE UP on MAKERS' MARKS

Virtually all Clarice Cliff and Susie Cooper ceramics are stamped. Clarice Cliff's work usually has her facsimile signature, together with the name of the pattern and the name of the manufacturer. Likewise, Susie Cooper's ware is usually marked with her name somewhere on the back.

Clarice Cliff's famous facsimile signature, featured on most pieces.

An early piece made by Susie Cooper at the Crown works, after she left A E Gray & Co in 1930.

Fine hand-painting like this is the unmistakable mark of an original work.

A Susie Cooper piece made at the Crown works.

This Fantasque stamp was used by Cliff from 1929 to 1934.

Ray Duns

build up a set by buying odd pieces of the same design, since most of her popular designs were made in large quantities.

Although most designers were overshadowed by her fame, Clarice Cliff designs aren't the only examples worth collecting. Susie Cooper's work is often thought to be much more sophisticated. Her ceramics are usually cheaper and may prove a better buy.

It's worth looking out for other ranges produced in the art deco style. Although these sets are characterized by their somewhat less distinctive designs, they are no less authentic. A 21-piece tea set by the Shelley Pottery, for example, can be bought for a fraction of the price of an equivalent set by Clarice Cliff. Services by factories such as Wedgwood and Royal Doulton are also worthwhile buys, as are pieces by Carlton Ware and Beswick.

FAKES AND REPRODUCTIONS

Although most art deco tableware isn't worth faking, one exception is Clarice Cliff, whose more expensive pieces have been copied. Although the backstamp may be convincing, fakes can often be identified by a poor standard of painting, an uneven glaze and an unglazed bottom rim that may be thinner than that found on genuine pieces. Reproductions aren't such a problem because they will be marked as such, but they are of little value.

One of the main factors to consider when buying ceramics is condition – whether you're buying a single piece or a complete service, it should be as close to perfect as possible. While some scratching of the glaze is to be expected, chipping or cracking obviously detracts from the value. Colours should be clean and bright, although allowance should be made for slight fading through use. Clarice Cliff's dark blue colouring is particularly prone to fading.

CHILDREN'S CHINA

With their colourful illustrations and nursery rhymes, children's crockery and bedroom ornaments are just as popular with collectors as they are with children themselves

Attractively illustrated china, made especially for children, reached the height of its popularity in the inter-war years.

Rabbits, cats, dogs and cartoon characters were frequent guests at nursery meals between the wars – they all featured on every child's favourite crockery. Once you had eaten up your greens, a familiar face or scene would be revealed as a reward. There were also china night-lights, bookends, money boxes, ornaments and toilet sets, and their charming designs ensure that they are still popular today.

Educational plates decorated with worthy advice and nursery rhymes had been popular in the 19th century but, by the early 20th century, children's china had taken on its modern form – popular children's characters were featured and the emphasis was on fun. A tea set featuring characters from *Alice in Wonderland*, which Royal Doulton first produced in 1906, was still available in the early 1930s. Although this and Royal Doulton's other lines did well, they were overtaken when, in 1934, the Bunnykins design was introduced and became popular enough to overtake them all.

BUNNYKINS

The artist behind Bunnykins was Sister Mary Barbara, a nun who taught history at a convent school. She was the daughter of Cuthbert Bailey, General Manager of Royal Doulton at Burslem. On the look-out for new designs for children, he remembered his daughter's doodles of playful rabbits, and by 1939 there were over 60 Bunnykins designs.

These original Bunnykins characters are still used, essentially unaltered, today. Other major potteries making children's ware at this time were Wedgwood and Shelley, and smaller makers abounded. Shelley used Mabel Lucie Attwell's designs and Susie Cooper drew characters for at least one Wedgwood line.

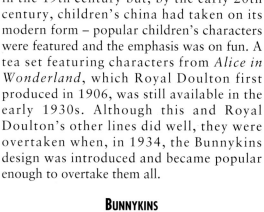

Ray Duns

Ronald MacKechnie

A children's alphabet plate made in Staffordshire around 1820 or 1830. The maxims in the centre come from Benjamin Franklin's 'improving' almanacs.

ORNAMENTS

For children who didn't have a real live pet, there were plenty of small china animals for company. Although not strictly made for children, Sylvac ware, made by Shaw and Copestake and first introduced in the late 1930s, found its way into many young hearts. The cocky little dogs sat on many a bookcase and dressing table, looking enquiringly at lifelike pussycats and stylized bunnies. These earthenware pieces were glazed in either pale green, buff, blue or yellow.

At the end of the day, a bedtime story would be read from one of the books kept neatly stacked between pretty china bookends. And after lights-out there was a china night-light that would glow comfortingly in the dark. Royal Doulton made a Bunnykins night-light, while several Staffordshire potteries made them in the shape of cottages, from which the light shone out through the open windows.

FOX TERRIER 4
made by Shaw and Copestake in the 1930s.

SYLVAC TERRIERS 4
in green and buff, with characteristically coy expressions and heads cocked to one side.

CERAMIC BOOKENDS 4
made in Germany. The boy and girl are dressed in 18th-century costume.

CERAMIC PLAQUE 4
with a setter's head gazing out soulfully from a ring.

A SYLVAC BUTTON TIDY 3
in the popular shades of brown and green. Impressed underneath is the Sylvac backstamp.

A PAIR OF SMALL SYLVAC RABBITS 4
in subtly different styles. Note the stylized herringbone pattern on the green bunny's ears.

FROM THE SYLVAC 3
range, these two long-necked cartoon dogs were made by Shaw and Copestake.

CERAMIC MONEY BOX 3
in the shape of a rabbit. The nose, eyes and claws are all hand-painted.

SYLVAC CAT 4
dating from the 1930s, with realistic tortoiseshell fur and bright green eyes.

4 **ALABASTER BOOKENDS**
with reclining ceramic figures. One little girl holds a camera, the other a rose.

Ronald MacKechnie

83

CROCKERY

Tableware decorated with favourite characters from children's books and cartoons cheered up many a meal in the nursery. Large sets had been fashionable in the 19th century, but by the 1930s children's crockery was often bought in single place settings. Many were made especially for tiny hands. Tea sets were often given as christening presents and can still be found in perfect condition with the original presentation box.

Royal Doulton's nursery-rhyme and Bunnykins patterns and Shelley's Mabel Lucie Attwell designs were both popular. Other names to look for are Paragon, Susie Cooper, Sylvac Pottery and Grimwades. Most were transfer printed on top of the glaze, although some have printed outlines which were coloured in by hand.

SOUP PLATE
illustrated with a Mabel Lucie Attwell design and distinctive rhyme.

PORCELAIN CHILDREN'S BEAKER
from the Simple Simon tea service, first produced in 1920 by Royal Doulton.

BUNNYKINS SET
comprising porridge bowl, plate and two egg cups. The plate shows a Bunnykins Santa Claus.

PART OF A PLACE SETTING
with matching 'Your Licence Please' illustrations.

A CUP AND PLATE 4
from the 'Alice in Wonderland' tea set by Royal Doulton, based on Tenniel's original drawings.

A SET OF THREE PIECES 6
from the Heath Robinson range of designs, based on the 'Cat and the Fiddle' nursery rhyme.

NURSERY RHYME 4
jug with simple black and white illustrations. It was made from 1907-34.

'OLD MOTHER 4
Hubbard' is illustrated on this nursery rhyme mug. It was made from 1903-39.

NURSERY RHYME 4
mug designed by Ann Anderson.

A BOWL 4
made by Paragon featuring Mickey and Minnie Mouse at the piano.

CHRISTOPHER ROBIN MUG 3 4
by Ashtead Potters and a child's pusher, spoon and fork in electroplated nickel silver.

Ronald MacKechnie

85

COLLECTOR'S NOTES

Even the best-behaved child had momentary lapses in table manners, so complete sets of children's china are rare. Examine individual pieces to make sure that there are no chips, cracks or scratches and that the transfer printing has not been rubbed or marked. The maker's mark should also be clearly visible. Earlier pieces with hand enamelling over the glaze tend to chip very easily.

Most people who collect children's china either specialize in the work of a particular designer or factory, one type of piece such as teapots or night-lights, or a theme such as scenes of children at play.

LEADING MANUFACTURERS

The most collectable factories are the most famous ones like Shelley, Royal Doulton and Wedgwood, but prices for these pieces can get rather high. Royal Doulton examples, for instance, are much sought after by collectors in the USA. On the other hand, Sylvac pottery, although it has now become well-known, can still be bought for a few pounds.

Famous designers' names – such as Eric Ravilious, Mabel Lucie Attwell and Leslie Harradine – are sure to push up prices. Clarice Cliff, renowned for her exotic art deco pottery for grown-ups, also designed children's tea sets, and these are just as popular with collectors as her other work.

Teapots are always popular but undamaged

CLOSE UP on IDENTIFICATION

The Bunnykins backstamp (above) was designed by Hubert Light for Royal Doulton.

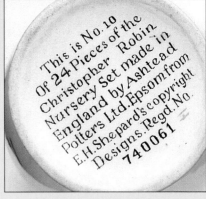

Extraordinarily detailed backstamp from Ashtead Potters (below).

This is No.10 Of 24 Pieces of the Christopher Robin Nursery Set made in England by Ashtead Potters Ltd. Epsom from E.H.Shepard's copyright Designs. Regd.No. 740061

This Sylvac impressed backstamp (above) was used before 1946.

Mabel Lucie Attwell's little elves, known as the boo-boos (below), were designed in 1926.

Ranald MacKechnie

COMPARE & CONTRAST

Ranald MacKechnie

Bunnykins children's china is still made today and designs have hardly changed from the originals produced in the 1930s. However, many of today's models tend to have a more rounded, modern shape.

1930s Bunnykins mug (left) and its modern equivalent (right).

ones are elusive. A Bunnykins teapot in the shape of a rabbit, if it is in very good condition, is one of the most expensive pieces of children's china available.

The Bunnykins series, still being added to today, is one of the most popular of all for collectors. Barbara Vernon's drawings were adapted for transfer printing by Hubert Light. He also introduced the chain of rabbits chasing one another around the rim and the backstamp of three bunnies in red jackets below the Doulton mark. Pieces from the 1930s can be recognized by their facsimile Barbara Vernon signature in blue.

SPOTTING A FAKE

Although prices for children's china are increasing, few pieces are known to have been faked on a large scale. Good forgeries, however, can be virtually indistinguishable from the originals and the best advice is to beware of suspiciously low prices for rare items, and to check with an expert or buy from a reputable dealer.

WADE WHIMSIES

Some of the miniature animal models made by the Wade Group of potteries were literally given away in the 1960s, but now attract a lot of interest from collectors

Ray Duns

Though they were not aimed specifically at children, the porcelain models in the Wade Whimsies series were particularly enjoyed by little girls. Some attempted to collect the whole series, while others gave a favoured few pride of place on the bedroom window-sill. The endearing animal subjects, posed and modelled for maximum cuteness, ensured their appeal, while their smallness added to their toy-like charm. The largest was 5.4cm/2⅛in tall, and several of them are less than half that size.

A total of 109 Whimsies were released in two bursts of activity. The first ones were made in 1953, when falling orders and cancelled contracts for industrial ceramics led the Wade group to develop new retail lines. They had already had a success in the cheap porcelain giftware market with the miniature Wade Porcelain figure series in the 1930s, and Whimsies were a logical step.

They were made in two potteries, one in Ireland and the other in Staffordshire, and were sold in boxed sets of five (or, in one case, four). The factories took turns at producing new sets – the competition between them probably contributed to the quality of these early models – until 1959, when the tenth and final set was put on sale.

Whimsies continued to be made in the 1960s, but were not sold directly to the public. Instead, they were packaged as 'giveaways' or premiums with various products, and also found their way into several brands of Christmas cracker. They proved so popular that, in 1971, Wade began to market a whole new series of Whimsies as a retail line.

This time, each model was boxed and sold individually, though it was still possible to buy the full set of five models packaged together in their original boxes. New sets, twelve in all, were issued regularly until 1980 (though none appeared in 1973), and existing sets continued to be produced until 1984, when Whimsies were taken off the market to make way for new miniature lines.

Whether they came in the boxed sets of the 1950s, or the individual packets of the later series, the small but appealing animal models in the Wade Whimsies series were welcome Christmas stocking fillers or birthday gifts for legions of young girls building up their own mantelpiece menageries.

THE FIRST TEN

All the Wade Whimsies from the original run in the 1950s were well-modelled, with the feet and legs moulded separately and distinctly. The colours are soft, pastel and more varied than the later series. All the models were hand-painted.

The first five sets had a general selection, while the latter five had a theme, respectively polar animals, pedigree dogs, a zoo, North American animals and farm animals. The most difficult models to find in mint condition, and hence the most valuable, are the shire horse and swan from set 10, while the kitten, dachshund and bull from set 2, the beagle from set 5 and the foxhound from set 10 are close behind.

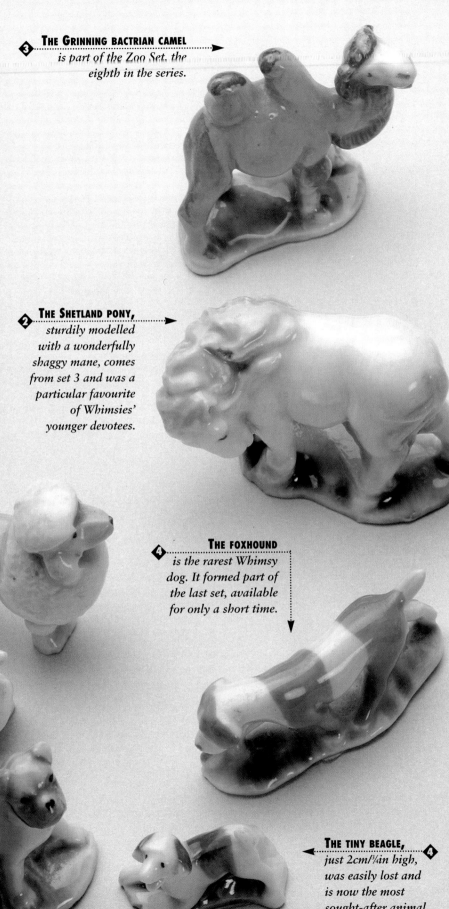

3 THE GRINNING BACTRIAN CAMEL is part of the Zoo Set, the eighth in the series.

2 THE SHETLAND PONY, sturdily modelled with a wonderfully shaggy mane, comes from set 3 and was a particular favourite of Whimsies' younger devotees.

3 THE FRENCH POODLE was included in the first set of Whimsies.

2 THE GREY SPANIEL, its docked tail held aloft, was another of the favourites from the first set of Whimsies.

4 THE FOXHOUND is the rarest Whimsy dog. It formed part of the last set, available for only a short time.

2 THE BOXER comes from set 7, of pedigree dogs.

4 THE TINY BEAGLE, just 2cm/¾in high, was easily lost and is now the most sought-after animal from set 5, which was issued in 1956.

Ray Duns

88

◆3◆4 **FARM ANIMALS WERE A FAVOURITE THEME.**
The snorting bull from set 2 and the piglet from set 10 attract the higher price, and the mare from set 5 – the only Whimsy set with four pieces – the lower.

◆3 **THE MONKEY**
from set 4, which was all zoo animals, although not marketed as such, is the only model to feature two animals together.

◆3 **THE FIRST 10 SETS CONTAINED FOUR BIRDS.**
The king penguin was the only Antarctic denizen in the Polar Set, while the snowy owl was in set 9.

◆2 **THE BABY SEAL**
was part of the Polar Set of 1956, in part inspired by the popularity of London Zoo's polar bear cubs.

◆2 **ZOO FAVOURITES,**
the rhino and the baby elephant both appeared as part of set 4 in 1955. The price guide is per model.

BEARS AND PANDAS, **◆2**
and particularly their cubs, made very winsome subjects for models.

89

THE SECOND SERIES

The new Whimsies made between 1971 and 1984 are noticeably less well-moulded than those made in the first series. The modelling is not so well defined and the feet and legs are blocked in to the base. The colours are not as vivid, either, although all the pieces were still hand-painted. About 25 models from this era were previously made as premiums – most notably for a Canadian brand of tea – in the same colours as the retail sets. After the series was discontinued, they continued to be used for premiums, but were given a single colour glaze to save on painting costs.

Most of the figures in the second series currently attract only small sums. The most sought-after model, the seahorse from set 9, released in 1978, is still only price guide 1.

Ray Duns

THREE PRIMATES APPEAR *in the second series. The strangely coloured chimp is from set 4 , the red-faced orang utan from set 10 and the gorilla from set 7.*

SEA CREATURES *appeared for the first time in set 9, released in 1978, in which the dolphin, seahorse and angel fish seen here were joined by a turtle and a pelican. The freshwater trout is from set 3.*

DOGS ARE AS COMMON IN THE SECOND SERIES *as in the first. This winsome puppyish trio of setter, mongrel and cocker spaniel all come from the first three sets.*

FARM ANIMALS FEATURED STRONGLY.
The cow, sow, horse and lamb
are all from set 6 and the ram from
set 8. Made to roughly the same size,
rather than scale, they can look odd
when they're displayed together.

A PELICAN, TWO OWLS AND A DUCK
are some of the birds from the second series.
The owls are recognizable as a barn owl and
a tawny, and the duck is mallard shaped,
though the colours are not life-like.

THESE VERY SMALL BIG CATS
include the lion from set
4, the stalking leopard
from set 7 and a demurely
posed and rather under-
striped tiger from set 10.

THESE ZOO ANIMALS
from the 1970s are not
as well-modelled or
realistically coloured as
earlier ones, though the
giraffe is an exception.

COMPARE & CONTRAST

The difference between the 1950s models and those of the 1970s is apparent when they're placed side by side. The grey squirrel on the right is from the very first set of Whimsies. The modelling is crisp, especially in the hands and acorn, and the colour realistic. The field mouse on the left lacks a little definition, and both mouse and ear of wheat are given the same colour glaze.

boxed set from the first series, but strangely enough this doesn't seem to carry much weight with collectors; the original box adds little to the value. Figures are almost always sold singly. Even if you do find a boxed set, you'll probably already have two or three figures out of it, so you won't need the extras. Besides, much of the fun in collecting Whimsies is in the search, and in gradually building up a collection by buying just one or two pieces here and there.

WHERE TO FIND WHIMSIES

Whimsies are sold in a variety of places; in with mixed lots at smaller auctions, at antiques fairs and flea markets, jumble sales, car boot sales, and in charity shops. Some dealers (not many, though) specialize in them, and they are your best bet for finding the higher priced figures from the 1950s.

Because of their collectability, some models have been remade in a similar, though not identical fashion, so take care. Backstamps and mould marks are an important guide to

COLLECTOR'S NOTES

Wade Whimsies have many attractions for a collector. They don't take up a lot of room, are easy to display and aren't prohibitively expensive – even a complete collection should be within most people's price range.

The models were made and sold in some numbers, and are not too difficult to find today. Generally speaking, those introduced late to a series are rarer than earlier ones, as they were not made over so long a period.

It would be unusual to find a complete

You may find models from the second series still housed in their individual boxes. Unlike many collectables, though, Whimsies aren't worth any more if sold with their packaging.

identification. Unfortunately, not all of the models are marked, and those that are, vary considerably. Some from the first series are marked in ink, some with a transfer print, and others with a moulded mark. Sometimes the mark is on the side or bottom of the base, and sometimes it's on the animal's feet.

As the moulds were used over a long period of time, figures can differ greatly in definition. Avoid pieces with a rather blurred look about them. Go instead for ones with cleaner, sharper moulding. Any Whimsies which have cracks or chips are immediately devalued, especially those from Series 2, which can be found quite abundantly.

Many collectors also search flea markets for the wooden trays once used by printers, made up of shallow compartments of varying height and width. Cleaned up, polished, and hung on the wall, these trays make ideal display cases for Whimsies.

CLOSE UP *on* MARKS

Ray Duns

Many Whimsies were unmarked. A few of the first series are transfer-stamped under the base, while others are mould-marked WADE on the edge of the base. Some have MADE IN ENGLAND added. Second series models are mould-marked WADE ENGLAND on the side of, or sometimes below, the base.

1950s TABLEWARE

*With the ending of wartime austerity conditions,
potters in the 1950s were free to indulge themselves
in new shapes and colours for everyday wares*

During and after World War 2, there were severe restrictions in the British pottery industry. Undecorated white or cream 'Utility Ware' was all that was available to the public. The only decorated wares that could be made were for export. Any sold on the home market were seconds or export rejects. The lifting of these restrictions in August 1952 led to a flood of new designs in tableware, as potters gleefully experimented with shape and colour.

In the vanguard of this experimentation was the Burslem firm of W R Midwinter. Roy Midwinter, the firm's head, visited the USA in 1952 and was greatly influenced by that country's more relaxed attitudes to dining and by their informal tablewares, some with a harlequin or mix-and-match attitude to colour. British attitures to eating were getting less formal, too. Convenience foods and take-away meals other than fish and chips became available for the first time.

Another major influence on pottery designers was the 1951 Festival of Britain, intended to show off the achievements and industrial might of the Empire. One of the strong design themes that emerged from the Festival was the use of angular, spiky graphics, and these were incorporated into the shapes and patterns of ceramics.

THE STAMP OF APPROVAL

In 1956, the Design Centre was opened in London, with the aim of promoting designs showing 'good materials and workmanship, fitness for purpose and pleasure in use'. Designers could submit their work, on payment of a fee, to a panel of judges who selected the best to bear the label 'Design Centre Approved'. This element of competition helped the expansion of new ideas.

Technical innovations also had an effect. Johnson Matthey introduced a new method of producing transfers, known as serigraphy or screen printing, which allowed for the reproduction of thick, flat-colour designs, which were often layered.

This made it look as if the motifs had been

Roy Duns

printed over the design, not incorporated into it. Printing was sometimes deliberately 'off register', with the colour overlapping the outline of the design. The method also lent itself well to the duplication of the hand-painted patterns favoured by many designers.

The dominant style of the 1950s was for simple shapes decorated with bold patterns or all-over colour glazes.

NEW STYLES

The new tableware was designed to appeal to the smart, young, middle-class market. Top designers were commissioned, especially by Midwinter, who employed freelances Terence Conran and Hugh Casson, and Jessie Tait as a house designer. Perhaps the company's most outstanding range was Stylecraft, which was designed by Roy Midwinter himself and introduced in 1956.

Designs were often naive in form. The Homemaker range by Ridgway Potteries had a simple black and white pattern of contemporary household furnishings, while Swinnertons's Springtime featured silhouette figures following country pursuits. Carlton Ware relied on asymmetrical shapes, often sparsely decorated, as in their leaf-like Windswept pattern. Terence Conran also used leaves as the basis of Nature Study, while Jessie Tait used them in another Midwinter pattern, Primavera. Textiles were another source of inspiration, with patterns such as Tweed, Gingham, Plaid and Homeweave, while scientific and technological motifs were the source of abstract designs.

RIDGWAY'S HOMEMAKER
pattern, with drawings of 1950s furniture, was the creation of a young designer, Enid Seeney. The price is for both the jug and the tureen.

HUGH CASSON
designed the screen-printed Riviera range, which reflected the first stirrings of Britain's foreign holiday boom, in 1954.

JESSIE TAIT'S ZAMBESI
pattern, represented here by a cup and saucer and three sizes of plate, featured black and white zebra stripes. The price is for all five pieces.

THE APTLY-NAMED SALADWARE ❸
was designed by Terence Conran. This plate, with its cheery, screen-printed pattern of vegetables, is typical of 1950s tableware.

TERENCE CONRAN DESIGNED CHEQUERS, ❹
represented here by a cup, saucer and side plate, in 1957. The price is for all three pieces.

ELEGANT SIMPLICITY ❻
of shape typifies Midwinter ranges. The price is for coffee pot and six cups and saucers.

FESTIVAL TABLEWARE, ❷
designed by Jesse Tait for Midwinter, was loosely based on scientific illustrations of the structure of crystals.

JESSE TAIT'S DESIGNS ❷
include Toga, represented here by a plate with a typical 1950s shape, part square and part circle.

Ray Duns

95

COLLECTOR'S NOTES

Tableware from the 1950s is still fairly underrated by collectors, though pieces by famous designers are sought after. Flea markets and jumble sales will often yield a rich harvest, and specialist dealers in shops and at antiques fairs are well worth visiting. Large auction houses will not feature it, but lots can sometimes be found at local auctions.

Midwinter's Stylecraft range is perhaps most evocative of the period. It can be found in many different combinations of shape and pattern. A harlequin collection could be built up without too much expense. Look out, too, for Ridgway's Homemaker pattern, decorated with drawings of contemporary furnishings.

Carlton Ware is very collectable and can prove very expensive, though prices are more reasonable for items from the 1950s. The same goes for china by Susie Cooper, whose pieces are normally signed and marked with the name of the pattern on the base. Flower patterns such as Gardenia, Parrot Tulip and Wild Strawberry are perhaps less exciting than the almost abstract designs such as Black Fruit, Green Feather and Charcoal Skeleton Leaf. She also favoured delicate polka dot or star decorations on the outside of cups which had pastel interiors.

DOTS AND DASHES

Grimwades manufactured a breakfast set in Royal Winton which had red plates with a white polka dot. The same colour scheme in reverse was used for toast racks, cups and other hollow ware. Crown Staffordshire, by contrast, favoured fine lines running down at random to decorate their Queensberry range.

CLOSE UP *on* FAMOUS NAMES

Design was a buzzword of the 1950s, and some designers became household names. Midwinter wares, in particular, usually named the designer in a printed stamp on the base.

Ridgway Potteries, founded in 1955, did not name their designers (left), but Midwinter made sure their famous names, including Jesse Tait, Hugh Casson and Terence Conran, were fully credited. Every Midwinter range also had its own distinctive logo.

Styles reflected changing social conditions. Part of Bewick's Circus range was a sandwich plate with a recess for a cup, made for those who wanted a handy snack in front of the TV.

Ray Duns

As with all china, items should be carefully checked for cracks and chips. Examine the handles of jugs and cups for damage. With teapots, pay special attention to the handles, spouts and the inner rim.

Tableware was expected to have a short life, and the new on-glaze transfers did not stand up so well to frequent use, so check for wear and rubbing. Knife marks often spoil the look of plates. If the tableware is of the mix-and-match or harlequin type, check the bases to see the various items really do match and that they are not a marriage of different sets.

COMPARE & CONTRAST

Burgess and Leigh, a well-established Staffordshire firm, entered the modern market in the mid-fifties with their popular Fantasia pattern, printed in black and white.

The plate on the left is genuine Fantasia. The cup and saucer below, with a slightly different design, are a modern pastiche.

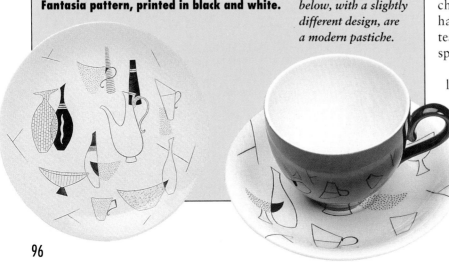

CIGARETTE CARDS

*Surprisingly informative and often beautifully illustrated,
cigarette cards offer the collector the thrill of hunting down
that elusive card to complete a set*

It is unlikely that anyone could have foreseen the day when a single cigarette card would fetch as much as several hundred pounds – of course, cards that do are particularly rare and there are plenty of others available at a fraction of that price.

Because cigarettes were sold in such flimsy packets in the 19th century, they were packed with a piece of card for added protection. Manufacturers soon realized the card's potential as a way to encourage brand loyalty, and the first British cigarette cards – which had calendars on them – came in the 'Richmond Gem' brand in 1884, although the oldest surviving card is from 1887. One of the longest-running series was launched in 1894 by the Liverpool firm, Ogden's. The 'Golden Guinea' and 'Tabs' series ran to 20,000 cards.

In 1901 the American Tobacco Company bought Ogden's and 13 British manufacturers joined forces to fight off the new American challenge. In the resulting trade war almost every single one of the 150 British cigarette companies issued cigarette cards as a way of holding on to their share of the market. By the time this fierce battle had ended, cigarette cards were firmly established and the golden age for card collectors had begun.

COLLECTOR'S NOTES

Some collectors specialize in themes such as film stars or sport, whereas others concentrate on particular periods. Another specialist area is the collecting of 'cards' made from materials other than paper, notably silk. Look out for unusual shapes such as circles and ellipses, and the sectional series which built up into one large picture for framing.

Ideally, cigarette cards should be kept in plastic wallets to prevent creasing or soiling. If cards have been stuck down in an album, they are worth less than loose sets.

Popular themes for men included sport, the military and transport. For women, flora and fauna were popular. In the 1930s, special penny albums were produced, in which collectors could stick their ready-gummed cards. The opened album below details the best Air Raid Protection methods and costs £10.

Lyndon Parker

PACKS OF CARDS

PLAYER'S 'USEFUL PLANTS AND FRUITS' SERIES
from 1902. This card features cinnamon.

Taddy's 'Clowns', which came in a set of 20, are Britain's rarest: just one card sells for over £600. Fewer than 20 sets have survived, and those that have are proofs with blank backs because the company closed down just before they were due to be released. A complete set is worth as much as £10,000.

Cards from before 1902 are very rare and even Edwardian cards fetch relatively high prices. More affordable are the cards produced in the 1920s and 30s, when they were produced by the million.

• Coloured cards tend to be more popular and more expensive than black and white.

• Sets are generally worth a little more than the sum of their parts, but if the cards have been stuck down they will be less valuable than loose cards.

• Only buy damaged cigarette cards if they are particularly rare.

MILITARY AIRCRAFT
series from Wills's, with facts on back.

KING EDWARD VII,
a biographical card from Ogden's, with information on the back.

RADIO CELEBRITY,
Geraldo, (left) from Wills's, and Gracie Fields, from Player's film star series.

BLACK EYE.
BLACKFEET SIOUX.

BLACK EYE
from a series on American Indian Chiefs, by Allen & Ginter, c1888.

FAMOUS PEOPLE
series from Carreras – aviator Sir Alan Cobham.

THE HOUSES OF PARLIAMENT,
which came with Ogden's Guinea Gold cigarettes.

JIGSAW-STYLE CARD
from WD & HO Wills. From a set of 48.

THE GREAT BEAUTIES SERIES
that came with Wills's 'Scissors' brand.

TADDY'S 'CLOWN'
series – Britain's most valuable cigarette cards. The price is for one card.

A COATS OF ARMS SERIES
in silk from the BDV Cigarette Company.

KENSITAS EMBROIDERED
sunflower c1930. There is a poem on one side and an advertisement on the other.

SUNFLOWER
(Adoration; Fidelity; Constancy.)

Lyndon Parker

SEASIDE POSTCARDS

*Seaside postcards have a special place in
the collector's heart, not least because
of their variety and affordability*

Postcard collecting, or cartology, is nearly as popular today as stamp collecting. But only in recent years has the enthusiasm for postcards matched the levels achieved in the first two decades of this century. At that time collectors were keenest on publishers' first editions, whereas today the most sought-after cards are the oldest and rarest.

During the heyday of the seaside resort, British holiday-makers who travelled to the coast had a unique and colourful choice of postcards to send home. Although continental resorts also produced the standard topographical card depicting a famous local scenic view or landmark, the British seaside postcard, with its unique graphic style and saucy humour, is instantly recognizable.

Humorous cards were not normally tied to a particular location and often the same basic design was overprinted with words appropriate to different resorts: 'Greetings from Blackpool' or 'Greetings from Brighton' for example. These cards are associated above all with the name of Donald McGill whose saucy designs came to dominate the seaside market after World War I. McGill is said to have designed some 3000 cards and his most popular ones regularly sold over one million copies or more.

The major publishers of seaside postcards at this time were Davidson Brothers, and J Bamforth & Co of Huddersfield, both of whom were famous for their comic cards; Valentine's of Dundee , a long-established printing firm, and Raphael Tuck, a London manufacturer of greetings cards since the 1870s, were the best-known producers of the seaside topographical postcard.

Bathing belle cards (above) were the forerunners of the pin-up. Edwardian seaside postcards (below) were varied and colourful.

Duncan Smith

FUN IN THE SUN

Postcards designed by cartoonists or commercial artists tend to command higher prices than purely topographical cards, and certain artists are more collectable than others. Look out for Donald McGill, whose well-rounded women, henpecked husbands and *double entendre* captions were immensely popular with generations of holiday-makers.

Other well-known designers of the period include Tom Browne, John Hassall, Dudley Hardy and Phil May. Browne and Hassall were signed up by Davidson Brothers, a pioneering publishing house in the production of humorous and satirical cards at that time. Louis Wain, also of Davidson Brothers, is another artist worth collecting.

Keep an eye out for leather albums filled with postcards. These were popular in Edwardian times and many are often still in mint condition.

Ordinary topographical cards, showing scenic views of resorts, were produced in their thousands and are therefore very cheap. Some people even buy them to send, instead of modern postcards.

A 1930s PULL-OUT. *Make sure the folds fall neatly into place and tuck tidily into the retaining flap.*

BUXOM WOMEN *are frequent sights on British seaside postcards This one dates from the 1950s.*

"GREAT FUN THESE RUBBER TYRES—AREN'T THEY, MRS RAMSBOTTOM?"

'PASSIVE RESISTANCE' *– this design by G Thackeray from 1910 was used for many different seaside resorts.*

THIS UNUSUAL *'envelope' postcard probably once contained a feather.*

PASSIVE RESISTANCE.

HAVE BEEN VERY MUCH TICKLED BY THE ENCLOSED **at Eastbourne**

AND THINK IT WILL TICKLE YOU.

Lyndon Parker

100

THIS EDWARDIAN *cartoon postcard was no doubt thought very risqué in 1910.*

THE APPEAL OF McGILL'S *somewhat vulgar humour is clearly obvious in this postcard.*

"The sand is gold,
the sky is blue,
You can see my ass
But it can't see you!"

"I can't get my winkle out
Isn't it a sin?
The more I try to get it out
The further it goes in!"

A TYPICAL CARD *by Donald McGill, who became known as the 'Leonardo of the saucy postcard'.*

'SEASIDE COMFORTS' *by Tom Browne. Browne had made a name for himself as a Punch cartoonist before he began designing postcards.*

ESCAPE *from a woman's traditional role was only temporary!*

"THE ONLY **WORK** I'M DOING THIS WEEK IS **WORKING UP AN APPETITE!**"

HAVING FUN *was what a seaside excursion was all about, as this card shows.*

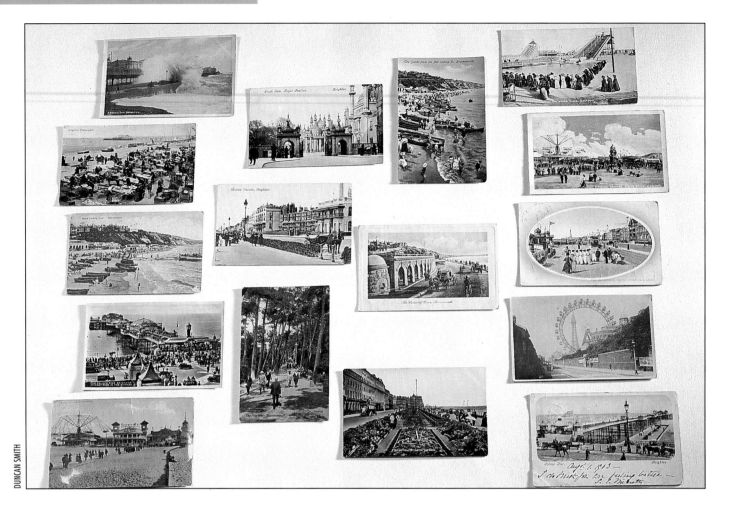

DUNCAN SMITH

These topographical postcards were printed from hand-tinted photographs.

COLLECTOR'S NOTES

There are many ways in which you can organize your postcard collection. Some people choose particular places or themes, while others stick to certain artists.

Cards that show people and/or transport at seaside resorts are very collectable. These show changes in style or fashion and are collected for historical interest.

The dating of cards is important – those bearing clear, dated postmarks will have the edge over the unstamped card.

Make sure that the postcard is in good condition. Cards should not be folded, creased or dog-eared, and the corners should be intact.

WHERE TO FIND CARDS

There are many places where postcards can be bought. Antique, junk and second-hand bookshops often include postcards among their wares and there are now specialist dealers in this field who advertise in collectables magazines (although rare or particularly sought-after cards will be keenly priced). Postcard fairs (some of them very large) are also held regularly in London and the provinces and collectors of unusual or very specific cards can often find these a real treasure trove; fairs are likewise advertised in various magazines.

Postcards also come up for sale at auction but most collectors will want to become familiar with other sources first in order to find out how postcards are valued.

CLOSE UP

Cards by well-known artists such as Donald McGill, Tom Browne and John Hassall are obviously more collectable than others. After you have looked at a few of their designs, their individual styles will be instantly recognizable. Most also signed their work, so look for a signature or initials on the bottom of the card.

Donald McGill always signed his name in full, with three dots marking the beginning and end of his Christian and surname.

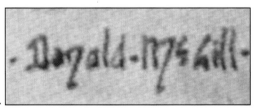

Tom Browne, whose humour was a little more sophisticated than McGill's, simply used the signature 'Tom B'.

PUB BOTTLES

Pub bottles, ranging from stoneware ginger-beer bottles to dark glass beer bottles and plain glass mineral bottles, can form a fascinating and inexpensive collection

Two of the greatest Victorian manufacturers of stoneware bottles were Doulton & Co and Joseph Bourne. Throughout the 19th century their factories produced bottles in all shapes and sizes for gin, whisky, vinegar, ginger beer, mineral water and other drinks. For the most part, the bottles were simple and functional, plain stone in colour with an occasional tan-coloured top. Originally each bottle was incised with the manufacturer's name and the contents, but by the late 19th century most were decorated with underglaze or transfer printing.

GLASS BOTTLES

In the mid-19th century low standards of manufactured food and drink were becoming a problem. Manufacturers responded by packaging their beverages in clear glass bottles so the contents could be readily seen, and glass began to undermine the stoneware monopoly.

As demand increased, so bottle manufacturers became conscious of the need to speed up production. In 1823 a Bristol manufacturer, Henry Ricketts, patented a moulding machine that not only produced more bottles but also made them to a uniform size, something even a skilled glass blower could not achieve. It also marked the beginning of embossing, which was to become a feature of glass bottles.

Although clear glass had been made for centuries, it was rarely used for bottles, as the duty on a clear glass object was considerably more than on coloured glass. But in 1845 the tax was lifted, and companies began to add manganese to their glass as a decolourant.

BOTTLING THE FIZZ

The first carbonated drinks appeared in the mid-19th century and a completely new range of clear glass bottles was produced specifically for these brightly-coloured, fizzy beverages. One of the greatest problems was retaining the drinks' fizz, as without a tight stopper they soon went flat. Corks were of no use unless kept moist and it was difficult to persuade retailers to store bottles on their sides.

In the late 19th century, Hiram Codd, a Camberwell manufacturer, patented an ingenious solution for bottling fizzy drinks. It used a captive glass marble and a rubber washer, which were forced against the lip by the pressure of gas in the bottle. The stopper was released by a wooden cap with a small dowel which pushed the marble down into the neck of the bottle. Codd's method was so successful that such bottles were still used in the 1940s.

THE WORLD'S BEST STOUT

WHITBREAD'S

Dennis Barnard

Competition between brewers has always been intense and one good way of differentiating their product has been to sell it in a distinctive bottle with an eyecatching label.

STONEWARE AND GLASS BOTTLES

The strength and durability of stoneware bottles made them ideal for all manner of drinks. Stoneware bottles, unlike glass ones, were always hand thrown, making each one unique. Designs changed remarkably little over the years.

The most familiar stoneware bottles were plain with a tan-coloured top, but occasionally brighter colours were used. Early bottles had incised lettering, but later innovations led to a variety of labelling methods, including sand blasting, underglaze printing, stencilling and transfer printing.

The range of glass bottles made for wines, beers, spirits and mineral waters throughout the 19th century was enormous. Before the 1820s, wealthy merchants commissioned personalized wine bottles with special shoulder seals. When moulds were introduced, it was found that such bottles could be embossed automatically, and although wine bottles remained fairly sober, almost all other bottles were gaily decorated with attractive lettering.

In the 1930s, Public Health Authorities complained about Codds (and stoneware ginger-beer bottles) being difficult to clean and re-use, and so manufacturers were encouraged to produce simpler shaped bottles. Although these were more hygienic, they were not as attractive as 19th-century bottles and so relied on eye-catching labels in order to sell their wares. Luckily, enough old bottles have survived for us to be able to appreciate their beauty.

A BEER BOTTLE produced by Barrett & Co in about 1920. Details of the manufacturer are heavily embossed on the glass.

A WORTHINGTON'S BOTTLE from the 1920s. It is complete with its untouched India Pale Ale, its stopper and an unbroken paper seal.

AN UNUSUAL BLUE GLASS BOTTLE which, although it has its cork, appears to have lost its dandelion and burdock stout.

NON-ALCOHOLIC
'Cheerio', a drink brewed in Manchester. The contents (almost certainly undrinkable now) have been preserved.

A BOTTLE OF KING'S ALE
brewed by Bass & Co in February 1902 to mark the accession of Edward VII.

A STONEWARE BOTTLE
from the 1920s that once held ginger beer. It has a screw top and is of a simple design with just the maker's name on it.

STONEWARE BOTTLE
in classic colours. It has a transfer-printed label that warns against refilling the bottle.

A HOP BITTERS
bottle filled with a non-intoxicating beverage by Duckworth & Co of Manchester.

DEALER'S TIPS

• Price is dependent on condition – a stained or broken bottle may be cheaper but is not a good investment.
• When bottles have been dug up, clean them carefully. Don't use hot water as this could crack glass or stoneware which has been accustomed to cold, damp conditions.
• Most stains respond to a long soak in a solution of soda. Rubbing with an abrasive cleaner may result in scratches.

Ray Duns

COLLECTOR'S NOTES

Bottles can be bought but they have the added attraction of being something you can dig up yourself. Millions were produced during the 18th and 19th centuries and those that were not recycled were consigned to huge urban rubbish tips or smaller country tips. For many years, keen collectors have been sifting through well-known tips, in search of more unusual specimens. However, finds dated before 1860 are rare, as the Victorian poor often sorted the rubbish and were paid a small sum for anything which could be re-used.

THE BEST FINDS

Digging up bottles can be more satisfying than scouring antiques markets. You can find information pinpointing the areas of old dumps on large-scale maps from your local library. For those who prefer cleaner pursuits, many stallholders now deal in old bottles.

Among the rarest and most desirable of all bottles are those manufactured for mineral water and carbonated drinks by Hiram Codd. Although millions were produced, children found the glass marble stopper

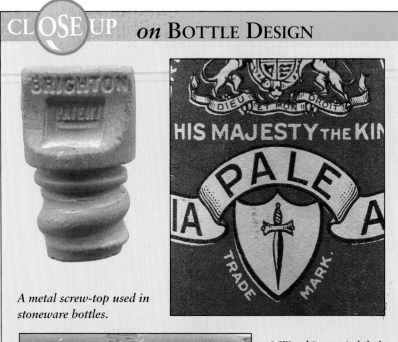

A metal screw-top used in stoneware bottles.

A Worthington's label. From the mid-19th century all beer bottles had to have labels.

Patent marks and other information were embossed on moulded bottles after 1823.

COMPARE & CONTRAST

These two stout bottles reveal just how much bottle design changed in the 19th century as new manufacturing techniques were introduced by brewers and others to satisfy public demand.

This stoneware bottle in traditional colours has a transfer-printed label. Such bottles are rarely used now.

A screw-topped embossed glass bottle with a printed paper label. Bottles like this are still in use today.

irresistible, and many were smashed to get at the plaything inside. Codd produced not only clear bottles but also a range in a variety of rich tones. Avid collectors are forever searching for fine-coloured Codds which are now worth large sums. But the amateur must beware – Codd's famous bottle was pirated many times and what seems like a charming original may be a recent copy.

DATING YOUR COLLECTION

With a little research, most glass bottles are easy to date because of the embossing on the neck and body. The manufacturer, area and contents are usually displayed in bold lettering across the front.

The most commonly found stoneware bottles are those for ginger beer. Their bold lettering is either incised or transfer printed, revealing the manufacturer and the place of origin. As stoneware was hand-thrown, it frequently has a potter's mark on the base.

In the 1870s, screw tops were introduced, followed by the hinged wire china stopper and the crown cork still in use for beers today. The search for cheaper production methods continued, and in 1903 the first fully automated bottle-making machine – and the forerunner of current bottles – came into use.

Ray Duns

COTTAGE BRASS

The decorative brassware that added rustic charm to many homes in the 1920s and 30s has made a comeback with present-day collectors

The quantity of brass produced this century is matched by the great variety of objects it was used to make. The bells, bowls, candlesticks and fire irons – and the figures with no other purpose than to please – all make attractive collections.

Although brass has been around for a long time – the Elizabethans used this alloy of copper and zinc to make cannons – it wasn't until the 19th century that new steam-powered rolling mills could produce sheet metal and the huge expansion in manufacturing began.

Bristol and then Birmingham became the centre of brass working, and companies such as John Jewsbury, Pearson-Page and Crofts exported their wares all over the world.

After World War 1 brass was used widely for decorative domestic objects, particularly good-quality reproductions of the household items of earlier days. Fire irons were very popular and many old patterns were revived.

Trivets – stands used for supporting cooking vessels over or next to the fire – were part of the inter-war passion for brasswork. The brass and copper pans and kettles that would have stood on the trivets were also popular. Most of these are strictly ornamental since, unless their insides are lined with unalloyed tin, they are highly poisonous to cook with. Nevertheless, they all help establish the cottage parlour look that was so popular at the time of their manufacture.

A range of decorative brass from the 1930s, of which many are copies of Edwardian items. From the left: an engraved Chinese bowl, a toasting fork, a single candlestick, a pagoda bell, a pair of open-twist candlesticks, a kettle, a chestnut roaster (hanging up), an oilcan, two handbells, a candle holder and a snuffer.

Michael Michaels

BRIGHT AND BRASSY

In the 1920s and 30s it was fashionable to display brass ornaments on the mantelpiece, their bright metal echoing the flames below. Letter holders, candlesticks and snuffers (once used to extinguish the candle's flame), ashtrays, pipe racks, boxes, trays and small figures were all popular and retain their charm today. Brass pipe stoppers, which had a small, flattened disc at one end for tamping down pipe tobacco, were also popular.

Other small brass items found on the mantelpiece included warming pans, sets of scales with tiny weights once used for weighing coins, letters or precious stones and metals, and musical handbells tuned to cover an octave or more.

If there is a drawback to collecting a lot of brass, it is the cleaning. The lacquer or varnish that protected antique brassware has usually worn away by now and the surface of any piece of brass will gradually blacken. In general, if you are cleaning it yourself, use a good-quality proprietary cleaner. Ornate decorative brassware should be cleaned with a toothbrush. This will ease out traces of previous cleaner (seen as a white deposit on the brass) and the piece can then be polished to a high shine.

THIS MATCHBOX HOLDER, ◆ 3
made in the early 20th century, was designed to hang on the wall. It is decorated with a variety of engraved and cast patterns.

BRASS PEN TRAYS
4 ◆ *often have ornate floral designs and rests at each corner for holding pens and pencils.*

A PAIR OF BRASS CANDLESTICKS
5 ◆ *probably dating from the Edwardian period. Many Edwardian designs were copied in the 1920s and 30s.*

A LETTER HOLDER FROM THE 1930s.
A brass handle and decorative punched sides are fixed to a wooden base. Such pieces became increasingly popular in the early 20th century.

A BRASS SKIMMER WITH COPPER RIVETS
made early this century. Skimmers were originally used for lifting the cream off milk when making butter.

CL OSE UP *on* BRASSWORK

Make sure that rivets, traditionally made of brass or copper, are in good condition.

A brass figure, made by casting, but hand-finished to provide finer detail.

A 30s 'open-twist' piece. A certain amount of pitting can be expected.

BRASS BELLOWS 5
are still very popular with collectors. Many, like this one, are decorated with designs that have been stamped on to thin sheets of brass.

A LETTER HOLDER 4
designed to hang on the wall. It has three intricately patterned brass pockets.

THIS COAL SCUTTLE, 4
made in miniature, was produced between the wars as a purely decorative item.

AN ASHTRAY 4
decorated with an Egyptian figure. The ashtray itself can be removed for cleaning.

BRASS ORNAMENTS FROM THE 1930s 2 3 2
are easy to find and reasonably priced. From the left: a tortoise button tidy with hinged shell, a lady bell and two solid brass pigs.

All photographs Michael Miller

COLLECTOR'S NOTES

The big problem with brass is how to tell whether a piece is original, say from the 19th century, or a more modern reproduction. Just to add to the confusion, before mass production many original moulds were re-used over a long period of time. However, earlier brass is generally paler in colour than the 'brassy' modern variety and it is also generally much thicker. Also, few fakes were made until the 1940s and reproductions made between the wars have their own value.

WEAR AND TEAR

The best advice when buying is to use your common sense. Consider the object's original function and, if the dealer claims it is an old piece, check that it has the appropriate amount of wear and tear. Remember that an uncleaned piece can look deceptively old. Reproduction brassware is usually made from thinner sheets of metal than earlier items. They dent easily and this leads to a false impression of age.

Brass tankards and flagons are rare, as are genuine antique bowls and dishes. Brass candlesticks are more common – particularly reproduction Georgian ones. Check the base of a candlestick. If it is rough and unfinished, it is probably reproduction, although more modern copies may have been turned for a smoother finish. Ridges and more widely spaced turning give these away. Candlesticks should also be checked for repairs – look out for clumsy soldering at the joints.

Brass jardinières or planters are often dirty and water-stained inside, but can be easily cleaned. Dents can be gently beaten out but splits downwards from the rim will

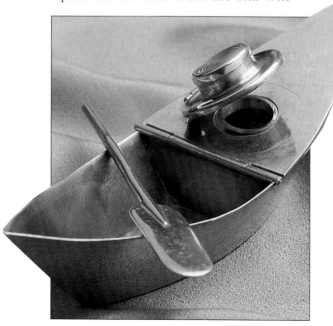

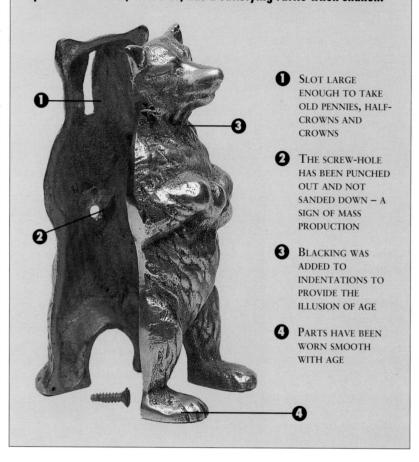

DESIGN IN FOCUS

MONEY-BOX BEAR

Money boxes were first produced on a large scale in the 19th century. Mostly aimed at children, they were frequently made in the shape of animals. This brass bear, dating from the 1930s, is in the same tradition. Cast in two halves, it is secured by a screw – very convenient when you want to get your money out. This piece actually holds very little money – a few of the old pennies would have filled it up – but the metal, of course, has a satisfying rattle when shaken.

❶ SLOT LARGE ENOUGH TO TAKE OLD PENNIES, HALF-CROWNS AND CROWNS

❷ THE SCREW-HOLE HAS BEEN PUNCHED OUT AND NOT SANDED DOWN – A SIGN OF MASS PRODUCTION

❸ BLACKING WAS ADDED TO INDENTATIONS TO PROVIDE THE ILLUSION OF AGE

❹ PARTS HAVE BEEN WORN SMOOTH WITH AGE

A decorative brass inkwell in the shape of a gondola. Its functional yet ornamental design is typical of reproduction brassware from the 1920s and 30s. Note that the deck is hinged to allow the ink bottle to be replaced.

detract from the piece's value. Fire bellows should have their original nozzles, and the leather should be sound. Studs holding the stamped brass covering to the boards should be intact and not modern replacements. It's also worth checking the screws. Modern, machined screw threads indicate, at the least, restoration work on the piece.

CLUES TO DATING

There are certain manufacturers' marks that can help in dating brassware. The word 'patent' stamped on the metal means it was made after about 1750. A stock number on the base indicates a date of 1850 or later. The words 'Limited' or 'Ltd' date the object from after The Companies Act of 1862; a trade-mark also indicates that it was made after 1862. The stamp 'England' was used after 1891 and 'Made in England' means that the piece was made in the 20th century.

HORSE BRASSES

*Collecting horse brasses first became popular in the
1920s and there are now several thousand designs to
choose from*

In the days when knights used to joust, their warhorses were decorated with plumes, cloths and elaborate harnesses. In due course, working horses of all kinds had their leather harnesses embellished, this time with decorative brasses.

Original horse brasses, which were perhaps made as early as the 16th century, were hand-hammered from sheets of brass, using a hammer, a punch and a file. From 1830 they were cast in sand moulds that were created from patterns skilfully carved in close-grained pearwood. And from 1870 to the present they have been produced by die-stamping designs into a thin sheet of brass.

Apart from the fact that they are attractive and enhanced the look of a horse, there were other reasons why they came into use. Some were certainly used for identification purposes, bearing the coat of arms of the horse's owner or a name with some kind of decoration. In time the ornamental side became more important. By 1900 some 2000 different designs appeared on Britain's horses.

LUCKY CHARMS

There are those that argue that horse brasses have a deeper significance. Certainly they have long been regarded as lucky charms. Those that incorporate crescents and stars may relate to ancient worship of heavenly bodies and a wish to ward off the 'Evil Eye'. Whatever their origins, horse brasses were being widely used on harnesses by the 19th century.

Cast brasses were filed and polished by hand before being sold. Short stubs on the reverse, that allowed the brass to be held in a vice, were filed off but traces of them can still be seen on some brasses.

The colour of the brass might be altered in several ways. A sequence of immersions in acid solution mellowed the colour. Other brasses were coated with lacquer which altered the colour and stopped oxidization.

Polished horse brasses, whether displayed on a leather harness or hung singly, look very good against a beam or on a white wall.

Michael Michaels

A MODERN souvenir brass, featuring a tree and stamped 'Milton Keynes'. It is of poor quality.

TWO REPRODUCTION brasses. The skull and crossbones is a masonic motif and the original brass is very rare. The other brass is from Pendeen in Cornwall and depicts tin mining.

DECORATIVE BRASSES

After World War 1, as the use of working horses declined, people began to take an interest in brasses for their own sake. By the 1920s, original brasses and those manufactured purely for decorative purposes began to appear on the walls of pubs, hotels and homes. They were mounted on horse leathers or hung directly on the wall or on a beam in groups or lines.

Many designs depict birds or mammals, including such unlikely species as pelicans, camels and elephants. Others incorporate heraldic devices, inn signs, trees, flowers, hearts or sun and moon emblems. The variety is almost endless, providing huge scope for collectors. You can build up a very interesting collection by specializing in one particular type of design.

THE HART APPEARS IN THE CRESTS *of several landowners. Horse brasses from the Duke of Westminster's estates, for instance, include a hart's head.*

TWO MATCHING PAIRS *of brasses on a brass-riveted martingale. The central brasses are popular stamped patterns; the other two are sun flashes.*

THREE 1930S BRASSES. *From left, a tarnished brass depicting a central heart within rayed piercing, a Sussex-type horse within a drilled rim and a military brass with a cock on a bugle.*

REAL  FAKE

Poor modern reproductions on mock leather (bottom) have little detail and are badly finished when contrasted with good old ones.

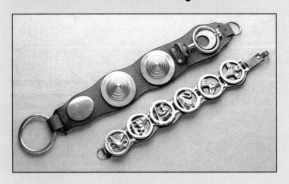

A HORSE BRASS ❷
showing a coracle fisherman carrying a coracle on his back. It is probably of Welsh origin.

❺ TURN-OF-THE-CENTURY BRASSES
on harness. The swinger at the top was worn between the horse's ears. Below it are sun flashes to reflect the sun's rays.

THE HORSESHOE ❷
is usually downturned in horse brasses. This design, with the horse's head and neck looking left, is a very common one.

FOUR BRASSES FROM THE 1930s: ❷
from left, Tower Refuge on Conister Rock in Douglas Bay (Isle of Man), a Sussex agricultural brass depicting a shepherd, a diamond playing-card motif and a Jamaica Inn brass from Cornwall.

❺ ❼ TWO STRINGS OF BRASSES
on harness. Both have moon brasses and the one at the top, made in the 1930s, has an eight-pointed star in a patterned surround.

Michael Michaels

113

COLLECTOR'S NOTES

Horse brasses are relatively inexpensive but if you want to collect genuine Victorian ones, that were actually used on horses, you will need some experience of looking for the correct signs of wear from the harness. Such 'real' horse brasses are usually well finished on the inside and show signs of having been frequently polished over the years. The majority of brasses on sale have been made since 1920 and have always hung on a wall.

WAYS TO CLEAN

The lacquer or varnish that protected antique brassware is usually worn away now. A slow oxidizing process takes place on the surface of brass, and if the oxide is very old, a caustic solution will be needed to remove it. This is a job for the professional. Acetone, however, will remove old cellulose, the commonest lacquer.

For general cleaning of brass yourself, a piece of lemon dipped in fine salt is as effective as any of the proprietary spirit-based cleaners – if a little messy! To polish your brasses use one of the manufactured liquid or paste polishes or impregnated non-scratch wadding. Apply polish with a soft brush and buff the brass with a soft duster. Brass is a soft metal that can be scratched by fingernails, so wear rubber gloves or soft gardening gloves if you want to prevent this.

REPAIRS

Simple repairs to brass objects can be effected with silver or lead solder, but anything complicated should be carried out by a professional. Members of the British Artist Blacksmiths' Association are well qualified to

CLOSE UP *on* HOW THEY ARE MADE

You can tell a great deal about the age of a horse brass from the quality of its manufacture. Victorian brasses for use on working horses were cast in solid brass and have a flat back. They are well crafted and well finished. Wall brasses, die-stamped from a thin brass sheet, are lighter.

Rear view of a modern wall brass (above), showing how the design has been stamped into a thin sheet of brass.

Souvenir brasses with place names (above) are almost certainly from the 1930s or later.

A flat back (right) indicates that the brass was cast – the usual 19th-century method.

Michael Michaels

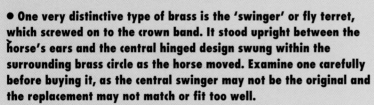
carry out excellent restoration work on valuable antique pieces.

Remember that reproduction brassware is almost always made from thinner sheets of brass. This is easily dented, which can give a false impression of age.

FINDING GOOD BRASSES

Antiques shops and bric-a-brac shops usually have a selection of brasses. They are the sort of thing that can also be picked up at car boot sales, street markets and jumble sales. Part of the fun is in hunting them out and, if this proves thirsty work, you can always pop into a pub and check out their collection.

CANDLESTICKS

Over the centuries, candlesticks have been made to the same basic design, but in a dazzling and ever-increasing array of patterns and materials

An attractive collection of brass, tin and enamel chambersticks, brass candlesticks and brass snuffer sets (these consist of snuffers and snuffer trays).

As late as 1939, one quarter of British homes had no electricity – so candlesticks have remained a vital household supply until very recently.

Almost all early candlesticks were made of metal; the first models had a pricket – a flat plate with a pin on it – on which the candle was impaled. Socket-style candlesticks appeared in the 17th century and quickly became the most popular design, though pricket candlesticks survived for use in church and have reappeared in some modern designs.

In the 18th century, people began to use glass and porcelain to make candlesticks and the 19th and 20th centuries saw the use of every material from silver to Bakelite. Elaborate silver and gilt candelabra with fluted columns were very popular for the dining room. Solid silver designs were also made in silver plate; Dresden china was used for the more ornate sticks, while cheaper ones were made of brass. There were glass candlesticks with slender plant motifs from the French and Austrian glasshouses, and candlesticks of gleaming, polished wood.

But these elegant designs were intended for the rooms downstairs. Upstairs in the bedroom, a different style prevailed.

CHAMBERSTICKS

Chambersticks were short-stemmed holders with drip trays and handles, especially designed for carrying between rooms and lighting the way to bed. They were made of brass, pressed glass, earthenware, iron or wood. The simplest of all were of enamelled tin, often in pale blue. Chambersticks often formed part of the dressing table set, and and there were pairs of squat sticks on straps for draping over mirrors.

As the 20th century advanced into the age of electric lighting, chambersticks were largely forgotten. Candlesticks have remained as popular as ever, though more for decoration than for function, and modern examples come in as wide a range of designs as those of the Victorians and Edwardians.

Without light shining through, this glass stick looks black. It is one of a pair, dating from the late 19th century.

Ray Duns

MARBLE, GLASS AND WOOD

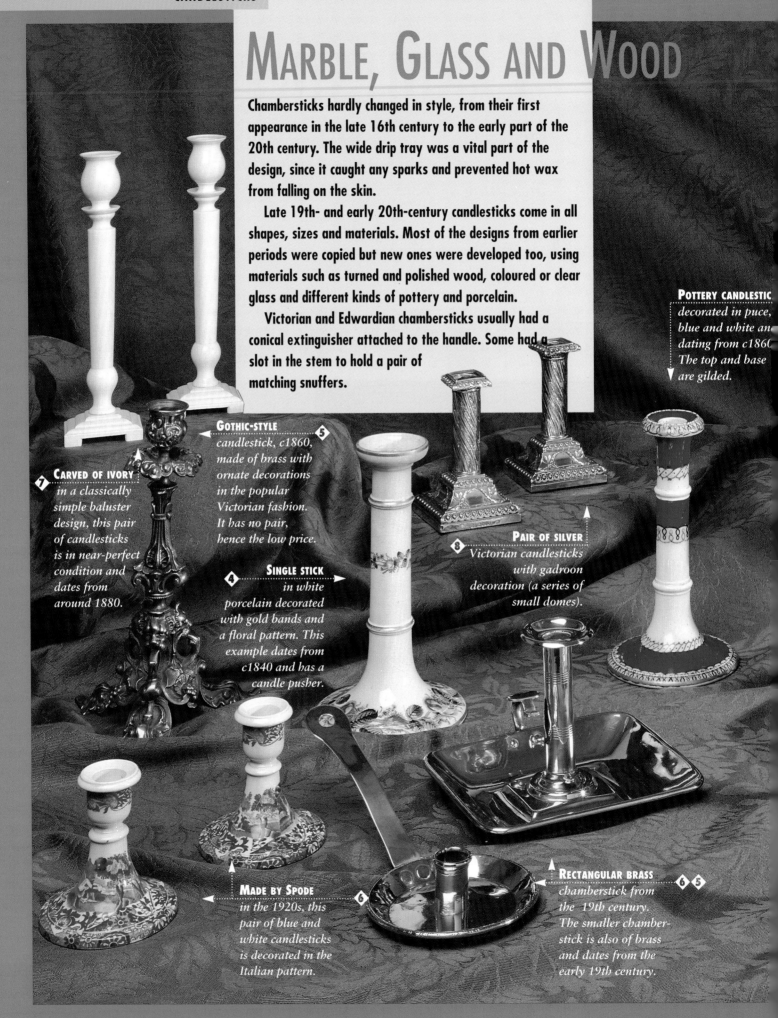

Chambersticks hardly changed in style, from their first appearance in the late 16th century to the early part of the 20th century. The wide drip tray was a vital part of the design, since it caught any sparks and prevented hot wax from falling on the skin.

Late 19th- and early 20th-century candlesticks come in all shapes, sizes and materials. Most of the designs from earlier periods were copied but new ones were developed too, using materials such as turned and polished wood, coloured or clear glass and different kinds of pottery and porcelain.

Victorian and Edwardian chambersticks usually had a conical extinguisher attached to the handle. Some had a slot in the stem to hold a pair of matching snuffers.

POTTERY CANDLESTIC
decorated in puce, blue and white an dating from c186C The top and base are gilded.

GOTHIC-STYLE 5
candlestick, c1860, made of brass with ornate decorations in the popular Victorian fashion. It has no pair, hence the low price.

CARVED OF IVORY 7
in a classically simple baluster design, this pair of candlesticks is in near-perfect condition and dates from around 1880.

SINGLE STICK 4
in white porcelain decorated with gold bands and a floral pattern. This example dates from c1840 and has a candle pusher.

PAIR OF SILVER 8
Victorian candlesticks with gadroon decoration (a series of small domes).

MADE BY SPODE
in the 1920s, this pair of blue and white candlesticks is decorated in the Italian pattern. 6

RECTANGULAR BRASS 6 5
chamberstick from the 19th century. The smaller chamberstick is also of brass and dates from the early 19th century.

ENGLISH SILVER-PLATE ⑧ candlesticks, c1855. They are in an elegant baluster design with foliate (leaf-shaped) decoration.

1920s BRASS ⑥ candlesticks in the popular barley sugar twist design, which first appeared in the previous century.

ONE OF FOUR ⑦ oak sticks in the Arts and Crafts style, c1890. Price is for the set of four.

PAIR OF EBONY baluster candlesticks, from the late Edwardian era.

IN CLEAR GLASS, ③ this matched pair of short-stemmed candlesticks was made in the 1920s.

THREE CHAMBER- ④ sticks in (left) tin c1860, (right) white enamel c1870 and (front) china with crimped edge c1900.

COLLECTOR'S NOTES

Candlesticks and chambersticks come in all shapes, sizes, styles and materials, and can make a beautiful and fascinating collection.

Chambersticks may have been more mundane pieces than tablesticks when they were first made, but as they were not kept when electricity took over, they are now less common and are increasing in value. Look for chambersticks in the best possible condition; most will be dented and scratched as they were heavily used and are likely to have been dropped a few times. The most valuable examples are those which still have the original extinguisher and snuffers.

SILVER, BRASS AND PEWTER

Tablesticks were often made of more expensive metals such as brass or silver and, of course, as each one took far more metal than a chamberstick they are likely to be more expensive. Liberty's produced both tablesticks and chambersticks in pewter for their Tudric range and in silver for the Cymric range – these now fetch hundreds of pounds at auction.

Early 19th-century silver candlesticks from makers like Matthew Boulton of Birmingham were not used for everyday purposes and are now very valuable indeed. A set of 12 Matthew Boulton candlesticks made in 1803 fetched £28,000 at auction.

Both brass and silver should be polished with a non-abrasive polish and washed in soapy water from time to time, then wiped with a chamois leather. Wooden sticks should be regularly dusted and occasionally rubbed with a suitable oil – almond oil, for instance. Porcelain and glass candlesticks can be washed

Ray Duns

DESIGN IN FOCUS — ALTAR CANDLESTICKS

Church candlesticks retained the old-fashioned pricket design after socket-style sticks were introduced. In this case, the pricket is formed by a threaded screw which runs the full length of the candlestick and protrudes from the wide drip tray to hold the candle. It is secured at the base with a butterfly nut. These sticks have been cast in three main sections with two decorative rings dividing the column from the top and base. The separate sections are held in place by the threaded screw. The drip tray has three decorative supports in the shape of griffins (a mythical beast, half lion and half bird). The base rests on three clawed bird feet, each grasping a ball. The candlesticks are made of brass and would cost around £1800 for the pair.

1. THREADED END OF RETAINING BOLT FORMS PRICKET
2. DRIP TRAY WITH GRIFFIN SUPPORTERS
3. DECORATIVE RINGS AT TOP AND BOTTOM OF COLUMN
4. BASE CAST IN ONE PIECE WITH GRIFFIN MOTIF
5. BALL AND CLAW FEET

Though this looks like a candle holder, it is in fact a lamp fuelled by vegetable oil. The silver snuff is exactly like a candle snuff, in both design and function. This rare example dates from 1819 and was designed by Matthew Boulton.

by hand in soapy water and carefully rinsed.

When buying, check for holes caused by excessive polishing of thin silver and avoid any metal sticks with signs of welding or soldering. Fakes are best detected by experts, but in the case of brass, watch out for modern pieces which have been 'distressed' to age them. Victorian brass is lighter in colour than modern brass. Silver pieces have sometimes been recast – examine the hallmarks carefully.

Always buy candlesticks in pairs whenever possible – single sticks can be worth as little as an eighth of the value of a pair.

PRESERVING EQUIPMENT

The equipment needed to preserve summer produce for the cold winter months was much the same in Victorian times as now, with preserving pans, scales, ladles and jars all put to good use by the busy cook or housewife

Peter Reilly

Today, refrigeration and air transport have made the effects of the seasons almost negligible but in the 19th century, one of the cook's tasks was to preserve gluts of low-priced summer produce and store them for the winter.

To enable the Victorian cook to capture the delicious tastes of summer in jams, jellies and chutneys, a large preserving pan, with straight or outward-sloping sides, was essential, to allow excess water in the fruit to evaporate quickly. The pan was made in a metal of good conductivity, such as silver, copper or brass, so that the jam cooked evenly.

As well as the preserving pan, scales for weighing the ingredients were needed, along with brass or iron trivets to rest hot pans on,

wooden spoons, a metal ladle and funnel for pouring, and containers for storing. A perforated skimmer with a long handle was used for removing the foam, which was much more copious with the loaf sugar used in those days.

The handsome kitchen scales, with their range of weights and big, wide pan, were made of brass or brass and cast-iron. The containers used were often stoneware jars, sealed with thick greaseproof paper and goose grease or mutton fat. However, glass came more and more widely into use during the period; wide-necked jars and narrower bottles were made of clear or palest blue-green glass, shot through with tiny air bubbles. They were sealed with cork and wax.

Before the age of refrigeration, preserving summer fruit and vegetables by bottling them or turning them into jams and jellies was an essential task for almost every Victorian household.

PANS & JARS

The type of equipment used for preserving has changed little, if at all, over the years. The most important item was the preserving pan, still produced in the same shape today as it was more than 100 years ago. Although some households had treasured preserving pans which were handed down from mother to daughter over the generations, most people had new ones, and these still make covetable antiques today.

Cast-iron and brass scales are popular in today's kitchens and reproductions of Victorian styles can be easily found. Originals, however, complete with weights, are usually beautifully crafted and are functional as well as ornamental.

Ceramic preserving jars are likewise still produced today in Victorian styles.

5 **A FINE QUALITY SHEET COPPER**
preserving pan with two side handles of solid brass. Copper was a very efficient conductor of heat.

3 5 **A LONG-HANDLED**
ladle was ideal for use with a brass preserving pan.

5 **A HEAVY SHEET BRASS**
preserving pan with an iron swing handle.

③ STONEWARE ➡
and glass preserving jars from the 1920s and 30s are surprisingly inexpensive.

④ VARIETIES OF CERAMIC
preserving jars extensively used in the 19th century included (left to right) flat-lidded salt-glazed stoneware and flat-lidded drabware versions.

⑥ DECORATIVE VICTORIAN SCALES
in good condition, complete with original weights, are much sought after by kitchenalia collectors.

④ FUNCTIONAL LATE VICTORIAN
iron and brass scales, with a complete set of weights. ▼

⑤ HANGING SCALES, ⬅ ②
such as this one dating from the 1940s, could weigh large amounts of fruit and vegetables.

Photographs by Peter Reilly, Roy Duns, Chris Barker and Rosemary Weller

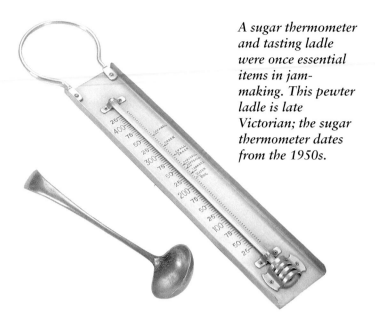

A sugar thermometer and tasting ladle were once essential items in jam-making. This pewter ladle is late Victorian; the sugar thermometer dates from the 1950s.

COLLECTOR'S NOTES

There are specialist dealers in kitchenalia from whom you can buy really fine quality copper or brass preserving pans as well as wonderfully decorative iron and brass kitchen scales. But many of these pieces, like some of the ones we've shown you, will be fairly expensive, having been cleaned and polished up and, in some cases, carefully restored.

However, lots of kitchen equipment can be found at car-boot sales, in junk shops and market stalls and in auctions of house clearances, where a miscellany of kitchen items might be sold in a number of different lots.

Most of the pieces you will find probably date from the 1930s or 40s on but, if they are still functional and in relatively good condition, they can be bargains at only a few pounds and pence. Sturdy ceramic preserving jars and glass Kilner-type or screw-top jars fall into this category, as do ladles, spoons, skimmers and thermometers.

GLEAMING BRASS AND COPPER

Because they are so attractive, brass and copper pots and pans have always held their value and you're unlikely to find them at rock-bottom prices unless the metal is so tarnished and dirty as to be unrecognizable. But even if you pay a fairly high price for these, it can still be worthwhile because they are highly durable and will last for generations.

Most people nowadays do not use their brass and copper pans for making preserves but rather as decorative objects in a kitchen, dining or sitting room, to create a warm, cosy, country-cottage effect.

Cast-iron and brass kitchen scales can also be found at fairly reasonable prices but, if you intend to use them rather than just display them, make sure you have a complete set of the weights that go with them.

CLOSE UP on PAN METALS

In Victorian times, most cooks preferred copper preserving pans because they were excellent heat conductors, even though the metal dented easily; a metal of good conductivity ensured that the jam cooked evenly and reached its setting point quickly. Copper saucepans were generally lined with tin, as copper can react and be toxic with some foods, but preserving pans were never lined.

There were two reasons for this: first, the large quantity of sugar in the jams and jellies rendered the copper completely safe; and secondly, the melting point of sugar is only just above the boiling point of sugar.

Brass pans were cheaper and were the choice of women on lower budgets but were less efficient heat conductors.

Brass preserving pans were more common, and cheaper, than copper ones. Silver pans were used by a wealthy few.

Ray Duns

ROLLING PINS

At first glance simply a basic piece of kitchen equipment, rolling pins were once highly prized love tokens given by sailors to their sweethearts

Many rolling pins are surprisingly attractive, with ornate decoration including enamelling, gilding and transfer printing. Also to be found are 'sailor's charms', hollow glass rolling pins which were filled with sweets and given to wives or girlfriends. Although some decorated rolling pins were used in the kitchen, many were considered beautiful enough to be displayed.

Rolling pins as we know them first became popular from the 17th century, when they were made in glass, porcelain or wood. Among the earliest designs were those made from coarse glass, which had the two qualities essential for making good pastry – they were both cool and relatively heavy.

But among the most collectable of all rolling pins are those of coloured glass. A large number were made at the Nailsea glassworks near Bristol, from the end of the 18th century. The first colour to be used was a rich dark blue, although the range soon included bottle green, black and opaque white.

Special effects like blue and white marbling, mottling, speckling and stippling were also particularly popular and by the 1850s ruby, turquoise and amethyst had been added to the range. Glass rolling pins were then also being made at glassworks in London, Shropshire, Yorkshire and Stourbridge.

Wooden pins are a cheaper alternative to other materials and cost from £10. They come in a variety of woods, most of which are either stained or lightly polished. Some have an extra roller, carved with an intricate pattern, which was used to impress a pretty design on to biscuits.

Duncan Smith

COLLECTOR'S NOTES

Although many people collect rolling pins purely for their decorative value, they can be put to use if they are not particularly delicate.

Because of their superior decorative qualities, glass rolling pins are more collectable than either wooden or ceramic ones. Most expensive are deep blue Nailsea pins dating from 1790-1810, followed by those with a marbled effect from 1810-30. These can cost up to £200. But the most colourful and interesting glass rolling pins date from 1830-60.

One popular decorative technique was enamelling, which produced attractively simple designs in one or more colours. Gilding produced a much more sophisticated look, particularly on dark colours, where simple designs could be picked out to striking effect. But it was a time-consuming process and uneconomical for the mass market.

Perfect for cheaper reproduction was transfer printing. This was a quick, easy – and above all cheap – method of decorating both china and glass and the majority of Victorian rolling pins are decorated in this way. At the top of the range are those with intricate scenes and verses, and those with dates which were specially made for births or marriages.

Duncan Smith

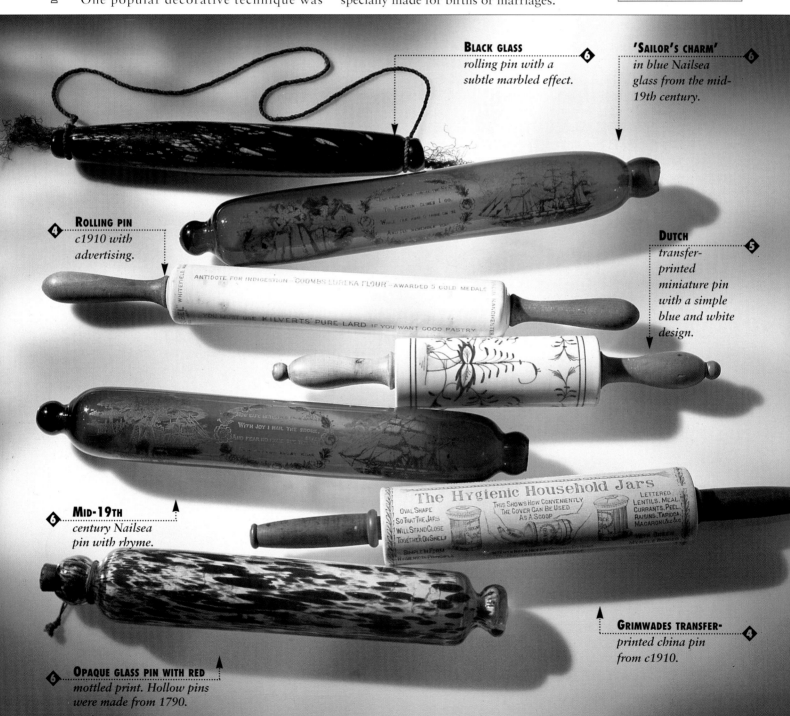

BLACK GLASS *rolling pin with a subtle marbled effect.* ◊

'SAILOR'S CHARM' *in blue Nailsea glass from the mid-19th century.* ◊

ROLLING PIN *c1910 with advertising.* ◊

DUTCH *transfer-printed miniature pin with a simple blue and white design.* ◊

MID-19TH *century Nailsea pin with rhyme.* ◊

GRIMWADES TRANSFER- *printed china pin from c1910.* ◊

OPAQUE GLASS PIN WITH RED *mottled print. Hollow pins were made from 1790.* ◊

ANTIDOTE FOR INDIGESTION — COOMBS EUREKA FLOUR — AWARDED 5 GOLD MEDALS

YOU MUST USE KILVERTS' PURE LARD IF YOU WANT GOOD PASTRY

The Hygienic Household Jars

JELLY MOULDS

No large 18th- or 19th-century house would be without a selection of moulds for shaping various desserts and savoury dishes for presentation at table, and these make a decorative and very useful addition to a modern kitchen

Spike Powell

The great variety of shapes available means a collection of antique jelly moulds is always an interesting subject for a display, whatever they are made of. These ones are all in creamware.

Jellies have been around a long, long time, from the 14th century at least. Originally they were savoury rather than sweet and were made by boiling up such unpromising bits and pieces as sheep's heads, cows' or pigs' feet or, in the case of hartshorn jelly, shavings taken from the antlers of a deer.

The resultant goo was clarified with egg white, strained, flavoured with wine, herbs and spices, and poured into moulds that were embedded in ice to set. Jellies took many hours to make and were very much food for the rich. As gelatin was such a co-operative material, readily flowing into ridges, ribs and twists, moulds could be as fanciful as the maker's ingenuity could devise, and several were used to build up elaborate tableaux for banquets. None of these medieval moulds, though, has survived to the present day.

The earliest examples we have are from the 1730s. By this time, sugar from the West Indies was readily available and jellies and other shaped confections were popular desserts, artistically presented and coloured with natural ingredients such as cochineal (red), syrup of violets (blue), spinach (green), saffron (yellow) and chocolate (brown).

FLUTES, FRUIT AND TURKS' CAPS

At this time, moulds were made of thinly-potted, white salt-glazed stoneware. Later in the century, creamware and pearlware were used. There was a huge variety of shapes; Wedgwood alone produced many different piped and fluted moulds, turks' caps, castles, suns and moons, wheatsheafs, Egyptian motifs, fruit, classical urns, religious subjects and national emblems, among others. They were often sold in 'nests' of graduated sizes, and large kitchens would have several dozen.

In the 1830s, copper jelly moulds became popular. Hammered or die-stamped into shape and lined with tin to prevent verdigris poisoning, copper moulds were more likely to have abstract shapes than representational ones. When polished, they looked very well in a kitchen, and often doubled as cake moulds.

In the 1840s, a heavy brown salt-glaze stoneware was increasingly used for moulds, and various earthenware finishes were literally pressed into service in the 19th century.

Pressed glass moulds were introduced in the 1880s. The best ones were made by Sowerby in Gateshead. The majority were shaped as fluted circles or ovals, though crouching rabbits, tortoises and other animals remained a popular subject in the 20th century, when many pressed glass moulds were imported from Czechoslovakia and the USA.

A FEW COPPERS

Copper jelly moulds are decorative as well as useful, and much sought after for display in period kitchens. As a result of this, large, heavy moulds – which tend also to be earlier in date – tend to fetch the best prices of all copper moulds, while those with decoration or other marks, including the names of retailers, coats of arms or the owner's initials – especially those of a well-known person – on the outside, attract an additional premium. Retailers' names to look for include Jones Bros(suppliers to the Duke of Wellington), Benham & Sons (who used the St Paul's cross trade mark) and Adams & Son.

In addition to the standard mould shapes, you may also come across ring moulds, which produced a hoop of jelly, the centre of which was filled, according to taste, with cream, fruits or something savoury, and small aspic moulds, made to present single portions of savoury treats in a clear jelly. These small copper moulds are often more detailed, and were made in a wider variety of shapes, than larger ones.

THE CLASSIC CASTELLATED DESIGN ◊
is well suited to copper moulds, which can generally supply a sharper edge than glass or earthenware. This is a fairly early Victorian example.

MOULD DESIGNS ◊
bearing relief decoration of stylized versions of plants, plumes and other natural objects were almost as common as castellated designs. This example is mid-Victorian in origin.

◊ **THE SCALLOP SHELL DESIGN**
could be used to make sweet jellies or other desserts, but was more usually used to shape savoury portions of seafood in aspic.

❻ **THIS LATE REGENCY MOULD**
is a standard shape, but has a fine, warm patina. It was probably made in Birmingham, the centre of copper production at the time.

MUCH BRIGHTER ❻
and more new-looking than it should be, this cleanly-modelled mould gains interest through its star shape.

❻ **VINE LEAVES AND GRAPES**
decorate this unusual box-shaped mould of the mid-19th century.

❻ **THIS EARLY MOULD**
is sized for an individual serving. The hole in the top leads to a tube going the depth of the mould, creating a hole that could be filled with some other delicacy.

THE DUMPY MELON SHAPE ❻
was a favourite for blancmange. Less cohesive than jellies, blancmanges tended to be shaped in less extravagant moulds to ensure that they emerged in pristine condition.

Roy Duns/Peter Greenhalf

127

GLASS AND CREAMWARE

Sowerby glass moulds from the late 19th century are highly collectable, but the great majority of glass moulds to be found today are very reasonably priced, and represent good value if you're looking for something with which to shape desserts.

The price of creamware moulds is determined by their age and complexity. Early pieces by Wedgwood tend to fetch the best prices. The cream of the crop are two-piece Wedgwood 'core' moulds. The inner part, shaped like an obelisk, cone or wedge, was finely painted; its cover, in the same shape, had a hole in the top, through which clear jelly was poured. Once the jelly was set, the coated core was used as a table decoration which shimmered attractively in candlelight. The jelly was never eaten.

Marked earthenware moulds tend to attract a slight premium, particularly those of top makers such as Booths, Copeland & Garrett, Davenport, Grimwades and Minton. Some 20th-century pieces by makers such as Shelley and Maling, particularly those showing art deco influences, will also fetch a good price.

THE LITTLE PEG FEET
seen on this creamware piece would have ensured a flow of air around the bottom of the mould to aid setting. Made in 1820, the mould has a bunch of grapes design.

INDIVIDUAL PORTION MOULDS
like this do not cost much less, and may cost more, than larger ones. Price is more to do with age (this is an early example) and the quality of the modelling than size.

THIS FAMILY-SIZE MOULD,
made in the first half of the 19th century, features a wheatsheaf. This may have meant that it was intended for something cereal-based rather than for jellies, but the sheaf is just as likely to symbolize plenty and prosperity.

VARIATIONS ON THE CASTELLATED FORM ❷
popular for copper moulds are seen on the majority of 20th-century pressed glass examples. Such moulds are almost always unmarked. Many were made in Czechoslovakia and the USA.

THIS CASTELLATED MOULD ❸
is a little more elaborate than the other two illustrated on this page, and much more cleanly pressed, hence the higher price.

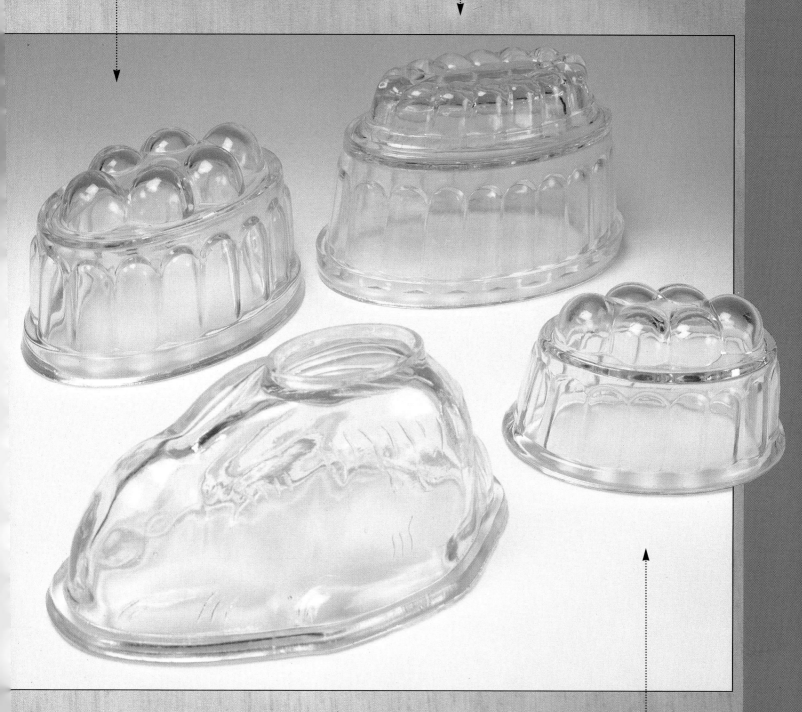

❷ **THE FAVOURITE ANIMAL SHAPE**
for jelly moulds – certainly in the 20th century – is the rabbit, perhaps because of its basically timorous, quivering nature. Nostalgic associations with childhood help to increase their desirability, though this 20th-century example is not particularly well modelled.

❷ **ANOTHER 20TH-CENTURY MOULD**
of a castellated design. For technical reasons, it's difficult to make pressed glass moulds with sharp inner edges, so the towers and battlements seen on copper castellated moulds have degenerated into fluting and vague blobby shapes.

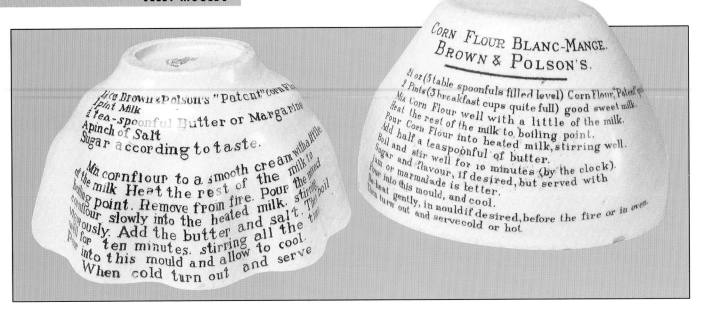

The recipes transfer-printed on these earthenware bowls identifies them as blancmange moulds made for the firm Brown & Polson, manufacturers of the important ingredient, cornflour.

COLLECTOR'S NOTES

Jelly moulds are decorative, useful and, on the whole, cheap, making them an excellent subject for a collection, particularly if you enjoy cooking and catering. Though jelly is now seen today as a nursery food - as shown by modern plastic moulds, usually shaped like teddy bears or other toys – it need not be. Old cookbooks will provide many recipes for savoury and sweet treats, including other types of moulded dessert such as flummeries thickened with oatmeal, creams flavoured with lemon and rosewater, and blancmanges. Even cakes and puddings were shaped.

Moulds were very common in the 19th century. Various gelatin preparations and the use of isinglass (derived from fish or seaweed) rather than boiled animals as a base encouraged their use. As a result, many have survived. Look for them at jumble and boot sales, in job lots at house sales and small auctions, and in junk and antiques shops.

CHOOSING

The sort you buy will depend on whether you want them to use or to display. Copper moulds are good to look at, but you should have them professionally re-tinned, to be on the safe side, before you use them. Ask about this when you buy. Glass is functional, but rarely beautiful. Creamware and earthenware can meet both needs; earthenware moulds are often decorated with transfer printing.

When buying copper, test the weight in your hand. Thin, light moulds are probably reproductions. Copper dents easily, and small dents are acceptable; caved-in moulds, of course, are not. Look for ones with a good, soft patina, and beware pieces that have been split and resoldered. Not only do they usually look unsightly, they are likely to split again.

Glass moulds are generally so cheap that you can safely reject any that are in any way chipped or cracked, but slight damage of this kind will not make much difference to an early creamware or earthenware piece. Look on earthenware moulds for marks, including Registered Design marks, which will help in dating the piece. Avoid earthenware examples which have become stained inside.

COPPER ASPIC MOULDS

Aspic moulds were made for single servings of savoury dishes, including meat, poultry, fish, eggs or game in aspic jelly and various savoury mousses. Some were shaped for specific dishes; fish moulds for fish mousse, scallops, crabs and lobsters for seafood in aspic, and so on. Another use for these small moulds was to build up elaborate edible dining-table centrepieces for special occasions.

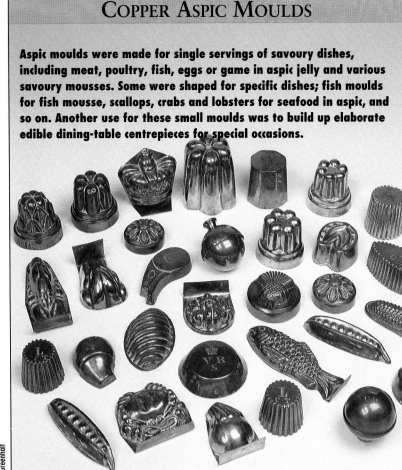

Peter Greenhalf

PLASTIC TABLEWARE

*Renowned for its bold colours and striking 1930s designs,
plastic tableware is growing in popularity with collectors who
appreciate its rather unusual visual appeal*

John Hollingshead

Because collecting plastic tableware is a relatively new phenomenon, it is still widely available and may even be found at jumble sales. A whole collection like this can be worth hundreds of pounds, a single plate £5.

Early plastics are relatively new to the collector, but they are becoming more and more popular, both for their stylish deco designs and for what they reveal about the development of the plastics industry. Some plastic collectables are now surprisingly expensive and out of the reach of the average collector, although tableware is still accessible. Some of the cheaper items available include napkin rings, ashtrays and picnicware.

Plastics can be defined as natural or synthetic materials that can be moulded by heat or pressure. Natural plastics like horn have been used for snuff boxes and decorative trinkets since the 18th century, and the modern plastics industry evolved from 19th-century experiments to find cheap substitutes for such rare and expensive natural materials.

Alexander Parkes invented Parkesine, the first semi-synthetic plastic, in 1862. However, the first real breakthrough came with the introduction of Bakelite, a plastic with good insulating and water-resisting properties which was patented by Leo Baekeland in 1909. This was the first totally man-made plastic and the trade name 'Bakelite' is now used to describe all formaldehyde plastics (where a by-product of the coal industry is mixed with phenol to form a resin). They all share its distinctive mottled brown, red or green appearance.

BAKELITE AND BEETLE

Bakelite was suitable for a vast range of goods including hairdryers and radios, its heat resistance making it ideal for anything electrical. But there were drawbacks – the first Bakelite beakers gave an unpleasant smell and flavour to hot liquids, and they were restricted to dark colours because of the special wood fillers needed to strengthen the resin.

It was the introduction of 'Beetle', or thiourea formaldehyde (a cast resin without a filler, made of urea formaldehyde and thiorea), that finally satisfied the need for a plastic suitable for food. It was tough, clean-smelling, and available in a wide range of colours.

Plastic goods first reached the mass market between the wars. In 1926 Harrods had a window display of the latest range of plastic tableware known as Linga Longa and Bandalasta. It caused a sensation. By the early 1930s, plastic tableware had proved to be an acceptable – and hardier – alternative to ceramics, and companies all over Britain were making it. Plastic was used for everything from condiment sets to cocktail shakers.

Plastic tableware soon graced every fashionable kitchen, perfectly complementing a whole new range of other plastics, including draining boards, toasters, utensils and plate racks.

DECO PLASTIC

In the late 1920s and early 1930s, as plastic designs broke away from their earlier imitation of traditional ceramic shapes, they began to follow a style all of their own. Profiles took on a much more streamlined and elegant look.

The largest manufacturer of plastic tableware in England was the Streetly Manufacturing Company, who produced Beetleware, a best-selling and affordable plastic line, sold mainly at Woolworth's. Bandalasta, made by Brookes & Adams from 1927-32, was one of the first and most expensive lines.

• Never stand plastics in direct sunlight or near hot lights – they may fade or crack.

• Scratched or cracked plastic is worth less – only buy top quality.

• A rub with metal polish will bring the gloss back to dull Bakelite.

• Soak in sterilizing fluid to remove stains.

BANDALASTA TEAPOT with green and cream marbled design. This was created with a mixture of coloured moulding powders.

BEAKERS c1930 made in thiourea formaldehyde (a sturdy resin introduced in 1921).

ORANGE SQUEEZER and toast rack, both made in urea formaldehyde.

John Hollingshead

BEETLEWARE BREAKFAST SET ❹
of plates, bowls and milk jug (some pieces are missing).

FRUIT BOWL ❸
made in Thetford Pulpware – a wood pulp covered in shiny plastic.

MOTTLED BLACK AND WHITE ❷
salt pot from the 1930s, made in urea formaldehyde.

BEETLEWARE JAM POT ❸
in orange thiourea formaldehyde.

BANDALASTA BREAKFAST SET ❻
in marbled orange and cream with a cream perspex toast rack, set on a mottled brown tray.

CUPS ❺
and saucers with matching egg cups taken from a set. They are made in mottled brown thiourea formaldehyde.

133

COLLECTOR'S NOTES

Street markets are one of the best places to search for plastic tableware. You'll usually find plenty of small mouldings such as eggcups, napkin rings and beakers.

The larger and often more decorative items of tableware, including cake stands and fruit bowls, are becoming increasingly difficult to find. This is partly because interest in collecting plastics has escalated in the last few years, and also because decorative tableware is prized above the more utilitarian pieces.

Unfortunately, a lot of plastic tableware has long since been relegated to the dustbin, and it was never manufactured on a scale to rival the most popular ceramic lines. Many surviving pieces have been chipped or cracked, and some have even partially disintegrated after heavy use or prolonged contact with hot liquids.

TOP OF THE RANGE

Bandalasta ware, undoubtedly the Rolls-Royce of the plastics industry, is the most sought-after trade name today. It has a certain solidity and a substantial feel which some of the later paper-filled urea plastics lack.

Brookes & Adams, who manufactured Bandalasta, also used extremely good quality steel dies; the pieces were given a high degree of finish. The thin lines of plastic which seeped out at the joints, known as 'flashings', were tooled away, unlike other companies' models.

The beautiful marbled colourings were unmatched by any other manufacturer and because of the way it was produced – with different coloured powders mixed in varying proportions and sprinkled into the moulds –

Ray Duns

DESIGN IN FOCUS

JAXONITE BISCUIT BARREL

Although most plastic tableware was specially designed to be practical and durable, one particular range was produced with a more decorative purpose in mind. This was known as Jaxonite, which combined a dark mottled body of urea formaldehyde, as used for Bandalasta Ware, with beautifully crafted silver-plated fittings. The effect this produced is typical of the art deco fashion for using contrasting colours and textures to create a dramatic visual effect. Large Jaxonite bowls or biscuit barrels were often bought as wedding presents and could be matched with a whole range of tableware. This biscuit barrel would cost around £35.

John Hollingshead

❶ AFTER SETTING, MOULDINGS WERE TRIMMED AND POLISHED

❷ DIFFERENT COLOURED POWDERS WERE MIXED FOR A MOTTLED PATTERN

❸ THE SILVER TRIMMING IS MARKED 'EPNS' (ELECTRO-PLATED NICKEL SILVER)

❹ THIS MARBLED EFFECT REMAINED POPULAR UNTIL THE MID-1930S

Cruets were particularly popular with manufacturers of novelty goods. These hand-painted plastic figures depict Mr Peanut (who was the trademark of the American Planter's Peanut Company) and date from the 1930s.

no two pieces are exactly alike. Bandalasta is often twice as expensive as other makes – look for the trademark on the base. You should also expect to pay high prices for large fruit and rose bowls. Colour also affects the price – Bandarouge, a rich mixture of red, orange, blue, green and yellow, is more collectable, and more expensive, than other colours.

Other high-quality trade names to look out for are Beaconware and Beetleware, both moulded by the Streetly Manufacturing Company, and Linga Longa.

OLD CORKSCREWS

Whether collected purely for their visual appeal, or as practical objects, corkscrews are available in a huge range of materials, designs and prices

Ray Duns

Corkscrews are one of those fun collectables that can be not simply collected but also used to great effect for their original purpose. They make great conversation pieces – especially if you collect novelty designs – and, though perhaps less good than modern counterparts, still open a bottle of wine efficiently.

At the end of the 17th century, vintners discovered that wine matured better when it was taken from the cask and sealed in a bottle with a cork. A device for the cork's removal thus became necessary and so began the history of the corkscrew. In the three centuries since, a great deal of ingenuity has gone into making the extraction of the cork effortless. However, no matter what shape or form a corkscrew has taken, its constituent parts have hardly changed. They are the worm, or screw; the shaft, extending upwards from the screw; and the handle.

The earliest surviving corkscrews, dating from the beginning of the 18th century, have a very short worm with a circular or ovoid handle. In many of them, the worm could be

neatly folded back into the handle, so that the corkscrew could be conveniently carried in a pocket or travel bag. By the end of the 18th century, the familiar T-shaped corkscrew had become the standard type.

The age of numerous inventions and devices began in 1795, when the Reverend Samuel Henshall launched his 'Button Screw'. This was a conventional T-shaped corkscrew with a metal button threaded between the worm and the shaft. The button pressed on the cork as the worm was driven home, helping the screw to grip firmly into the cork. The cork could now be rotated in the neck of the bottle, greatly easing its extraction.

NEW DESIGNS

After Henshall's invention the floodgates opened and more than 400 different designs of corkscrew were registered or patented in the 19th century. One of the most popular types, patented by Edward Thomason in 1802, was known as 'Thomason's Screw'. A metal barrel fitted over the worm and lodged atop the neck of the bottle, providing leverage. With the worm driven into the cork, turning the handle further activated a counter-threaded screw that drew the cork out of the bottle.

The 'King's Screw' was another popular 19th-century device. It was similar to Thomason's, but it had a smaller handle fixed at right angles to the main handle; this was turned to extract the cork after the worm had been twisted home. Both Thomason's Screw and the King's Screw were usually fitted with a small cleaning brush, almost a standard feature in 19th-century corkscrews. Some were also equipped with a small ring in the top of the handle by which they could be suspended when not in use.

Another variety of corkscrew, first made in the late 18th century but popular throughout the 1800s and into Edwardian times, was the ladies' corkscrew, designed for opening perfume bottles. The worm was generally of silver and was protected by a silver sheath. Ladies' corkscrews often formed part of a matching set of implements for the dressing case.

VICTORIAN CORKSCREWS

Steel was almost always used for the worm and shaft of corkscrews of whatever period or design. Handles, however, have been made in a wide variety of materials. Many 18th-century folding corkscrews had a silver handle, but this tended to be replaced by cheaper materials such as nickel or electroplate in the 19th century.

The greatest variety of materials is found among 19th-century T-shaped corkscrews. Most handles were of polished wood turned on the lathe. Bone, also turned on the lathe, antler, horn, tusks, and teeth were other materials used for handles. These – like wooden ones – were occasionally trimmed with brass. Some of the most decorative and delicate handles were of mother-of-pearl and porcelain. Rarest of all – and often exceedingly attractive – are those made of colourful millefiori glass. These date from the late 19th century or the early years of the 20th century.

A love of gadgetry also gave rise to the combination corkscrew, equipped to perform more than its primary function of opening bottles. The 'scissor' corkscrew, for example, was also a wirecutter, useful for dealing with champagne bottles, and often incorporated a hoof pick, a glass cutter or a tin opener. In the same way, corkscrews were sometimes incorporated in other objects, even the handles of walking sticks and umbrellas. Many pocket tool kits would also include a small corkscrew in their range of portable items.

A SIMPLE CONCERTINA CORKSCREW *known as 'Armstrong patent lazy tongs'. Made of steel, it has a bladed worm, a retaining circle that fits the bottle top and a T-shaped handle.*

THE PATENT LEVER *is an English cast-iron cork drawer in two parts. The worm is screwed in, then the handles are attached and levered apart to draw the cork from the neck.*

TWO INTERESTING DESIGNS *known as pocket folding corkscrews. A tool kit is included with the corkscrew. One is steel, one brass.*

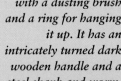

A T-BAR CORKSCREW *with a dusting brush and a ring for hanging it up. It has an intricately turned dark wooden handle and a steel shank and worm.*

AN ADVERTISING CORKSCREW *designed to promote the soft drink Bovril which had no need of a corkscrew to open its jars. It is a simple design with a short worm.*

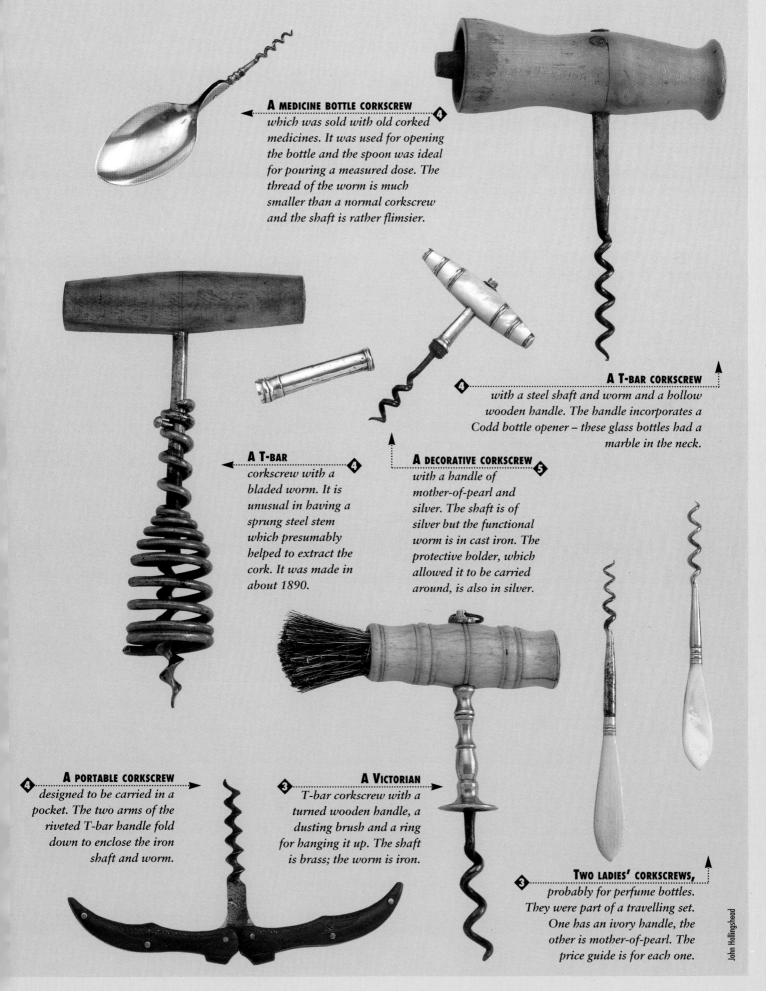

A MEDICINE BOTTLE CORKSCREW ◄ 4
which was sold with old corked medicines. It was used for opening the bottle and the spoon was ideal for pouring a measured dose. The thread of the worm is much smaller than a normal corkscrew and the shaft is rather flimsier.

A T-BAR CORKSCREW ▲
with a steel shaft and worm and a hollow wooden handle. The handle incorporates a Codd bottle opener – these glass bottles had a marble in the neck.

A T-BAR ◄ 4
corkscrew with a bladed worm. It is unusual in having a sprung steel stem which presumably helped to extract the cork. It was made in about 1890.

A DECORATIVE CORKSCREW 5
with a handle of mother-of-pearl and silver. The shaft is of silver but the functional worm is in cast iron. The protective holder, which allowed it to be carried around, is also in silver.

A PORTABLE CORKSCREW 4
designed to be carried in a pocket. The two arms of the riveted T-bar handle fold down to enclose the iron shaft and worm.

A VICTORIAN ►
T-bar corkscrew with a turned wooden handle, a dusting brush and a ring for hanging it up. The shaft is brass; the worm is iron.

TWO LADIES' CORKSCREWS, 3
probably for perfume bottles. They were part of a travelling set. One has an ivory handle, the other is mother-of-pearl. The price guide is for each one.

John Hollingshead

137

20TH-CENTURY CORKSCREWS

After the amazing ingenuity of the Victorian period, the basic design of the corkscrew changed little in the early 20th century, and the familiar T-shape remained as popular as ever. The main change was in decoration, reflecting new styles such as art deco, which was all the rage in the 1920s.

One of the favourite types of corkscrew in the 20th century has been the type in which the handle is the body of an animal and its tail is replaced with the worm. Cats, dogs, donkeys, mice and various other animals have all been used in this way. Often their bodies were stylized into chunky shapes in tune with the art deco fashion. Like their 19th-century counterparts, these animal corkscrews were made in brass and copper, but the 1930s versions were usually plated with fashionable chrome. Small ashtrays and dishes were also produced to match.

Souvenir corkscrews are another type that have been very popular in the 20th century. They often feature local emblems such as the Cornish piskie, along with county and other place names and perhaps the line 'A souvenir from ...'.

TWO STEEL TERRIER corkscrews of different designs. Though quite amusing, the ones with a worm for a tail had less leverage than a T-bar.

A T-BAR CORKSCREW with a steel shaft and worm. The curved and tapered orange handle is of dyed bone.

A T-BAR CORKSCREW of a very solid and workmanlike design, intended to provide maximum leverage. The shaft and worm are of steel and the turned handle is in stained wood.

AN ADVERTISING CORKSCREW given away by the makers of Perfecta waxed corks. In a T-bar design, it is entirely in steel with a bladed worm.

"PERFECTA" WAXED CORKS

AN ART DECO CORKSCREW in gleaming chrome. When you want to carry it around, the worm can be protected by the addition of a screw-on cover. The handle is a plump cylinder.

A MULTI-PURPOSE TOOL KIT from the pre-war period. In addition to a corkscrew, this British-made implement incorporates a bottle opener, a spike and perhaps a glass cutter.

FOUR BRASS DOGS ◆
with a corkscrew worm in place of their tail. They are all loosely modelled on terriers and probably date from the 1920s or 1930s. The price guide is for each one.

A NOVELTY ◆
corkscrew in steel, depicting the full figure of a top-hatted man with a hooked nose. There is an inscription on the base. The shaft and worm appear to fold away into the handle.

A TRAVELLING SET ◆
shown assembled (near left) and in parts (far left and centre). In addition to the corkscrew, there is also a screwdriver and a gimlet.

A MONOPOL-TYPE CORKSCREW ◆
in cast steel with a bladed worm. It has a short barrel that fits over the wine bottle's neck and allows the cork to be withdrawn as you make several further turns of the screw.

A CAST BRASS ◆
corkscrew in a novelty design depicting an Irish terrier. The worm is in bladed steel.

A NOVELTY BRASS CORKSCREW ◆
featuring a figure with a pig-like face and an unusual hat. He was perhaps a demon or a creature from myth or fairy-tale.

139

COLLECTOR'S NOTES

From a practical point of view, the most important feature of any corkscrew is the worm. The best worms have a sharp point and edges and are about as long as the average cork. The handle, whether on a manual or a mechanical model, should give a firm grip; novelty handles, designed to be visually striking, can be awkward to pull on, although many are collected solely for their visual appeal. A cleaning brush in the handle adds to the value of the item, as does any inscription, decorative engraving or brass trim.

BUILDING A COLLECTION

As they were made in such large numbers throughout the 19th century, even the best mechanical corkscrews are not particularly rare today. Less popular types, overshadowed by the more famous ones, are worth looking out for, even if they are less efficient. The engagingly impractical, the gimmicky, or 18th-century models, whose short worms make them difficult to use, can make an interesting collection if you simply want to display them rather than use them.

In the late 19th century there were some particularly complex designs and these are worth looking out for as notable examples of

An attractive cocktail set comprising corkscrew, bottle opener and cocktail sticks, dating from the 1930s. The delicately worked cocktail sticks are made in electroplated silver and are designed in the shape of various fruits. The base of the stand, the bottle opener and the corkscrew are all fashioned in chrome and black Bakelite.

splendid Victorian ingenuity.

Trade corkscrews, such as those given away with medicine bottles, are now very rare, as most people threw them away. However, it is still possible to find corkscrews made by brewers and distillers to advertise their brands.

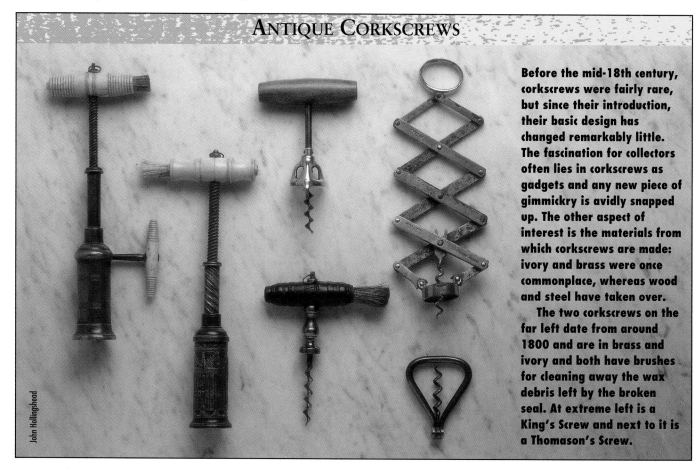

ANTIQUE CORKSCREWS

Before the mid-18th century, corkscrews were fairly rare, but since their introduction, their basic design has changed remarkably little. The fascination for collectors often lies in corkscrews as gadgets and any new piece of gimmickry is avidly snapped up. The other aspect of interest is the materials from which corkscrews are made: ivory and brass were once commonplace, whereas wood and steel have taken over.

The two corkscrews on the far left date from around 1800 and are in brass and ivory and both have brushes for cleaning away the wax debris left by the broken seal. At extreme left is a King's Screw and next to it is a Thomason's Screw.

John Hollingshead

OLD KEYS AND LOCKS

Locks and keys have been around for centuries and the Egyptians even had massive wooden keys and wooden locks well before the time of Christ

The earliest locks were of wood, with a horizontal sliding bar which was fastened by vertical pins that dropped into holes in the bolt. The lock could only be opened by inserting a key which had corresponding pegs. It was such a successful design that it lasted, with variations on the theme, for over 4,000 years. In fact, wooden pin locks were still being used on some English country furniture until the mid-19th century.

The Romans fashioned locks and keys of bronze and iron; their more elaborate designs were decorated with brass and ivory. Metal locks were first made in England as early as the 9th century.

By the 13th century, locksmithing was an established trade in London. Locks on chests were faced with decorative lockplates. By the 16th century, locks were designed with wards – fixed projections on the inside plate of a lock which could only be moved by inserting a key with a corresponding pattern. Some of the finest keys of this period came from France, where locksmiths produced steel keys with intricately cut wards and fancy fretted tops. Elaborate chest locks were made by the Germans, sometimes with a whole series of bolts held in place by springs set in the lid.

Sue Baker

GREATER SECURITY

External lockplates gradually disappeared during the late 17th century, to be replaced by locks recessed into the wood. The keyhole was protected by an escutcheon – a brass plate – which prevented the wood being damaged. When used on drawers, the inset lock was known as a till-lock, till being an old name for a drawer. The till-lock was also used on cupboards, where it was placed vertically.

Robert Barron invented the double-action tumbler lock in 1788, where the key had to bypass the wards and lift both tumblers. A little earlier, in 1784, Joseph Bramah had designed his 'invincible' lock. This replaced the fixed wards with a series of movable levers. The makers had such confidence in their new product that they offered 200 guineas to the first person to pick the lock. The prize remained unclaimed for 60 years.

The next innovation came with Jeremiah Chubb's 'detector' lock in 1818. It was also claimed to be unpickable, as any tampering disturbed the mechanism of the six-lever lock, signalling to the owner that there had been interference. The Yale cylinder lock was patented by Linus Yale in the 1840s. The barrel contained a cylindrical plug with a grooved keyway which was turned by a flattened key.

The variety of keys is extensive, as locksmiths have attempted to keep one step ahead of thieves with a talent for lock-picking. Seen here are (top) a French night-latch key, (left) an English lift-up night-latch key, (centre) a chest key and (bottom) an English safe key.

KEY MONEY

Keys have three parts: the ward which activates the lock, the shaft and the bow (the top of the key). By the 16th century, keys had either simple kidney- or heart-shaped open bows or were ornately fretted. Shafts varied in length and were either plain or decorated with fluted or spiral grooving. French keys were finely chiselled from steel, while German keys tended to be heavier with repetitive patterns to the wards.

By the 18th century, keys had become even more decorative. Bows were ornately cast in silver or silver-gilt and bore monograms or cyphers, sometimes surmounted by crowns. Others had pierced bows decorated with scrolling foliage, flowers or birds. Entwined dolphins were also favoured. Some had figural bows that were beautifully designed. Shafts were finely turned in baluster forms, or had spiralled flutes, bobbin turning, or V-shaped grooving.

Most keys fall in price guide 1-2 and even 500-year-old keys can be price guide 3-4 unless they have intricate warding or are particularly ornate. Antique locks, complete with keys, will be price guide 4-6.

1 AN EDWARDIAN KEY corroded with rust. It could be cleaned and polished; needle files are very useful.

1 A SMALL IRON KEY from the 19th century. It is in fair condition and has a dust stopper in the end of the shaft.

3 A LARGE KEY from the 18th century. It is well preserved.

1 A SMALL IRON KEY from the 19th century. It has lost its dust cap.

2 AN IRON KEY from the early 19th century. It has a collar on the shaft to prevent the pin (the end of the shaft) going too far into the lock.

2 A SIMPLE IRON KEY from the early 19th century. It has a typical open bow.

5 A SAFE KEY with an intricate ward. It is in fine condition, complete with its spring stopper. It was made by the Liverpool firm of Milner's.

3 A FRENCH LATCH KEY of c1800. They were invented by Odell.

2 A SMALL VICTORIAN KEY with an ornate bronze bow and a steel shaft or shank. It dates from 1870 and was probably the key to a small box or perhaps a drawer.

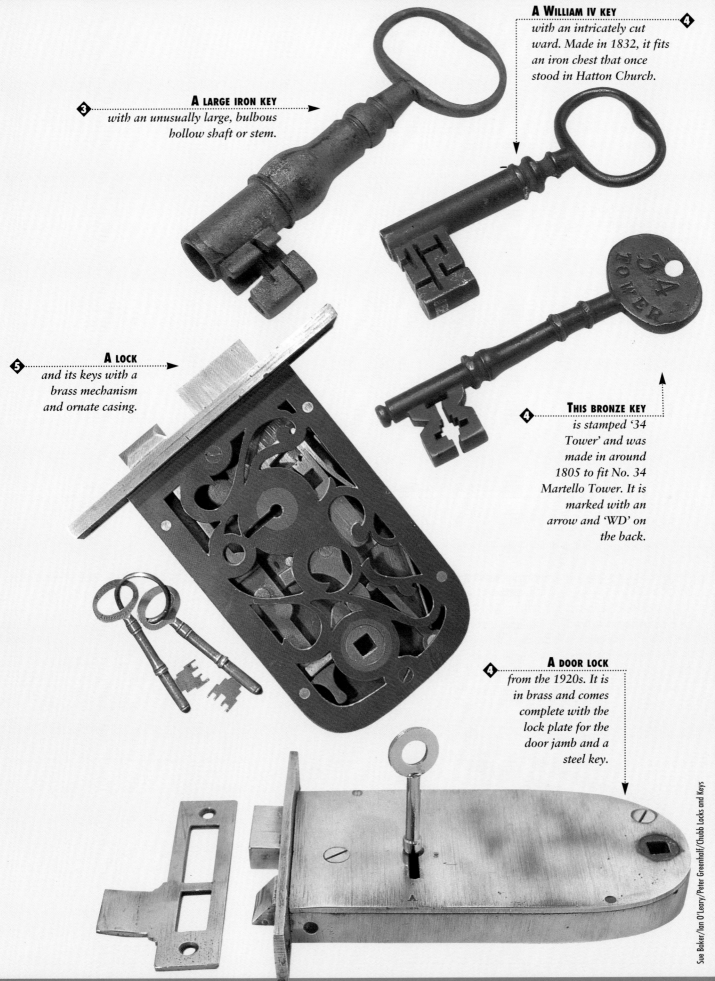

4 ◆ **A WILLIAM IV KEY**
with an intricately cut ward. Made in 1832, it fits an iron chest that once stood in Hatton Church.

3 ◆ **A LARGE IRON KEY**
with an unusually large, bulbous hollow shaft or stem.

5 ◆ **A LOCK**
and its keys with a brass mechanism and ornate casing.

4 ◆ **THIS BRONZE KEY**
is stamped '34 Tower' and was made in around 1805 to fit No. 34 Martello Tower. It is marked with an arrow and 'WD' on the back.

4 ◆ **A DOOR LOCK**
from the 1920s. It is in brass and comes complete with the lock plate for the door jamb and a steel key.

Sue Baker/Ian O'Leary/Peter Greenhalf/Chubb Locks and Keys

COLLECTOR'S NOTES

Old key and lock sets are rarely found together; keys tend to get lost over the years, and to remove a fine lock may ruin a handsome piece of furniture.

Keys turn up at antiques fairs, in multiple lots at auction, and can often be picked up at jumble or car boot sales. Locks are less easily found, being snapped up by furniture dealers to fit into restored furniture. Missing keys can be made for a lock by a good locksmith.

Locks are more easily dated than keys, although to have them in situ obviously makes the task easier. Elaborate escutcheon plates had been phased out by about 1770, becoming smaller or being replaced by plain brass keyholes. Locks in the 17th century were generally of steel, almost square in shape, upwards of 7.5cm/3in across, and held in place by nails.

By 1720, locks on domestic

Mounted for display on a wooden stand, this is a 'Patent Climax Detector Lock', designed by Edwin Cotterill. Manufactured in Birmingham, it was used in the 19th century on safes.

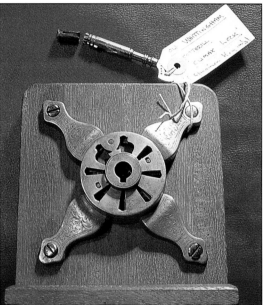

furniture were smaller, at 5cm/2in across. Steel and iron locks on quality furniture were replaced by brass in the mid-1700s and were secured by screws. The iron till-lock is still in use. Continental locks of the 18th century were usually longer than English locks from the same period.

Bramah's locks were frequently stamped with the maker's name, and a study of this stamp can reveal the date of manufacture. The keys were smaller than others of their time and were frequently lost. To replace an old Bramah key or pick the lock can prove almost impossible, but try contacting Bramah who are still trading in London.

Locks in the 19th century were patented and were impressed with the words 'secure' or 'patent', or were stamped with royal cyphers, giving an indication of age.

Dating keys is very difficult. The same patterns have been made for centuries and it is still possible to buy Continental keys based on Renaissance designs. Only frequent handling, perhaps visiting museums and studying collections, or buying from a reputable dealer will ensure a satisfactory purchase.

DESIGN IN FOCUS
A PRESENTATION KEY

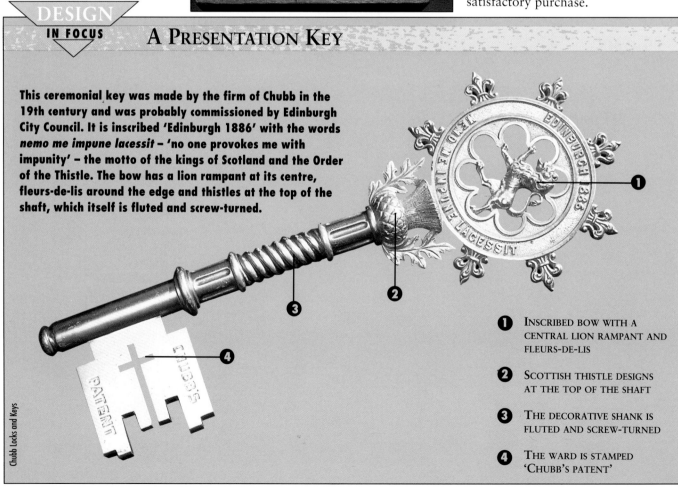

This ceremonial key was made by the firm of Chubb in the 19th century and was probably commissioned by Edinburgh City Council. It is inscribed 'Edinburgh 1886' with the words *nemo me impune lacessit* **– 'no one provokes me with impunity' – the motto of the kings of Scotland and the Order of the Thistle. The bow has a lion rampant at its centre, fleurs-de-lis around the edge and thistles at the top of the shaft, which itself is fluted and screw-turned.**

Chubb locks and keys

❶ INSCRIBED BOW WITH A CENTRAL LION RAMPANT AND FLEURS-DE-LIS

❷ SCOTTISH THISTLE DESIGNS AT THE TOP OF THE SHAFT

❸ THE DECORATIVE SHANK IS FLUTED AND SCREW-TURNED

❹ THE WARD IS STAMPED 'CHUBB'S PATENT'

TREEN

*Those who enjoy the look and feel of old wood will enjoy collecting treen;
the warm patina and worn surface that come only with age
and use are a large part of its spreading appeal*

Ian O'Leary

Literally speaking, treen is anything that is made from wood, but in a collectors' sense it's usually confined to small articles (no bigger than a spinning wheel) made from carved and/or turned wood and in everyday domestic, farm or trade use. It can include bowls, paperweights, spoons, cruets, platters, snuff and smoking aids, toys, pen boxes, lap desks, love tokens or tools, but not furniture or purely decorative 'art' objects.

Wood was for centuries the main material from which domestic objects were made. People ate off wooden trenchers and drank from wooden vessels. Wood was cheaper, more easily worked and more readily available than ceramics, glass, pewter or other metals.

Native woods – in England ash, elm and beech – were used for the more workaday pieces, while the more decorative ones were usually in fine-grained hardwoods, better able

to take carving. These included mahogany, yew, olive, sycamore and lignum vitae.

The latter was especially important because of its size. It could make large bowls, 40cm/16in across, without a join. The dark surface of the wood was suitable for both applied and inlaid decoration. Large 'wassail' bowls are a rare and expensive find today.

Other methods for decorating pieces of treen included covering them with designs in penwork, pokerwork or paint (particularly common on Scandinavian pieces), or using parquetry, marquetry and pieces of decorative metal, but the great majority were simply turned or hand-carved. Many pieces have an agreeably 'folksy' quality, and have developed a warm, attractive patina over the years, while others, such as the rare Georgian tea caddies carved in the shape of pieces of fruit from the appropriate fruitwoods, are precision pieces.

Collectors of treen include those interested in domestic and agricultural history, in tools and kitchenalia and in the rituals of taking tea or tobacco, as well as those who simply enjoy looking at, handling and using old wood.

TREEN

For lovers and collectors of wooden objects, treen has for a long time been very much a poor relation to furniture, fine carvings and highly decorated and ornamental veneered pieces. It's only in the last 20 years that it's been recognized as a collectable in its own right – rather than as part of a general collection of kitchenalia, toys, smoking requisites, tableware, Tunbridge ware (see issue 25, pages 597-600), Mauchline ware (see issue 21, pages 501-504) and so on – and though prices have begun to rise, many Victorian pieces can still be bought for price guide 4.

The main determinants of price are age (18th-century and earlier pieces are unusual and command a premium) and the quality of the craftsmanship. Unusual hardwoods such as lignum vitae tend to attract interest, while pieces with more elaborate carving also tend to fetch higher prices. These often originated in Europe, where wooden pieces were made for wealthy customers at a much later date than they were in Britain.

5 NUTCRACKERS
with a screw action preceded the scissor types. One of these has been carved as a squirrel. Price is per item.

3 A PLEASANT PATINA
adds to the utilitarian appeal of this pine Edwardian coffee grinder. Earlier ones in walnut are sought after.

4 MEASURING BOWLS
holding a pint or half-pint are made to stack away on top of one another when not in use.

4 ⬦ **A MORTAR AND PESTLE** *was standard equipment in kitchens, used for crushing nuts, herbs and spices. This early example has a mortar of lignum vitae.*

3 ⬦ **DAIRY ANTIQUES** *are a rich source of treen. These ribbed and moulded butter pats were used to shape and squeeze newly-made butter. Price is per item.*

LOOKING LIKE DRINKING VESSELS, *these are in fact Victorian pint measures. The one on the far left was probably used domestically, but the royal initials and the number 27 on the one on the near right suggest it was an offical measure made to be used in shops or markets.* ⬦ **4**

Sue Baker

COLLECTOR'S NOTES

The great majority of treen available today is Victorian or 20th-century work. That said, though, there is enough of it available to make building up a reasonable collection a fairly straightforward matter. It's increasingly sold at auction, often as part of a furniture sale, and is a staple of country house sales – often in mixed lots – and antiques fairs.

Treen is a very wide collecting field, taking in beautifully carved love spoons from Wales and Scandinavia, penwork boxes, Tunbridge ware trinkets and basic turned bowls. You can make a general collection or specialize in a particular type of ware, a favourite wood or a dceorative technique, such as pokerwork or turning. If you're looking for inspiration, Birmingham City Museum houses a collection of more than 7,000 pieces of treen dating back as far as the 16th century.

The increased popularity of treen has led to faking of expensive items such as Welsh love spoons. Modern copies are artificially aged by staining and distressing the wood. Cheaper pieces, though, are almost always authentic.

Unless a piece is actually broken, condition doesn't matter too much. Even the most battered, utilitarian pieces have a homely, hand-made quality that can be attractive, and

Paper-knives in wood make relatively inexpensive collectables, though the one at the top, commemorating Edward VII, is a little more valuable.

dents don't necessarily detract from their value, as they are seen as a sign of age and use. Disfiguring woodworm holes may also appear in old pieces. These should bring down the price. Never buy treen with new wormholes.

If the piece is in two or more parts, make sure you have them all. Check that hinges are secure and have not been replaced, and that lids fit tightly without sticking.

BUTTER MOULDS

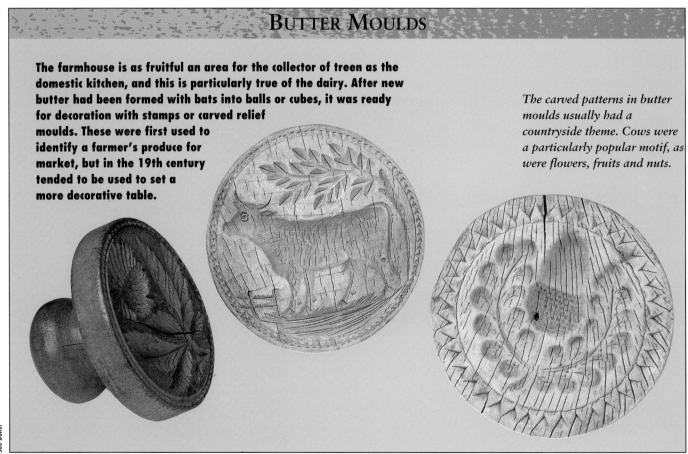

The farmhouse is as fruitful an area for the collector of treen as the domestic kitchen, and this is particularly true of the dairy. After new butter had been formed with bats into balls or cubes, it was ready for decoration with stamps or carved relief moulds. These were first used to identify a farmer's produce for market, but in the 19th century tended to be used to set a more decorative table.

The carved patterns in butter moulds usually had a countryside theme. Cows were a particularly popular motif, as were flowers, fruits and nuts.

TUNBRIDGE WARE

Some of the most decorative but useful small objects were made in Tunbridge ware, a range of wooden items patterned with a distinctive mosaic

Ray Duns

Many Tunbridge ware items were not simply decorative but were also very practical. The jewellery box here, decorated with a picture of a castle, sits on a 19th-century lap desk, designed for use by travellers.

Tunbridge ware is the name given to small wooden objects – boxes, trays and so on – decorated with a mass-production technique that imitated the effects of marquetry and parquetry. It is named after Tunbridge Wells in Kent, where the technique was developed in the late 17th century; in the 19th century it became so popular that it grew into a veritable industry.

Marquetry is a decorative veneer made of shaped pieces of wood (or other suitable material such as ivory) formed into a mosaic; parquetry is marquetry with a geometrical pattern. Both are very time-consuming and therefore expensive to produce. The manufacturers of Tunbridge ware solved the problem of creating similar designs that could be replicated comparatively cheaply.

The design was made from sticks of wood of various colours, glued together in bundles in such a way that the ends formed a picture or pattern. By slicing this bundle of sticks transversely (rather like a loaf of bread) a number of identical versions of the picture were created, thin enough to be stuck to the surface of the box, tray, or whatever else was to be decorated. Some highly skilled craftsmen could cut ten or even more slices from a 2.5cm/1in length of sticks.

Tunbridge ware manufacturers made a huge range of articles such as stamp boxes, cigar boxes, trays, needle cases, cotton reels and measuring tapes. In 1837, one company, Fenner and Co., advertised backgammon sets, tea caddies, inkstands, comb trays, thermometer stands and much more. At the height of the industry, more than 180 woods were in use. Sometimes these woods were boiled to enhance their natural colour, although the local oak was already a lovely green tone, thanks to a fungus that dyed the wood tissue.

POPULAR DESIGNS

The most popular Tunbridge ware articles were those intended as souvenirs, decorated with views of places such as Shakespeare's house. Floral motifs were also common, and butterflies, shells, dogs, cats and fish were other favourites. The mosaic veneer did not necessarily cover the entire article, often being laid in as an edge border or a central motif.

Despite the speed of production, Tunbridge ware items were finely crafted. Some makers combined various techniques in their wares. Mosaic borders might surround a transfer print or painting, or occasionally be mixed with traditional marquetry techniques. There were also craftsmen who experimented and developed their own techniques. George Wise, for example, rolled and pressed wood shavings into a thick glue; when this was dried and sliced, the effect was that of marbling.

BEAUTIFUL WOODWORK

The Tunbridge ware industry flourished for most of the 19th century, but mass production of household goods and cheap imports of decorative woodwork from India and Japan sent it into sharp decline; by 1902 only one manufacturer – Boyce, Brown and Kemp – was still operating. The industry briefly revived in the 1930s, when art deco enthusiasts appreciated the geometric patterned veneers, but production finally ceased when the factory was bombed in World War 2.

The most expensive of all Tunbridge ware is furniture. Chairs, tables and cabinets were produced, but these large objects never really caught on and examples rarely come on the market. However, some small items of furniture were more successful, notably a 'dainty work-table' made at Nye's Manufactory in 1850. This was an extraordinary example of patient, methodical workmanship and the ornate mosaic decoration was emphatically Victorian. All types of Tunbridge ware have risen in value and undamaged pieces are becoming difficult to find.

9 *A* **VICTORIAN LAP DESK**, *made in 1850, is decorated with a floral motif surrounding a picture of a ruined abbey. Around each image is a thin border of geometric design.*

2 *A* **LARGE BOX STANDING ON FEET** *with a decorated lid and a band of tapestry-like Tunbridge ware decoration around the sides.*

3 *A* **CIRCULAR BOX** *and a square stamp box, each decorated with lively geometric designs. The price given is for each one.*

4 **THREE CIRCULAR SEWING** *accessories. The one at bottom left is a thread winder.*

5 *A* **SQUARE PINCUSHION** *with purple velvet; the price given is for this. The boxes above and to the left are of similar value.*

5 **A CIRCULAR BOX** with a bold geometric design. Below it is a rare Tunbridge ware yo-yo (unpriced).

7 **AN OBLONG BOX** decorated with a picture of a castle and panels of tapestry-like mosaic. In front of the castle is a pincushion in lathe-turned stickware (unpriced).

5 **A NEEDLE CASE** with a simple but effective design and the word 'Needles' picked out in mosaic.

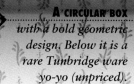

THREE OBLONG BOXES variously decorated with a geometric design around a postage stamp; a tapestry-like mosaic; and a butterfly. **5 6**

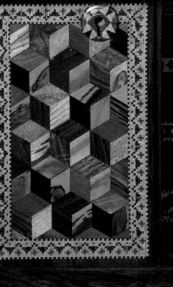

9 **A LADIES' JEWELLERY CABINET** of wonderful design in a rich, dark wood. The top, doors and drawer fronts are elaborately decorated.

4 **A LATHE-TURNED** cylindrical box, perhaps for needles. The ends are decorated.

6 **A TAPER STICK** of lathe-turned stickware on an extravagantly decorated circular base.

Duncan Smith

CL⊙SE UP *on* DESIGNS

This geometric pattern was made by cutting a thin slice through a bundle of carefully glued sticks.

This design of cubes, with its three-dimensional effect, is made from diamonds of different wood.

Elaborate floral borders, here built up as a mosaic, were very popular with the Victorians.

The square-sectioned sticks of wood that were glued together for this mosaic can be clearly seen.

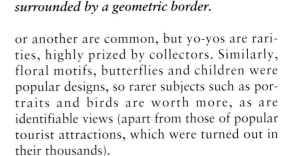

Ray Duns

A jewellery box made in 1870. The lid features a picture of a castle, surrounded by a geometric border.

or another are common, but yo-yos are rarities, highly prized by collectors. Similarly, floral motifs, butterflies and children were popular designs, so rarer subjects such as portraits and birds are worth more, as are identifiable views (apart from those of popular tourist attractions, which were turned out in their thousands).

COLLECTABLE PIECES

Among the other interesting items of Tunbridge ware you can look out for are candlesticks, pincushions, picture frames and bonnet stands. There were even examples of jewellery, including brooches and cuff links. Small items are not necessarily the cheapest. Some thimble cases, for example, were turned on a lathe to create a barrel shape, and the work involved is reflected in the price.

COLLECTOR'S NOTES

A huge amount of Tunbridge ware was produced during the 19th century and much of it still survives. However, it has now become so popular with collectors that pieces in pristine condition are becoming hard to find. The mosaic veneer is virtually impossible to repair, so the value of Tunbridge ware depends even more than with most collectables on the condition of the article. A scratched surface can be stripped and re-varnished, but if the veneer is torn or sections have peeled off, the object may be practically worthless.

RARITY VALUE

Apart from the question of condition, the price of Tunbridge ware will depend on the type of object and the nature of the decoration. Generally speaking, the more unusual the article and the more complex the design, the more expensive it will be. For example, boxes of one sort

A folding book rack, made around 1860. The mosaic picture is of Penshurst Place in Kent. The opposite end is decorated with the image of a stag and doe.

Duncan Smith

Duncan Smith

MAUCHLINE WARE

The attractive wooden souvenirs named after the Scottish town of Mauchline combined usefulness with fine craftsmanship, resulting in a wide range of popular goods

Rosemary Weller

Whether in brightly coloured tartan or the natural creamy-white of sycamore wood, Mauchline ware is highly collectable today. It reached its peak of popularity in the 1860s.

Mauchline (pronounced 'Moch'lin') ware was extremely popular in Victorian times. It takes its name from the small coastal town near Ayr that was the main centre of its manufacture, though not the only one. The town's most famous factory was the 'Box Works', run by the brothers William and Andrew Smith, which continued in business until closed by a fire in 1933.

So great was the brothers' repertoire that in 1850 Andrew Smith was able to say that his firm's products consisted of 'almost every article you can conceive it possible to make, from postage-stamp boxes to tea trays'. In the 1860s, at the peak of the trade, having taken over most of their competitors, and employing over 400 people, they opened a warehouse and a factory in Birmingham. By this time, the Smiths were turning out tens of thousands of pieces in hundreds of styles.

Items were often decorated with pictures of Scottish heroes like Robert Burns, who was associated with the town of Mauchline, or with illustrations of famous resorts and renowned views. There was hardly a town or a view in Scotland that was not immortalized in Mauchline ware, and there was scarcely a place in the British Isles where it could not be bought. It was also successfully exported to France, America, Canada and Australia.

TYPES OF DECORATION

Mauchline ware was usually made of sycamore, which is a creamy-white, close-textured wood, generally free of blemishes. Articles were first made up, then decorated. Early 19th-century, hand-drawn illustrations were followed by tartan decoration, which was itself hand-painted onto the pieces. Later, a machine was developed that drew the tartan pattern onto paper, which was then stuck on.

Tartan sewing eggs or étuis were especially attractive. These wooden eggs contained thread, needles and thimble, and were finished with tartan paper. Because paper cannot be made to cover a curved surface without creasing, it had to be stuck on in segments. Where the segments met, a fine line was carefully gilded, attractively masking the joint.

From the middle of the 19th century onwards, transfers were used. These were made from 'Japanese' paper which was laid onto a painted plate and then lifted off and placed on the article to be decorated. Actual photographs were also used as decoration, notably by Archibald Brown, a keen photographer and former employee of the Smiths, who set up the Caledonian Box Works at Lanark.

MAUCHLINE'S MANY DESIGNS

The earliest hand-decorated penwork boxes are the most expensive to buy and can cost between £100 and £250, depending on size and condition. Hand-painted tartan also fetches high prices, especially if the tartan frames a portrait of a Scottish hero such as Bonnie Prince Charlie or Robert Burns. Printed tartan is hardly less expensive and is much sought after; prices for good-quality items are only slightly less than penwork boxes.

Much 19th-century transfer ware has survived and pieces are reasonably priced, but expect to pay up to £250 for rare examples. Makers rarely put names or dates to their products. Retailers' names can occasionally be found, well hidden away, and these increase the value of pieces. Transfers were rarely updated, so the same ones were probably in use for 40 years or more.

5 THIS PHOTO ALBUM *features a delicate vignetted view of the church at Seaford in Sussex.*

4 A THREAD HOLDER *showing St Nicholas church, Newcastle; it was upgraded to a cathedral in 1882.*

6 THIS PAPERKNIFE *bears the name of the original two manufacturers of Mauchline and is thus a highly desirable object.*

THE BRIG O' DOON, *appearing on this box, is an old bridge across the River Doon. It has links with Robert Burns.*

154

Roy Duns

5 ◆ **A SOUVENIR** ▶
of the childhood
home of George
Washington, this
axe alludes to the
incident when he
is said to have cut
down his father's
cherry tree.

4 ◆ **THIS MONEYBOX**
features Saltaire Congregational
Church in Yorkshire.

5 ◆ **A NEEDLE CASE** ▶
with a view of Edinburgh
seen from the castle. Many
tourists bought this
type of object.

3 ◆ **A WARRIOR**
on horseback in a
daring pose enlivens
this box – an unusual
and spirited design.

2 ◆ **A PAPERKNIFE**
in a very simple
style, embellished
with a design of a
Welsh tea party.

4 ◆ **THIS CHEST-SHAPED BOX**
is a souvenir of Stirling
Castle, one of Scotland's
most famous historic
sites. It is dated 1889.

Rosemary Weller

This jewel box and ornamental bucket are examples of fern ware, in which the pattern was made with real ferns. Such objects were highly popular in the late 19th century.

Collector's Notes

Now that Mauchline ware has become so collectable, it can be found in many antiques shops and in bric-a-brac shops, though it is still not universally known. The pieces are small, easy to store and dust, and easy to display in glass cases or in the open. They

should, however, be kept out of bright sunlight which will fade their decoration.

Because Mauchline ware was manufactured in such huge quantities, using similar techniques for decades on end, pieces are inevitably difficult to date. Look out for commemorative pieces, as their origins are automatically easier to trace. A number of major exhibitions and royal occasions were marked by transfer views. The coronation of King George V in 1910 was probably the last occasion on which they were used.

FERN WARE

Carefully purchased and cared for, Mauchline ware pieces are a source of great interest, and are likely to appreciate in value over the years.

The range of products is so great – including such items as whist markers, parasol handles, lip salve cases and children's money boxes – that some collectors like to specialize in either a type of product or one of several styles of decoration.

A field of its own is fern ware, which began to appear soon after 1870. Real ferns were used to produce the surface decoration, and although the pattern was used on a much smaller scale than transfers or tartans, it still appeared on quite a range of articles.

Mauchline ware has its origins in early 19th-century penwork boxes, which were decorated by hand.

REAL ? FAKE

A close look at the transfer reveals that the egg cup was made in Germany, not Scotland.

Manufactured in Germany.

Like many other successful ventures, Mauchline ware soon had its imitators, although in most cases the quality did not reach the same high standards. Real Mauchline ware always used smooth, fine-grained sycamore wood, which has an attractive natural colour and is pleasant to handle. The grain of this egg cup, however, is much more coarse than that of genuine Mauchline products.

LLANDUDNO.

Peter Reilly

GLOVES

A wide variety of beautiful gloves can still be found today, ranging from simple white crochet to coloured silk with intricate embroidery or diamanté designs

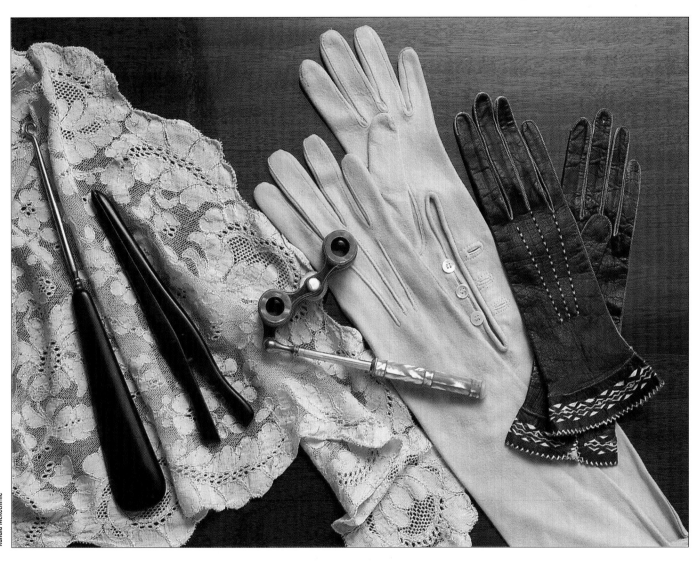

Ranald McKechnie

For the Victorians and Edwardians, gloves were an essential accessory, regardless of the weather. Most men, women and even children had several pairs which were selected according to the occasion and gloves were sometimes changed several times throughout the day, depending on the status of the wearer.

Those who were unsure about which gloves to wear on a particular occasion could refer to a book on etiquette. Ladies were informed that to appear in public without gloves was decidedly vulgar, and that dining with gloves on was simply not the done thing.

In the early 19th century gloves were quite plain. Men could choose from kid, chicken-skin, white cotton or silk. Ladies wore buff suede or white kid, which was sometimes delicately embroidered. Women of substance wore a new pair of gloves every day because pale calf skin stained so easily. Towards the end of the century, ladies' gloves were becoming more functional and the fine decoration seen in earlier decades began to disappear.

Glove collectors may also be interested in the range of glove accessories – glove stretchers were used to stretch tight gloves, and glove hooks prevented fingers from soiling the gloves when doing up the numerous buttons.

Many people who collect gloves also collect glove accessories. Glove stretchers and hooks are both popular. Examples such as these cost about £10 each.

GLOVES

A wide range of beautiful gloves is still available to the collector, from simple white silk, lace or crochet ones to coloured kid and silk with intricate embroidery or diamanté designs. More modern styles from the 1920s, 30s and 50s can add an unusual touch to a collection. Stylish art deco designs in rich colours and using fabrics such as felt, suede and new synthetic fabrics are increasingly sought after nowadays.

You may also want to include knitted gloves in both black and white silk or cotton in a collection. These were produced in the early years of this century around Nottingham and a great many survive. They can be found very cheaply in markets.

OFF-WHITE 1930s
gloves with a stylish knitted wrist and decorated inset.

WHITE KID 2
gloves with finely stitched stripe design.

BLACK SUEDE 5
gloves with diamanté pattern for stunning evening elegance.

RED GAUNTLETS 3
in deco style with wide wrists and fan tucks.

Ronald McKechnie

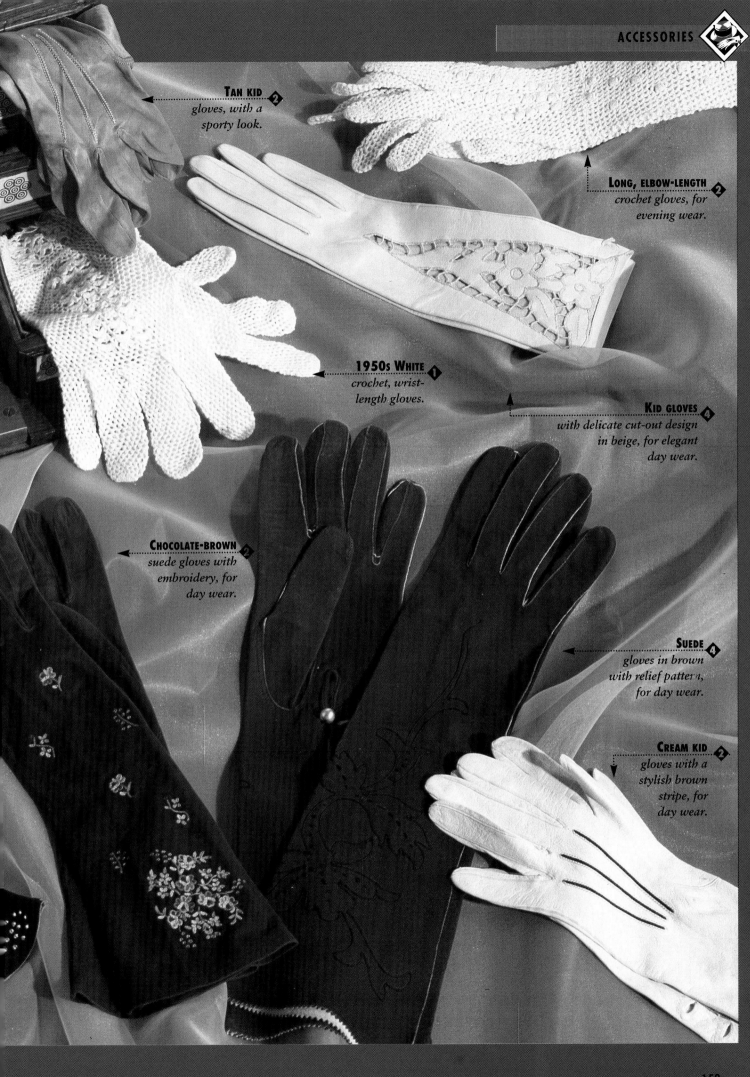

TAN KID ❷ gloves, with a sporty look.

LONG, ELBOW-LENGTH ❷ crochet gloves, for evening wear.

1950s WHITE ❶ crochet, wrist-length gloves.

KID GLOVES ❹ with delicate cut-out design in beige, for elegant day wear.

CHOCOLATE-BROWN ❷ suede gloves with embroidery, for day wear.

SUEDE ❹ gloves in brown with relief pattern, for day wear.

CREAM KID ❷ gloves with a stylish brown stripe, for day wear.

COMPARE & CONTRAST

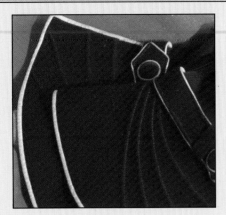

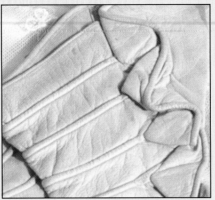

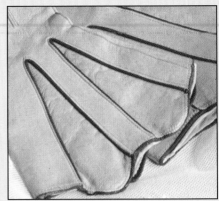

Wide-wristed deco gloves clearly modelled on early motoring gauntlets.

1930s gloves with a decorative feature of frilled and stitched kid.

Gauntlet wrist formed by fluted inset panels trimmed with brown.

COLLECTOR'S NOTES

Like many other fashion collectables, the price of a pair of gloves varies enormously. This largely depends on their age, workmanship and general condition. Rarity obviously also has a considerable effect on price. Earlier examples are, of course, harder to find and much more expensive. Evidence of a famous owner or the label of a well-known manufacturer may also enhance their value.

Tiny gloves from the early 20th century in leather, suede or cotton can still be found for as little as £2 a pair. Victorian kid gloves in good condition cost around £10. But if there is

This glove collection includes several from the 1930s, with gauntlet-style wrists, as well as one elbow-length pair in white kid for formal evening wear.

elaborate decoration such as embroidery or pearl buttons, gloves may fetch considerably more. Rare collector's items such as expertly crafted 17th-century gloves are in a different category altogether, costing as much as £600.

To avoid damage, old gloves should ideally be stored in flat boxes in a cool, dry place away from strong sunlight. Carefully wrap each glove in plain tissue paper or muslin – but never use coloured paper because it can stain.

Gloves from the 1920s, 30s and even 50s have become increasingly collectable and can now be found in antique markets and fairs. Depending on materials, condition and decorative details, these can cost up to £20. They are fairly keenly priced because many are bought as modern fashion accessories by young people. However, simple cotton or crochet ones should cost no more than a pound or two.

CONDITION AND VALUE

Condition is a particularly important factor when buying gloves. Colours, for example, should be bright and even; if not, the gloves have been inexpertly or too frequently cleaned. Gloves with obvious stains should be avoided. Kid and suede gloves are particularly difficult to clean and could be damaged if taken to other than a specialist cleaner. Gloves with recent repairs should also be avoided, although old repairs can add interest. If you do buy gloves in less than perfect condition, perhaps because the design or decoration interests you, make sure this is reflected in the price.

Glove accessories, such as stretchers and hooks, can often be picked up very cheaply in jumble sales and from market stalls. A specialist gloves dealer will also usually have a few accessories, often in fine quality materials such as ivory or tortoiseshell.

SCARVES

As fashion accessories, scarves have been in existence since Edwardian times when oblong lengths of lace, gauze or embroidered muslin were often worn, rather like stoles, over outdoor attire

Inspired by original Edwardian scarves, long, flowing scarves in silk or chiffon were produced by fashion designers in the 1920s. Among them were Poiret and Fortuny, following the championing of the scarf by Isadora Duncan who used them to add movement and texture to her somewhat daring dances (she was also killed by the scarf when the ends of one she was wearing became caught in the wheels of a Bugatti automobile).

The square scarf, so familiar today and which was at the height of its popularity from the 1930s through to the 1960s, has its origins much further back in time with the development of the kerchief or bandanna. This printed cotton workaday item was a male accessory but was hardly fashionable since it was used to soak up sweat and grime and was worn in the 19th century by all types of workmen, peasants and, in America, by cowboys, ranchers, railwaymen and even bandits.

THE RIGHT TACK

The square printed silk scarf as we know it was virtually invented by the harness-makers Hermes in the late 1930s. Their scarves, decorated with equestrian motifs, were made of the finest silk twill on to which some 40 different colours had been screen-printed. They were soon being worn by well-born French women, British royalty and international celebrities. Hermes scarves are still being made today and, as evidence of their enduring role as a status symbol, in the 1970s Queen Elizabeth permitted a photograph of herself wearing a Hermes scarf to be used on a British postage stamp.

Other couturiers were quick to follow Hermes' lead. Elsa Schiaparelli promoted her 'shocking pink' range of garments and perfume on several boldly designed scarves and, from the 1940s, designers such as Hardy Amies, Lanvin, Pierre Cardin and, in the 1960s, Emilio Pucci all produced 'designer' scarves.

Raoul Dufy was one of the first artists to produce scarf designs. One of his most famous was 'The Elephants' on which blue elephants are set amid red flowers and on which stags and leopards are depicted, all set against a

Sue Baker

pink ground with a blue border. Other notable artists who produced scarf designs were Matisse, Cezanne, Cocteau and Andy Warhol.

The vast majority of scarves that you'll come across are not these collectors' items but those produced in their millions during the 1950s and early 1960s for fashion-conscious women. Commemorative scarves for both the Festival of Britain in 1951 and the Coronation in 1953 can be found, as can travel scarves, with views of Paris, Rome and other cities, as well as scarves produced by airlines and cruise ships. Flowers, fruits and animals, particularly dogs, were favourite subjects but were often boldly treated and in bright colours.

Attractively designed scarves in soft or silky fabrics are always a joy to handle and a delight to wear.

KNOTTED UP

Most post-War scarves are relatively inexpensive. This is true even of the commemorative and travel scarves which are already sought after by collectors. Even cheaper are unsigned scarves from the same period depicting floral or fruit and leaf designs. The nature of the fabric also determines price. Finely-woven silk scarves of whatever design will cost more than those in cotton, wool or synthetic fabrics.

However, artists' scarves, especially those commissioned in London by the designer Zika Ascher in the 1940s, command high prices. Ascher worked with not only Matisse and Cocteau but also a number of British artists including Henry Moore, John Piper and Felix Topolski and personally oversaw the printing of these fine, limited edition scarves, of which between only 175 and 600 were produced. Collectors value these.

3 ▸ **A BALLERINA SCARF** decorated with images from Tchaikovsky's Swan Lake. *The swirling design is printed in two shades of pink with hints of grey and black.*

◂ **A SOUVENIR SCARF** **1** from London, printed in the 1950s with five of the top tourist attractions.

3 **THIS DESIGN** of stylized poodles in black and white is divided into four by Parisian-style lamp posts. This is a 1950s design in silk.

AN ITALIAN SILK SCARF ◆**3**

from the 1950s. Dogs were particularly fashionable at this time. This simple four-colour design features poodles around a central image of a leash and collar.

◆**1** **A WOOLLEN HEADSCARF** ▲

from the 1950s. It is printed in a green and white checkerboard design with a series of foxhunting scenes around the edges and horse and hound heads in the centre.

◄ **A FLORAL DESIGN** ◆**1**

from the 1950s, featuring chrysanthemums. The images have a loose, soft-edged feel and are printed on silk in six colours with a grey border.

Sue Baker

163

COLLECTOR'S NOTES

Old scarves are exactly the kind of thing that you might find in the attic, at jumble sales, second-hand shops, markets and auctions disposing of general household effects. Many women never throw out old clothes and fashion accessories until decades later so it's well worth asking relatives if you can rummage through their cast-offs. Few dealers handle scarves specifically but many specialize in textiles and it is from some of them that you will be able to get the more collectable items such as artists' scarves but at a price.

PRICES

Commemorative and travel scarves from the 1940s and 1950s are quite affordable, even from dealers, and generally fall into price guide 3. Early couturier ones are rather more expensive, depending on the maker, style and quality of the fabric, while Pucci scarves from the 1960s, with their bright psychedelic colours and geometric designs, will certainly fall into the upper range of price guide 5.

If you intend to form a collection of scarves, you'll probably need to be selective by choosing scarves from a particular period, ones on a particular theme or those produced by a particular designer. Sporty scarves, for instance, have already attracted a following and there are many collectors of commemorative scarves. Patriotic scarves from World War 2 were produced in large numbers to celebrate the Anglo-American alliance, the Anglo-French alliance, the liberation of Paris and other notable events, particularly VE Day. Some of the best have interesting typography and vibrant designs like those on wall posters.

CARE AND DISPLAY

As with all textiles, check scarves carefully for condition. Holes and stains seriously devalue any item. Scarves in absolutely mint condition are fairly rare; they were, after all, worn close to the face and covered the hair, so grease, cosmetics and perfume stains are likely to have affected the scarf at some stage of its life. Do not attempt to clean fine quality silk or chiffon scarves yourself without expert advice – you could do irreparable damage.

You may, of course, want to wear your scarves but if you intend to display them, simple clip-frames will show them off to advantage. Keep them out of direct sunlight which will fade their colours. If you are storing them flat, do not use plastic bags – they prevent natural fibres from 'breathing'; instead, wrap them in acid-free paper.

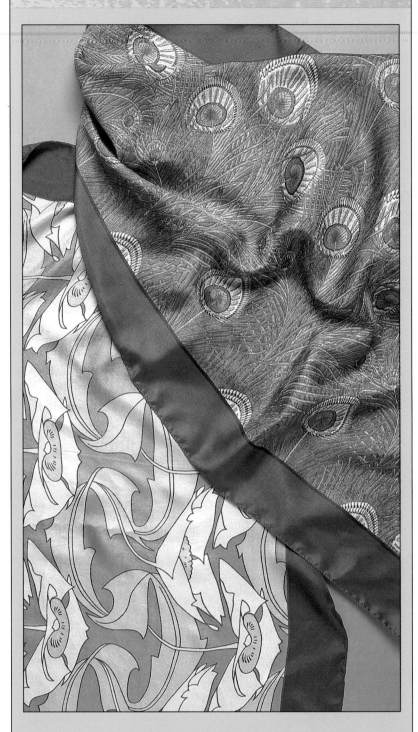

LIBERTY'S SILK SCARVES

Less well known than the Hermes scarves and the many sporty designs that were produced, but equally attractive are the fine silk scarves made by Liberty's of London in the 1970s. Their choice of designs was refreshingly different. They opted to reproduce their original fabric designs from the turn of the century, such as peacock feathers (designed by Rex Silver c1900) and lotus leaves; these make an interesting contrast to the deco and 1950s-style designs of most collectable scarves. The peacock feather was at one time the symbol of Liberty's. The scarves have a single-colour border, and 'Liberty of London All silk Made in England' is overprinted in a corner of the design. They are screen-printed in a range of five or six colours.

Sue Baker

HANDBAGS

Neat, elegant and practical, handbags were just as indispensable for the 1930s woman about town as they are today

Handbags of some form have always been an important ladies' accessory – for carrying both money and personal belongings. In the 16th century, a small pouch was suspended around the waist, either outside or underneath clothing, but by the late 18th century, when dresses were soft and flowing, a bulging pouch would have spoiled the line. Instead, decorated fabric bags with drawstrings began to be used. Women could now carry around a whole host of items – from letters and visiting cards to fans. The fashion was short-lived, however – when fuller skirts came in, separate pockets or small bags worn at the belt rendered these fabric bags superfluous.

But by 1870 large leather 'handbags' were becoming popular for visiting and shopping trips and, during the Edwardian period, new handbag styles appeared that reflected women's freer lifestyles at that time. Ladies could choose from practical, briefcase-style bags for daytime use, or more decorative, feminine bags for the evening.

After World War 1, as more and more women went out to work, the handbag had to adapt to holding all manner of things, ranging from lipstick holders and powder compacts to cigarette holders and lighters. The clutch bag was the favourite of the 1920s flapper and remains a popular handbag style even today.

COLLECTOR'S NOTES

Most antiques fairs and markets have at least one stall specializing in period costume and accessories, always popular collectables. But don't disregard car boot sales or jumble sales, since lucky finds can occur in the most unlikely places.

As a collector, it will help to specialize either in one type of handbag or a particular period. Areas to concentrate on include particular materials, monogrammed bags, evening bags or those with typically art deco motifs or chrome or plastic trimmings.

If you can afford it, focus on bags in good condition – it's much more satisfying to have a collection of five or six well-preserved and attractive bags than a dozen examples which are damaged, faded or torn.

Before attempting any repairs, get advice from a local museum or dealer – the bag may need to be treated professionally. Leather bags (but not suede) can be carefully cleaned with saddle soap, and most plastics respond to detergent on a damp, but never wet, cloth. Never use an abrasive substance on leather or plastic. As always, seek specialist advice if you are in any doubt about cleaning methods.

During the 1930s, handbags came in all shapes and sizes. Whether made of crocodile skin or ostrich feather, there was a bag for every outfit and occasion.

Ronald Mackechnie

BAGS OF STYLE

Fashionable handbag styles of the 1930s were varied and innovative. Made from a wide range of materials, bags were often decorated with abstract patterns based on sun rays, pyramids and scallops.

Day bags were usually made of leather, and were finished with a discreet clasp or flap. More expensive leather and suede bags even had matching handbag 'furniture' such as a purse or notebook.

Afternoon and evening bags were made of silk, grosgrain, crepe and artificial silk and were decorated with chrome, Bakelite, diamanté or marcasite for added glamour.

Towards the end of the 1930s handbag designers became even more inventive and celluloid and other new plastics were moulded, cut and applied in multiple layers to create more and more unusual designs.

PASTE JEWELS decorate the clasp of this green satin evening bag of the 1930s.

THIS MAROON French handbag with brass trim is made of antelope skin.

A TASSEL FINISHES off this beaded bag.

SQUARE-SHAPED handbag (right), covered in beads. The sequined bag (below) has filigree clasps and handles.

EMBROIDERED with delicate petit-point flowers, this bag has a brass filigree clasp and handle.

THIS LACE AND SILK BAG has an ormolu clasp.

MADE FOR EVENING wear, this handbag is decorated with paste jewels.

THIS UNUSUAL CYLINDRICAL compact bag from the late 1930s is covered in antelope skin.

THIS FOX-SHAPED HANDLE is made in Bakelite. The bag itself is made of pleated silk.

Lyndon Parker

MEN'S ACCESSORIES

*Social changes and the growing influence
of the USA strongly affected the way
men dressed between the wars*

The 1920s and 30s saw great changes in men's fashions. The formal dress codes of Victorian and Edwardian gentlemen had required an army of servants to maintain. However, the serving class all but disappeared after World War 1, and fashions changed along with the new social order.

Edward, Prince of Wales, led the way. His liaison with Mrs Simpson led to an interest in all things American, and particularly in the 'lack of pretension' that characterized the informal way American men tended to dress. Suddenly, casualness in dress and manner became the acceptable hallmark of a gentleman. This trend was reinforced further down the social scale by another strong American influence, Hollywood movies.

Fair Isle sweaters, tweedy suits, suede shoes, jaunty flat caps and stylish braces with a jazzy design all owe their popularity to the Prince. Morning suits and top hats, the old daytime uniform, became evening wear under the new regime. Colourful ties and soft shirt collars reflected the more relaxed attitude.

CLIPS AND PINS

The new fashions saw the introduction of a range of up-to-date accessories as well as the retention of some old favourites. Long neckties made an appearance, and tie clips and collar pins came with them. A collar pin was a gold or silver bar with knobbed or jewelled ends. These were attached to the collar and pushed the tie knot up and forward. Tie clips were worn further down and fixed the tie to the shirt front. These came in gold, silver or coloured enamel and were usually either plain or decorated with sporting motifs.

Turned 'French' cuffs had been popular since before World War 1, so cuff links were already established as an accessory. However, the art deco movement stamped them with its own distinctive style. Geometric and sunburst designs made an appearance.

Evening wear had its own set of accessories, which tended to be of better quality than daytime wear. There were thin evening watches worn on the wrist. The chain of the old fob

Ronald Mackechnie

watch was retained, but had other useful objects attached to it, such as silver or gold propelling pencils or cigar cutters.

Fred Astaire helped to keep the cane fashionable for evening use, along with the top hat. White silk scarves, with tassels, were draped around the collar of an evening jacket, coat or cape, while cummerbunds were usually made of coloured satin or silk.

A shop display to gladden the heart of a Bertie Wooster, with pins and links in the case and sporty ties, socks, scarves, sweaters, caps and braces under the counter.

DAY WEAR

In the 1920s and 1930s, wing collars and stiff detachable collars were abandoned for all but the members of a few formal professions such as the law. Long neckties, cravats, or jolly bow ties were worn with the new, softer-collared shirts. The collar could be either long and pointed or cutaway, a style favoured by the Prince of Wales.

Tie clips, which fixed the tie to the shirt, were fastened halfway down the length of the tie, just above the waistcoat, which itself often had a much racier design than the plain black or pinstripe affairs favoured by Edwardian men of substance.

Flat caps were just one of several accessories that were reminiscent of the golf course, where American styles made a big impression. Argyll socks and Fair Isle sweaters were further variations on the same sporty theme.

THIS YELLOW SCARF *with a red fringe would have been worn with a smart winter overcoat.*

PAISLEY PATTERNS *were popular through the 1930s. This cravat is in rayon, first made in the 1890s.*

ARGYLL SOCKS *were usually worn with plus-fours on the golf course or on country walks.*

BRACES, *though usually concealed under a waistcoat or jacket, still had showy patterns.*

Ronald Mackechnie

LEATHER GAUNTLETS
were for motoring, and would not have been worn about town.

GOGGLES AND A CAP
were de rigeur when taking a spin in the country in a sports car.

THIS GOLD WATCH
has a leather strap. The square face is in the deco style.

A SILVER HIP FLASK
like this would have helped to revive sagging spirits on a golfing or shooting weekend.

THREE SETS OF LINKS,
two in silver and enamel and one in gold.

STIFF WHITE COLLARS,
which were attached to shirts with studs, went out of fashion in the 1920s.

TIE PINS AND CLIPS
were plain or had sporty motifs: the three pins here have a horseshoe, a tiger tooth, and wishbone.

TWO COTTON TIES
with bold patterns. The paisley would have gone with a suit, the check with more casual wear.

169

5 THIS BLACK RAYON WAISTCOAT *would have been worn under a dinner jacket. White ones were also favoured.*

EVENING WEAR

Even the most sporty gentleman still dressed for dinner, the theatre or the opera in the 1930s, and needed something formal to complement his outfit. In many cases this simply meant more elegant, or at least more expensive, versions of his daytime accessories.

Dress shirts did not have their own buttons, but were fastened with a matching set of studs and links. The stud heads were typically mother-of-pearl or white onyx edged with enamel, silver or gold and set with a central garnet, ruby or semi-precious stone.

A cane was part of an ensemble that often included an opera cape and a monocle. Monocles were not always an optical necessity, but a popular affectation, immortalized by the humorist P G Wodehouse, creator of Bertie Wooster and Jeeves.

2 BOW TIES AND CUMMERBUNDS *were intrinsic parts of full evening dress. The bow tie is in white cotton, and the cummerbunds in pleated silk.*

5 THIS EVENING CANE *is in ebonized wood and has a gold-trimmed horn handle.*

5 A GOLD CIGAR CUTTER *would have been worn on a chain and tucked in a waistcoat pocket.*

2 MOST MONOCLES *were just magnifying glasses. This one was hand-held, rather than worn in the eye.*

1 THE STUD-FASTENING WING COLLAR *was in fashion only for evening wear in the 1930s. This one is made of white cotton.*

4 THIS GOLD COLLAR PIN *is in a typical style, and would have joined a cutaway collar below the tie knot.*

DEALER'S TIPS

• There are several styles of cuff link – chain links, dumb-bells, swivel shanks and fixed rings among them – but classic links should have two identical heads.

• Wristwatches with square or oblong faces tend to fetch better prices than circular ones.

• Look out for relatively inexpensive 1930s links and dress sets in bakelite, celluloid and other plastics.

A TOP HAT ⑤
in black felt was the ultimate evening accessory for men.

BUTTONHOLES ④
were kept fresh in silver holders like this, which were filled with water and clipped to a lapel.

WHITE SILK ②
was a favoured material for evening scarves, which were draped round the collar of a dinner jacket or overcoat.

FOUR 1930S PINS ④
set with different stones. From left to right, a pearl, a diamond, an opal and a clustered pearl.

GOLD JEWELLERY ⑤
was worn in the evening. A signet ring set with cornelian is shown with three sets of links.

A GOLD CHAIN AND FOB ⑤
was still worn across a waistcoat, but no longer had a watch on it.

171

REAL ? FAKE

Ronald Mackechnie

The immaculately-enamelled white gold cuff links on the left are from the 1930s, as confirmed by the hallmarks, while those on the right, although superficially deco in style, are a cheap imitation and were made in the 1970s.

replaced fob watches at the end of watch chains. They can be made of base or precious metals and prices will reflect this. Again, look for hallmarks. Check that there are no chips on any enamel pieces, and have a good look at jewel settings to make sure that any stones are firmly in place. Replacement of lost stones can be an expensive business.

At the cheaper end of the market are items of clothing such as scarves, ties, hats, braces, gloves and cravats. These can be fun to collect and to wear as they add that finishing touch of authenticity to present-day fashions, which are often based on 1930s styles.

Look out for signs of moth damage on woollen articles such as original Fair Isle sweaters. Old silk and cotton can rot; check creases and seams carefully. Old umbrellas, made of a silk and cotton mix, are hard to find in good condition for this reason, though they may be collected for their handles, which often bear fine decorative work.

COLLECTOR'S NOTES

Gentlemen's accessories can be sought out in specialist shops, though sharp-eyed collectors may find rich pickings in antique shops and markets. Prices vary wildly, depending on the quality of an article and the demand for it.

Wrist watches first became popular in the 1920s and 1930s, and fairly plain ones can sell cheaply. However, watches that display a distinctive art deco design can command hundreds or even thousands of pounds, especially when they are made of silver or gold. Working watches are obviously more collectable than broken ones, though many may need just a simple cleaning to get them going properly again.

Cigarette cases of the period can be cheap and cheerful or fabulously expensive objets d'art, made of precious metals and stones or enamelled with sunbursts or geometric designs (see pages 505-8). Make sure the hinges are in good working order.

MODERN REPRODUCTIONS

Cuff links, tie clips and pins are desirable objects to collect and need not impoverish the collector. Beware of modern reproductions, though, as they will be made of cheaper materials. Gold and silver items will be hall-marked; check the date from these. Tie pins can make good bargains, as they are not widely collected but often made of 18ct gold.

Cigar cutters, propelling and retractable pencils, pocket knives and swizzle sticks (used for mixing cocktails in the glass) often

CLOSE UP *on* TIE PIN HEADS

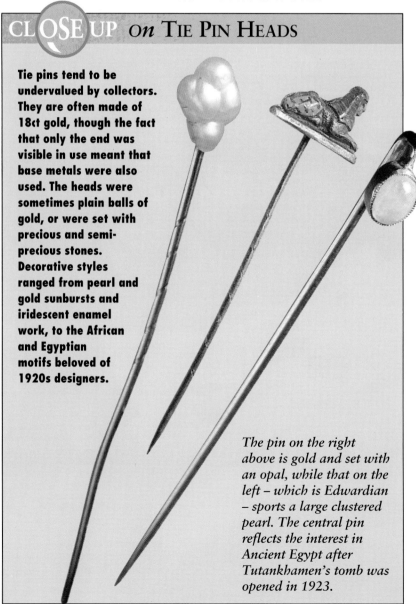

Tie pins tend to be undervalued by collectors. They are often made of 18ct gold, though the fact that only the end was visible in use meant that base metals were also used. The heads were sometimes plain balls of gold, or were set with precious and semi-precious stones. Decorative styles ranged from pearl and gold sunbursts and iridescent enamel work, to the African and Egyptian motifs beloved of 1920s designers.

The pin on the right above is gold and set with an opal, while that on the left – which is Edwardian – sports a large clustered pearl. The central pin reflects the interest in Ancient Egypt after Tutankhamen's tomb was opened in 1923.

SEWING ACCESSORIES

*Because of the popularity of needlework in the Victorian era,
sewing accessories in a wide variety of styles and materials are
still relatively easy to find today*

Sewing really had its heyday in the 19th century, when it was seen as an art form. Ladies enjoyed the hobbies of embroidery, beading, knotting and tatting. For some, needlework was also a social event, carried out in the company of friends. And as it became more and more popular, manufacturers were quick to produce sewing equipment with increasingly lavish designs.

By the Edwardian period, changing social patterns, combined with the growing popularity of the sewing machine, meant the decline of needlework as a hobby. This was reinforced by the introduction of high-quality embroidery and lace made in factories.

But there were still many who practised needlework at home, though the highly decorated sewing equipment of the Victorian era gradually gave way to simpler designs, more in keeping with Edwardian tastes. In this period the more decorative sewing accessories came from France, and were usually presented in flat leather cases covered in velvet or leather. Equipment also came in ladies' companions – square or rectangular boxes, which often also included a scent bottle.

Because ladies' companions and sewing cases were frequently given as expensive gifts, the decoration of the tools inside was often of very high quality. Tools in silver gilt, inset with coral or turquoise, or decorated in gold or filigree work, were all popular.

Beautifully crafted needlework tools are still popular, not least because they are bygones of a forgotten age, when sewing was seen as a social grace.

NEEDLEWORK TOOLS

Much sewing equipment forms a collector's field in its own right. Thimbles and thimble guards are a prime example – despite the fact that there is little variation in shape or size, they come in an amazing variety of materials and decorative finishes.

Embroidery scissors often come in boxed sets of three, in varying sizes. Those from the Edwardian era can be quite ornate, with fancy silver handles and steel blades. Scissors were very expensive – in 1913 a pair of small embroidery scissors cost over six shillings.

Tape measures were an indispensable part of any sewing kit. Wind-up tapes in carved wooden or ivory cases were very popular with the Victorians and Edwardians, and were often shaped in the form of miniature beehives or tiny barrels.

Cotton or thread winders, which were used to prevent embroidery silk from getting tangled, were also made in a variety of shapes and materials.

Silver pincushions in novelty shapes abounded, many from Birmingham.

SILVER PINCUSHION ◈6
modelled in the shape of a lady's shoe. Those modelled in the shape of birds and animals are also very popular.

◈4◈5 **SILVER AND IVORY THIMBLES**
are still relatively easy to find. Intricate decoration adds value, as do semi-precious stones. On the far left is a thimble guard.

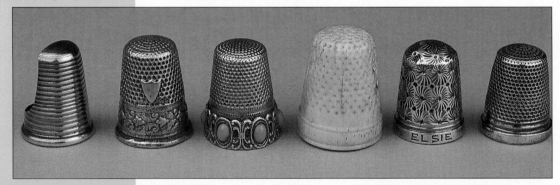

◈2◈4◈4 **THREAD WINDERS**
(far left) had simply carved wooden cases, while wind-up tapes (centre) were made with surprisingly ornate cases of wood or ivory. Thimble cases (far right) often came in novelty shapes such as shoes and acorns.

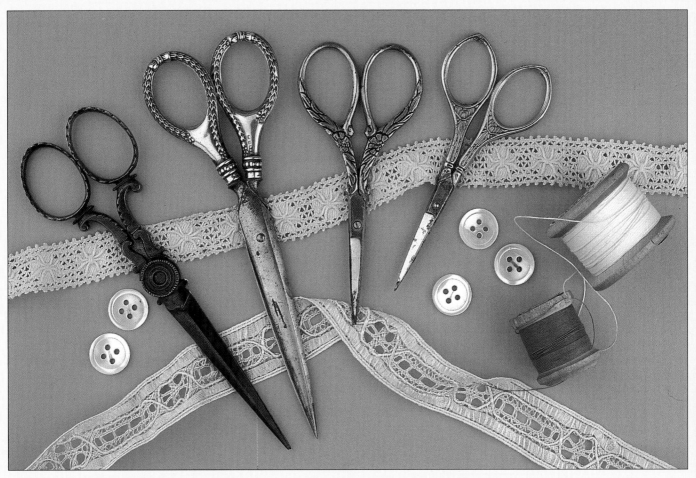

2 3 **EMBROIDERY SCISSORS** with daintily engraved handles so typical of the Victorian era. Handles were often either gilt-finished or silver-hallmarked. Sets of scissors are worth more in their original boxes.

HEMMING BIRD 6 tool, used to hold material while sewing. The clamp fixes the tool to the table, and the beak of the bird, which opens when the tail is pressed, grips the cloth. These were often given as love tokens.

Chris Barker

COLLECTOR'S NOTES

Because of the wide range of needlework equipment available, most collectors tend to specialize in one particular area. Some concentrate on a particular period such as Regency or late 18th century, while others restrict their buying to pincushions, scissors or thimbles. As with many collectables, the condition of sewing equipment is of great importance.

Novelty items can be surprisingly valuable. A tape measure cleverly hidden in a celluloid sailor, for example, can cost more than a 19th-century solid silver needlecase.

LIMITED EDITIONS

Thimbles are still made in great quantities today, especially in china. Some are produced as special limited editions, with the collector in mind. Modern examples are invariably easy to identify because of their clear markings; those in solid silver often have hallmarks near the rim, which give you a precise date.

Look out for scissors made in the shape of a long-beaked bird – cranes or storks were both popular. But be careful when buying scissors – modern examples are sometimes sold in antique boxes if the originals have gone missing, and antique-style scissors are also still being made in Germany and Switzerland. It's always a good idea to ask whether the piece is a genuine antique, especially when paying high prices. Avoid scissors with signs of rust.

Winders, clamps and pincushions are highly

COMPARE & CONTRAST

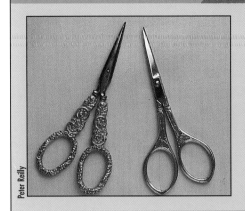

Scissors made for different purposes can be deceptively similar in appearance. The pair on the right are needlework scissors, but the pair on the left are grape scissors, used at the table for cutting grapes from a bunch. They were sometimes decorated with grape motifs.

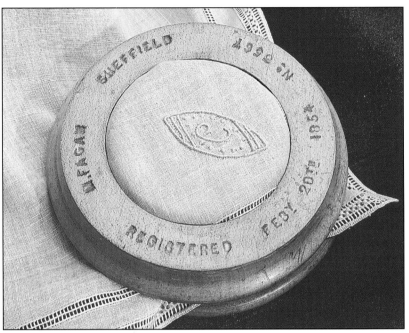

Wooden frames were used to stretch the material, to make embroidery easier.

collectable and are valued according to their rarity and the materials they are made from. Ornamental pincushions used to be given by sailors as love tokens. Frequently stuffed with sawdust, the baize backing was oversewn with coarse sailmaker's thread.

CARE AND REPAIR

Most sewing equipment is best left in the state in which it was purchased. Some tools were originally stained or painted and this decoration can easily be damaged if the object comes into contact with any liquid.

Silver pincushions with fabric pads need special care. The originality of the fabric is an essential feature and should not be tampered with. Cleaning very dirty silver can be speeded up by using a silver dip, but subsequent polishing should always be done with a cloth, otherwise the soft, oily sheen will be lost.

CL**OSE** UP *on* THIMBLES

Marks on thimbles provide a surprising amount of information. The number '3' (above) is a size guide, 'Dorcas' (above right) is a brand name well known to thimble collectors, and 'Elsie' (right) is simply the original owner's name.

FOUNTAIN PENS

*The first reliable and leakproof fountain pens
revolutionized handwriting; they are now collected
for their looks as well as their historical importance*

Steve Bisgrove

The traditional quill pen could be a sensitive writing implement, but it had drawbacks; it had to be replenished with ink every few words and needed constant trimming with a penknife. Attempts to add ink reservoirs to quill pens date back to at least the 17th century (when Samuel Pepys mentions such a device in his famous *Diary*), but it was not until the 1880s that the first successful fountain pen was put on the market. This was made possible by the refinement of the steel nib (which at first tended to be unpliable and liable to tear the paper), by the development of new kinds of ink (traditional types often corroded metal or clogged up the workings of the pen) and by the ingenuity of manufacturers in overcoming problems relating to filling, leakage and ink flow.

The two most famous manufacturers in the early days of the fountain pen are still household names today – the American firms of Parker and Waterman. J J Parker patented a fountain pen in 1823, but it was unreliable, and it was Lewis Edson Waterman who manufactured the first completely successful

fountain pen in 1883. Waterman had started out as an insurance salesman, but he changed career after a leaking pen ruined a contract and lost him an important deal. By 1888 his company was making pens in over 50 sizes and styles, all with a money-back guarantee.

British manufacturers who followed in the Americans' footsteps included Reliance and Co., who made a highly regarded pen with a 14-carat gold nib, tipped with iridium to improve writing performance. Like other early fountain pens, it was filled by means of a glass eye dropper, but in 1908 a breakthrough was made when the lever-operated rubber ink holder was patented.

This device set the seal on the success of the fountain pen, which by the time of World War 1 was regarded as indispensable. Barrels were made from a variety of materials, including mother-of-pearl, gold, silver, glass and plastics such as Bakelite and Parker's 'Permanite'. There were little pens for ladies' handbags, often with bands of gold, and the invention of the pen clip allowed pens to be put in pockets the right way up, reducing the risk of leakage.

It was not until the late 19th century that technological advances produced reliable fountain pens that did not leak. They came as a blessing to the writer and were soon to be found on the desktop of everyone who seriously put pen to paper.

177

FOUNTAIN PENS

There can obviously be fairly little variation in the size and shape of pens, but they were made in a great variety of materials and decorative finishes. At the top end of the market were those with barrels in precious metals, like the 'Swan' of 1900 by the New York manufacturers Mabie, Todd and Bard, which was gold-plated. One of the most common materials was vulcanite, a black substance made by heating rubber with sulphur; it was used to simulate jet, but is somewhat duller in appearance. There were also many accessories for the fountain pen. Blotting paper would have been placed in a leather blotter on the desk, where there would usually also be an inkstand and inkwell; fountain pens needed refilling with ink about once a week on average.

THE "SWAN" "EASY-FILI" FILLER
(Patented)

Fills and cleans Any Fountain Pen in a few seconds without unscrewing the parts.

Absolutely Safe and Clean.

Price, In Card Box : 2/-
Filled with "Swan" Ink.
U.K. Postage and Packing
1½d. each extra.

THE "LONGSHORT" STYLO
Long for the Hand. — Short for the Pocket.

"LONGSHORT" Stylos are so called, because, although they close up short for the pocket, they open to nearly double the length for comfort in writing.

Spiral Spring Needle.
Patent Ink Trap.

A very popular pocket stylo which may be carried in any position

Size A
In Black or Tan
Price 5/- Each.
Length open, 4½ ins. Closed, 3 ins.

Also Size B (larger). Price 7/6 each.
Length open, 5½ ins. Closed, 3½ ins. Black only.
(Insured Postage on Stylos, 3d. each extra).

Printed in England.

"THE BLACKBIRD" FOUNTPEN

2 AN ADVERT *from the 1930s for two Swan pens, the Stylo, a forerunner of the ballpoint, and the stylish 'Blackbird Fountpen'.*

5 A BAKELITE PEN, *dating from 1915, accompanied by a glass dropper for filling it with ink.*

3 A STURDY VELVATIP PEN *dating from c1910. The barrel is made of vulcanite, a tough material derived from rubber.*

5 A TRAVELLING INKWELL *in the form of a cricket ball (the exterior is covered with leather). It was made in the 1890s.*

7 THIS ELEGANT FOUNTAIN PEN *was made by the American manufacturer Conklin in about 1910. It boasts lavish 14-carat gold decoration.*

5 A SLIM GOLD-PLATED PEN *made by Mabie, Todd and Bard of New York in about 1910. It has a truly classic simplicity.*

Ray Duns

178

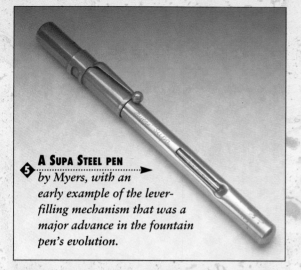

A Supa Steel pen 5 by Myers, with an early example of the lever-filling mechanism that was a major advance in the fountain pen's evolution.

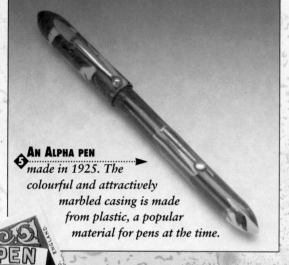

An Alpha pen 5 made in 1925. The colourful and attractively marbled casing is made from plastic, a popular material for pens at the time.

Parker Pens UK Ltd.

An advertisement for Parker pens 1 published in 1900. The pen was guaranteed not to leak and had a gold nib.

A box of nibs 2 made in Birmingham by George W Hughes. At the turn of the century nibs were often called 'pens'.

A 1930s Waterman USA pen. 4 The plastic barrel, with its gold decoration, contrasts with the marble-effect end and cap.

Inks 2 come in corked bottles with attractive labels.

A Parker pen 4 made in the 1930s. It is particularly appealing, with a geometric pattern on its plastic casing. Like most Parkers it had a gold nib.

Fountain pen nibs 2 often came in attractively styled boxes such as this and are now collectors' items in their own right.

A Waterman fountain pen 4 from about 1920, with a brown and black plastic body. The marbled design has long been popular with pen makers.

Fine Art Photographic Library

CLOSE UP *on* BARREL STYLES

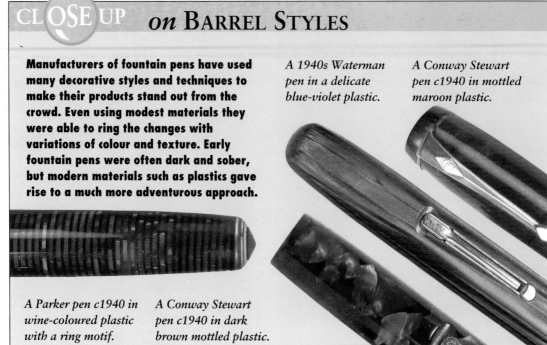

Manufacturers of fountain pens have used many decorative styles and techniques to make their products stand out from the crowd. Even using modest materials they were able to ring the changes with variations of colour and texture. Early fountain pens were often dark and sober, but modern materials such as plastics gave rise to a much more adventurous approach.

A 1940s Waterman pen in a delicate blue-violet plastic.

A Conway Stewart pen c1940 in mottled maroon plastic.

A Parker pen c1940 in wine-coloured plastic with a ring motif.

A Conway Stewart pen c1940 in dark brown mottled plastic.

This early example of a fountain pen (above left) dates from the mid 18th century; it comes with its original leather case (above right). The cap of the pen lifts off to reveal a quill nib.

COLLECTOR'S NOTES

Since the late 1980s there has been an upsurge of interest in vintage pens, with a consequent steep rise in prices. Pens are now an established specialist field, and auction houses sometimes devote sales exclusively to them. Many factors affect the price that a pen can command, notably age, rarity and condition. The material of which the pen is made is also obviously significant, for one in gold or silver will naturally tend to be much more valuable than one made from plastic.

In general, the most sought-after fountain pens are those from before the turn of the century, because of their rarity and historical importance. Even the most basic pens from this period are in demand, because few of the millions that were produced are likely to have survived in pristine condition – if a pen was not intrinsically valuable, it was likely to be scrapped as soon as it was superseded by a better model, in much the same way that we casually throw away cheap ballpoints today.

Whereas ladies' pens were usually made in a single size, pens for men were often available in a range of sizes, typically five. The bigger ones, with their 'macho' appeal, are generally worth more than the smaller ones. The American Parker firm made a range of pens known as 'Big Reds' between 1921 and 1932 and these 'status symbol' pens have been perennially popular with collectors. Nibs as well as pens were available in various sizes, and here also the bigger ones tend to command the highest prices.

Although many vintage pens are bought for display, some collectors like to use them, and there is no reason why they should not be functional as well as attractive. Often, however, pens will be sold in non-functioning condition, and this should be reflected in the price. Repairs can be expensive, so you should take this into consideration if buying a pen that is likely to need some attention.

Ray Duns

This elegant pen is of a type that was made specifically for ladies. It has hooks on the end of the cap rather than a pocket clip, as it was intended to be worn round the waist attached to a belt ring. The hooks were always on the cap end, so the pen was less likely to leak.

CIGARETTE LIGHTERS

To smoke was to be chic in the art deco period and pocket cigarette lighters were made in novel and imaginative styles which are now highly sought after by collectors

The 1920s and 30s were the age of glamour, symbolized by the modern woman who cut her hair, threw away her corsets and petticoats and took up smoking.

The sophisticated young woman with scarlet lips and bobbed hair, languidly smoking a cigarette in a long, slim holder, is one of the enduring images of the 1920s and 30s. A stylish cigarette lighter was a fashion essential for the modern girl.

Petrol had recently become available, so that a wick soaked in it could be used to make a flame – far more attractive than the old-fashioned smouldering tinder. Then a new type of 'flint', made of iron filings combined with the rare metal cerium, was invented. This gave a good spark when struck with steel, and the first 'striking' lighters were quickly developed. They were made of metal and filled with cotton wool soaked with a few drops of petrol and had a wick, a flint and a steel cap which struck the flint. It was not long before the cap was replaced by a steel wheel with a milled edge. The 'wheel-and-flint' petrol lighter quickly became the most popular design and is still widely used today.

DUNHILL'S UNIQUE

However, early lighters were a favourite butt of many music hall jokes because of their inefficiency and the strong smell of petrol which hung around them. It was Dunhill who changed their image with the introduction of the Unique lighter, launched in the early 20s as 'the lighter that changed public opinion'. Its clever design put an end to petrol evaporation – which solved the problem of the smell and meant that the lighter rarely needed filling – and it could be operated with one hand. With the introduction of the Unique, the lighter 'ceased to be a toy and became a necessity'. Everybody wanted one of these chic, stylish lighters and manufacturers fought to capture the market with ever newer and more striking designs for both pocket and table lighters. Cartier's Department S – the predecessor of today's Cartier 'Must' – was set up in 1926 and produced upmarket and expensive lighters throughout the art deco period. One pocket lighter made by them in 9-carat gold and black enamel folded neatly into its own case, while another example in 18-carat gold had a Cartier watch built into it. They also produced a number of novelty table lighters in the form of pistols, books and pencil cases.

But don't let these top-of-the-range names put you off. While they influenced the market, they were obviously only a small part of it, and there were plenty of firms catering for smokers who wanted stylish designs in more practical materials than gold and diamonds.

Advertising Archives

POCKET LIGHTERS

The standard material for most lighters was chrome-plated brass. Models from the middle of the price range were plated in silver or gold and on older lighters it is possible to see the brass faintly glowing through where the silver plating has been worn away.

Different firms pioneered different styles: Dunhill's lighters were generally quite restrained in the typically English style, often with no decoration other than texturing of the metal – though there were some spectacular exceptions. In the United States, the classic Zippo lighter – named after the newly invented zip – first came out in the early 1930s. Ronson's designs were in typically flamboyant American art deco style using chrome, enamel, brass and plastic. The Viennese firm IMCO sold lighters made from cartridge cases – an idea copied from the soldiers who fought in the trenches during World War 1. Colibri, named after a South African bird, made an automatic lighter with a sprung mechanism which struck the flint.

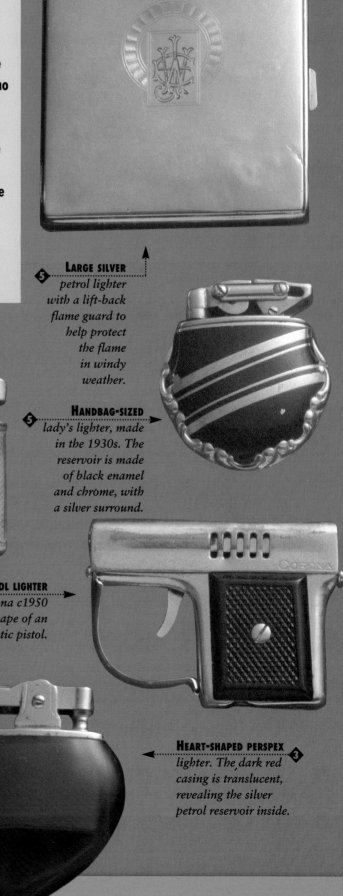

5 LARGE SILVER petrol lighter with a lift-back flame guard to help protect the flame in windy weather.

2 CHROME-PLATED LIGHTER in traditional style, decorated with an engine-turned pattern.

5 HANDBAG-SIZED lady's lighter, made in the 1930s. The reservoir is made of black enamel and chrome, with a silver surround.

5 SILVER LIGHTER for the handbag, etched and decorated with enamelled flowers.

3 NOVELTY PETROL LIGHTER made by Corona c1950 in the shape of an automatic pistol.

4 SILVER-CASED gentleman's lighter with elegant ribbed decoration and lift-off top.

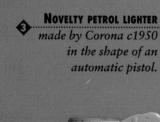

3 HEART-SHAPED PERSPEX lighter. The dark red casing is translucent, revealing the silver petrol reservoir inside.

BRASS LIGHTER ❷
with lift-off cap
and the typically
clean lines of deco
design. The metal
is polished to an
unornamented
matt finish.

RONSON FLINT-STRIKING LIGHTER ❷
made of brass and given away to
customers as a complimentary gift
from a motor supplies company.

CHROME LIGHTER ❸
in a characteristically art deco
design with a stark geometric
pattern in black and chrome.

A 'SUPER' BRASS ❹
novelty petrol
lighter. It has been
made in the shape of
a fountain pen with
a Parker-style clip,
bearing the name of
the manufacturer.

RARE PATENT AUTOMATIC LIGHTER ❹
made by Thorens. The case is
made of chrome with a matt finish
and flip-top lid. The button at the
side produces a spark when pressed.

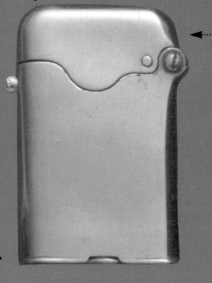

1930s LIGHTER ❹
in pale grey-green
enamel and silver
plate with an
airbrushed design.

ENGINE-TURNED LIGHTER ❹
by Mosda, bearing the Gibraltar
crest. A panel for the owner's
initials is included in the design.

RONSON LIGHTER ❸
made of chrome
with black leather
casing and a plaque
for the owner's initials.

A 1920s NOVELTY ❹
lighter made of brass in the
shape of an old-fashioned book
with heavy leather bindings.

THORENS LIGHTER c1930 ❹
with a stylish abstract design
on a dimpled background.

Ronald Mackechnie

COLLECTOR'S NOTES

Lighters were made in such a huge range of styles that you could easily base your collection on the products of one particular manufacturer or country. However, with lighters available at prices ranging from a pound or two to several thousand, this is a rich and exciting field for collectors and it could be more fun simply to base your collection on your own personal taste.

Models with strong deco features are particularly sought after. As well as having art deco patterns on the surface, some lighters are characteristically deco in shape. For example, Mouchon made one called Le Sphinx which had a stepped outline influenced by the Egyptian styles fashionable at the time. Some IMCO lighters were strongly deco in design, such as the Fit, which also had geometic, Egyptian-style decoration, and the Wendy, which was triangular, rotated out of a triangular sleeve for use and had an attractive tassel.

NOVELTY LIGHTERS

Examples by small manufacturers such as the British companies Polo and Orlik are very collectable, as are novelty lighters, which were produced by several makers in a wide range of imaginative designs – but beware modern reproductions of deco designs. Most will be fuelled by butane gas, which didn't appear until the 1960s. Dunhill's first ever lighter was produced in 1923, using a Colman's mustard tin as the prototype. It was called the Everytime Lighter because of its reliability. Their Compendium Lighter, today worth over £1000, appeared in 1937. Designed for men, it incorporated a watch, a cigarette case, an ivory memo tablet, a miniature card case, an inch measure, a penknife and a pencil. The ladies' model replaced the penknife and measure with lipstick, powder and a mirror.

Ronald Mackechnie

Prices for these luxury lighters would start from around £100. The one with the hidden watch was inspired by a South American who had one made in 1926 of solid gold. This model is worth over £1500.

Accessories are also available – these include such items as wick tongs, designed to enable the lighter owner to insert a new wick more easily, wheel cleaners and lighter fillers.

Table lighters offered the designer even more scope for imagination – an extreme example of this is Dunhill's 'Lighthouse Table Lighter'. It was made of 18-carat gold in the shape of a lighthouse 60cm/2ft high, standing on an island of amethysts. The whole lighter weighed 50kg/110lb and was sold at Christie's in 1987 for £37,500. However, most art deco table lighters were made in less ambitious forms, such as chrome aeroplanes, lady golfers or even cocktail bars with a waiter.

Touch-tip lighters were very popular. This design has a metal wand with a wick in one end. The wand is contained in a small reservoir of petrol in the body of the lighter. When the metal end of the wand is scraped across a ribbed metal striking plate, it creates a spark which ignites the petrol-soaked wick. The lighter function is frequently almost incidental to the design – for example, one model was made in the form of an art deco style 'bat girl' with outstretched wings, the lighter being housed in a column at her side.

DEALER'S TIPS

- **All lighters will be more desirable if they are in working order: ensure the wick and its holder are present in petrol lighters. The petrol-soaked cotton wool wadding inside will often need replacing, but this is not a problem and shouldn't affect the value.**
- **A petrol lighter will not operate unless the retaining screw which holds the spring for the flint and its mechanism is present.**
- **Check that the striking plate is present on touch-tip lighters and that the wand shows a spark when struck.**
- **It is often worth buying up old lighters at a flea market, boot sale or auction and cannibalizing them for spare parts.**

COMICS

Comics have a great deal to recommend them – they provide the collector with a reminder of a lost childhood, are an entertaining read and are affordable as well

The most valuable comic in the world, issue one of *Action* (1939) starring Superman, could fetch as much as £18,000. The collector's market has been dominated by American publications such as this in recent years, and values of certain comics increased even further with the advent of films like *Superman* and *Dick Tracy*. *Batman* comics trebled in value when the film was released in 1990.

British comics still provide a great deal of scope, however, and have the advantage of being much more reasonably priced, though the first issue of the *Beano*, dated 30 July 1938, could fetch up to £2000.

The majority of early British comics were actually aimed at adults, as publishers didn't think children would want to spend a halfpenny of their pocket money on a magazine. Among the first batch was *Comic Cuts*, published on 17 May 1890 by Alfred Harmsworth, which claimed to give 'one hundred laughs for one halfpenny'.

The first great heroes of the comics were two tramps, thin Weary Willy and fat Tired Timmy. They were created by the artist Tom Browne and appeared in *Illustrated Chips* (1896). Their simple style made them role models for comic characters in years to come.

CHILDREN'S COMICS

It wasn't until the turn of the century that comics specifically for children were produced. *The Rainbow* appeared in 1914, and from then on at least two or three were launched every year, each with a free gift such as a balloon, toffees, a cardboard cutout toy, as mask or a whistle.

In the 1930s, a new action-packed slapstick style was introduced and the old-style captions under pictures were replaced by American-influenced speech bubbles.

The Beano *and* Dandy *were among many a schoolboy's secret hoard of comics, for reading under the bedclothes late at night.*

Lyndon Parker

THE COMIC STRIP

Many favourite comics began in the 1930s, which really was the Golden Age of the comic strip. It was at this time that D C Thomson launched *The Dandy* (1937) and *The Beano* (1938), with their rebel characters Desperate Dan and Dennis the Menace, who are just as popular with children today as they were when they first appeared.

The Dandy and *The Beano* were the first British comics to adopt the now-familiar speech bubbles instead of captions. They are now among the most sought-after British comics around, with an issue one fetching up to £1500.

War-time comics *Adventure* and *Wizard* are filled with action-packed pages of adventure, science fiction, sport and detective tales.

Girl's comics have long been a neglected field, and most can still be bought quite cheaply. They first gained popularity in the 1950s with the advent of *School Friend* and *Bunty*, the longest-running girl's comic. *Bunty* started on 18 January 1958 and thrilled girls with the boarding school exploits of 'The Four Marys'.

Judy is rather more dynamic in content than *Bunty*. Another comic from the D C Thomson stable, it is filled with tales of adventure featuring the dare-devil do-gooder, Supergirl.

• Comics can be a good investment, but do be careful which ones you buy – values fluctuate according to what's in fashion.

• British weekly comics like *The Beano* and *The Dandy* are much more affordable than the American monthlies like *Flash, Marvel* and *Spiderman*.

THIS ADVENTURE ❷
comic from 1936 came with nine free gifts inside and originally cost two pence.

AN ISSUE OF ❷
The Beano *from 1946. One of Britain's oldest and most popular comics, it celebrated its 50th birthday in 1988.*

THE DANDY ❸
from 1944 with Korky the Kat on the front cover, just as he was in the very first issue in 1937.

WIZARD FROM 1938 ❷
sold itself on the front cover as 'the paper with "The Black Outlaw" and "Grey Ghost"'.

AN ACTION COMIC ① from 1983 – the magazine that launched one of the world's most popular comic strip heroes. Superman was introduced in the very first issue in June 1939.

④ AN AMAZING SPIDERMAN comic dating from the 1960s. It tells the story of photographer Peter Parker who turns into Spiderman after being bitten by a radioactive spider .

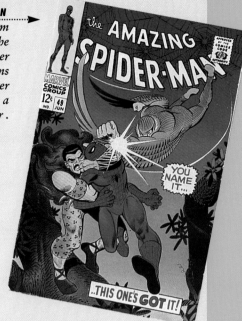

AN EARLY BUNTY ① from October 1958. It was launched in January of that year and was aimed at the younger schoolgirl.

AN AMERICAN ④ Marvel Mystery comic from 1942, graphically illustrating events at Pearl Harbour.

AN EARLY ISSUE OF ① the popular girl's comic, Judy, dating from 1960.

All photos Lyndon Parker

on DENNIS THE MENACE

Dennis the Menace and his dog Gnasher, two of Britain's most popular comic characters, are famous for their naughty antics. Dennis can now be found on everything from mugs to socks, and there is even a Dennis the Menace fan club.

COLLECTOR'S NOTES

Demand for comics fluctuates dramatically. People often collect them as a reminder of the good old days and the collectable titles inevitably change. Unlike many other bygones, the most valuable comics are usually no more than 30 or 40 years old.

There are so many comics around that the would-be collector is advised to have a focus before starting. Many people simply choose the magazine they read as a child. From this initial starting point you might branch out further, by concentrating on a particular artist, character or theme.

Once you have made this decision, look around different shops and markets to find the best price. Jumble sales, charity shops and car boot sales are good hunting-grounds for comics – you can often find great bargains.

WHAT TO LOOK FOR

With comics, good condition is essential. In the United States they are graded from mint through fine to coverless. A comic in mint condition is pristine, unread and uncreased. Comics with any writing, tears or printing faults are immediately devalued. The more tatty the comic, the cheaper it should be. Avoid comics repaired with adhesive tape since this causes damage as it ages. If mending, use special document-repairing tape.

COMPARE & CONTRAST

An issue of *Film Fun* from the 1930s, printed in black and white, showing text captions running under the pictures (left).
By the 1960s, *Film Fun* had followed the trend for two-colour printing (below) and featured American-style cartoons with speech bubbles.

Dealers sell comics in special plastic bags and this is how they should be stored. Ideally, they should be kept upright in a binder to avoid creasing and stored out of bright sunlight.

Availability is also a key to value. Comics from the war years are of particular value because they are so scarce, due to the hoards of newspapers and comics that were collected for recycling.

The first issue of a comic run is usually the most valuable, although one-off editions like a Christmas special are worth looking out for.

TOMORROW'S TREASURES

New comics are constantly being published, including many aimed at the adult market. This is probably due to the success of *Viz*, which was launched in December 1979. Unfortunately, however, not every new launch becomes a classic.

One that has is the science-fiction comic, *2000 AD*. Its dynamic hero, Judge Dredd, was the Dan Dare of the 1980s and continues to be a favourite. Even though it was only launched in 1977, it is already collectable.

Copies of 2000 AD dating from the late 1970s and early 1980s, now worth over £2 each, are a good investment.

Lyndon Parker

SUPERHERO COMICS

Comic-book heroes with strange and mysterious powers first appeared at the end of the Great Depression, and have since become an established part of American culture. Their early adventures are now hugely collectable

American comics have always been different. Where British ones tended to be loosely bound, monochrome creations, mainly aimed at children, their transatlantic counterparts were smaller, full-colour, stapled magazines ('comic books') that appealed to teenagers and young adults.

Comic books focussed on action stories, with tales of cowboys, detectives, soldiers or figures based on popular movie heroes. Then, in 1938, Superman, created by Jerry Siegel and Joe Shuster, made his debut in issue 27 of *Action Comics*, published by DC comics.

The immediate impact of the Man of Steel led other publishers to rush to create their own versions. What might have been a passing fad was given a boost when the USA entered World War 2 in 1941. Suddenly, rather than besting ordinary denizens of the underworld, superheroes faced the challenge of Japanese spies and Nazi saboteurs. The adventures of heroes like Captain America were followed by GIs as well as their younger brothers.

LITTLE HORRORS

The Golden Age of superhero comics came to an end in the late 1940s, when there was a fad for horror comics. These soon ran up against the innate conservatism of the 1950s; the resulting furore led to the setting up of a censorship body, the Comics Code Authority, in 1954. The Comics Code affected superhero titles as well as horror. Humour and romance comics flourished and the bland superhero comics that did survive – mostly from DC – were aimed at younger children.

The second coming of superhero comics – known to collectors as the Silver Age – was ushered in by Marvel Comics, who challenged the supremacy of DC's *Batman* and *Superman* in two ways. They set up a jokey rapport with their readers, addressing them directly, and introduced superheroes with personalities and problems; Spiderman's alter-ego, for instance, was a bookish, nerdy misfit who was shy with girls. Marvel also revived Golden Age characters such as Captain America with new twists to their personalities.

Ray Duns

The first comic in this new style, *The Fantastic Four*, was written by Stan Lee and drawn by Jack Kirby, the driving forces behind Marvel; both had been in the industry since the 1940s. DC responded in kind and American superheroes hit a new high of popularity, cemented when comic books – particularly mystical titles such as Marvel's *Silver Surfer* – were adopted by the hippy counter-culture at the end of the 1960s. They have since gone from strength to strength.

In the 1940s, superheroes won the war for the Allies many times over, but in the 1960s and after they took on mythic villains whose powers almost matched – but never surpassed – their own.

6 THE FLASH, FASTEST MAN ALIVE, and the Hawkman were both revived by DC comics in the Silver Age, but this comic detailing their early adventures is a relic of the 1940s.

SHAZAM! THE GOLDEN AGE

Some comics from the Golden Age (1938-1950) are golden indeed; only a handful of copies in good condition are known to exist, and these can fetch thousands of pounds on the rare occasions they are offered at auction. Early appearances by DC comic's Superman and Batman – who first appeared in 1939 – attract particularly lively interest, as does Fawcett's Captain Marvel. Most American-issued superhero comics of the period fetch sums ranging from price guide 6 upwards, though foreign and later reissues will sell for just a fraction of that.

British reprints of the period usually had the strips cut up and rearranged to fit the larger British format, and are nothing like as valuable. Original American comics were not commercially imported to Britain in the 1940s and 1950s, and are very scarce. The only source was those brought over by or for American servicemen, and these were readily available only around US air bases.

The great interest in Golden Age comics in the 1970s, when the collecting habit really took off, encouraged many companies to reissue the original comics in new covers or formats. Those intrigued by the artwork and stories, rather than rarity, will find these a much more attractive proposition.

BILLY BATSON, an orphan newsboy, became Captain Marvel when he said the magic word 'Shazam'. About 150 copies of his first appearance in Whiz survive. This is a reprint; originals are price guide 10.

AMAZON princess, Diana, became Wonder Woman in 1941 to get girls buying comic books. This is a 1974 reprint of a 1942 edition.

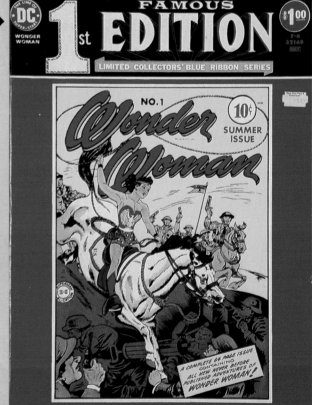

10 THIS ISSUE OF DETECTIVE COMICS, NUMBER 27, has the first appearance of Batman, and is the most expensive comic book ever, though copies very rarely come on the market. DC comics took their name from the initials of this title.

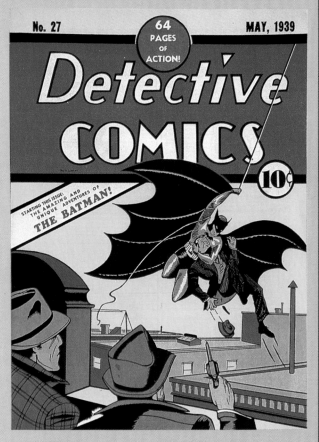

No. 27 · 64 PAGES OF ACTION! · MAY, 1939

Detective COMICS 10¢

STARTING THIS ISSUE: THE AMAZING AND UNIQUE ADVENTURES OF THE BATMAN!

THE DOLL MAN punched considerably more than his weight. Created by the prolific Will Eisner and published by Quality Comics, the diminutive superhero's adventures were reprinted in various British comic annuals of the 1950s. Unlike most popular heroes of the Golden Age of Comics, Doll Man has never been convincingly revived.

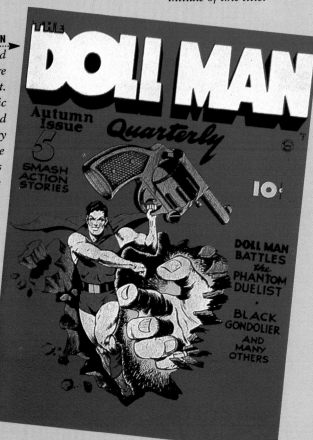

THE DOLL MAN Quarterly · Autumn Issue · 5 SMASH ACTION STORIES · 10¢ · DOLL MAN BATTLES the PHANTOM DUELIST · BLACK GONDOLIER AND MANY OTHERS

THE HUMAN TORCH AND THE SUB-MARINER **6** usually scrapped with each other when not repelling the Nazi menace. The rarity of this issue on Timely, a precursor of Marvel (who revived both characters in the 1960s), makes up for the comic's rather shabby condition.

SUPERMAN **1** soon graduated to his own magazine from the pages of Action Comics. All Golden Age Superman comics are very collectable, though this reprint of the first edition, published in the early 1970s, is easy to find.

SUPERMAN · 64 PAGES OF ACTION! · ALL IN FULL COLOR · THE COMPLETE STORY OF THE DARING EXPLOITS OF THE ONE AND ONLY SUPERMAN

ALL BRAND NEW FEATURES! · THE HUMAN TORCH also THE SUB-MARINER · 10¢ · SUMMER NUMBER · 40 THRILLING PAGES of HUMAN TORCH and TORO

Roy Duns

MARVELMANIA AND THE SECOND COMING

Comics from the Silver Age are much easier to find than those from the 1940s, and are generally much more affordable, though early Marvel titles and various 'cult' comics such as *The Silver Surfer* can be much pricier. DC comics (the initials come from Detective Comics, one of their earliest titles) were first widely distributed in Britain in 1959, Marvel a year or so later. Early issues were often shipped over as ballast, meaning that it's now difficult to find examples that aren't water damaged, and various distribution problems – the dock strike near the end of 1964, for instance – created several rarities.

While the price of Golden Age comics is fairly stable, the market for superhero comics published since 1960 can be very volatile. Even fairly recent issues from DC and Marvel are the subject of speculation. Some titles acquire a collector's value well over the cover price just a few months after publication, while others plummet. As distribution is no longer a particular problem, with networks of specialist shops all over the UK, high prices are generally the result of high demand for the work of fashionable writers and illustrators.

▲ **SWAMP CREATURES – BASICALLY ANIMATED GOO –** ❶
have been around since the heyday of horror comics. Marvel's version ran for 22 issues in 1974-75 and was revived in 1979.

◀ **GREEN LANTERN** ④
is a revived Golden Age character whose powers derive from a ring charged from a lantern given to him by a body of intergalactic crime fighters, the Green Guardians. This is an early issue of one of DC's enduring titles, which ran for 224 issues from 1960-1988.

MOON KNIGHT ❶
ran for 38 issues in its first run from 1980 to 1984. It's mainly noticeable for its striking art, seen to good effect in this atmospheric cover, which was the work of Bill Sienkiewicz, one of the hottest comic artists of the 1980s.

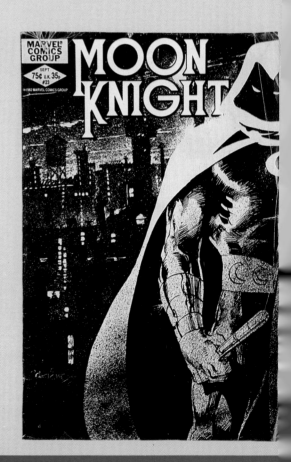

SUPERMAN ④ has appeared in numerous special editions over the years as well as in his own books. This, the first of DC's 80-page Giant Magazines, appeared in 1964 to celebrate the Man of Steel's silver anniversary.

INTRODUCING: THE POUNDING POWER OF **THE WRECKER!**

② **A VIKING GOD** may seem an unlikely superhero, but Thor of Asgard has wielded his hammer for Marvel for three decades.

③ **SPIDER-MAN AND THE FANTASTIC FOUR** are Marvel's longest-running titles and very early issues of both in fine condition attract some of the best prices of the Silver Age, price guide 6 and above. Slightly later issues like these are also collectable. The price is per comic book.

② **THE X-MEN, TEENAGE MUTANTS WITH SUPER POWERS,** became a cult when revived as the New X-Men in issue 94 in 1975. Over the years, the title has featured the early work of several fine artists.

Ray Duns

COLLECTOR'S NOTES

Though superhero comics do have an investment potential, it's a complex market, and if you don't have an interest in them as an art form, or simply a good read, you'd be better off not collecting them. If you are interested, though, they can make an absorbing hobby.

It can be fun to pick up odd issues of different titles, but most collectors settle on some particular favourite and try to amass a complete run. Some comics only had a short life, so this is fairly easy, but other titles are a real challenge; *The Amazing Spiderman* and *The Fantastic Four* are close to 400 issues, while Superman has racked up 500 appearances in his own title alone. It's possible to collect a favourite artist, though the best will have been associated with thousands of issues and dozens of titles in their careers.

TOMORROW'S HITS TODAY

Specialist dealers are the best place to look for collectable comics, as well as the new issues that may be the collectables of tomorrow. Comics fairs and mail-order sales and auctions are other good sources, while comic books sometimes still turn up in boot sales, jumble sales, flea markets and the like, though rarely in collectable condition. It may be worthwhile looking through attics and cupboards for old copies squirrelled away in childhood, though these will probably have deteriorated unless stored with care. Comics were printed as throwaway items, using very cheap grades of paper. They generally brown, chip and decay unless kept in a special environment.

Condition is very

There's more to enjoy in comics than the stories and artwork alone. The small ads appearing in Gold and Silver Age comics are a treasure trove of frankly bizarre novelty products.

THE SPIRIT

Early comic books were seen by newspapers as a promotional opportunity. Sales were boosted with comic supplements. One of the most successful was the weekly 8-page *Spirit*, created by Will Eisner, a great innovator as both writer and illustrator. The adult-oriented strip has since been reprinted in comic-book form.

Ray Duns

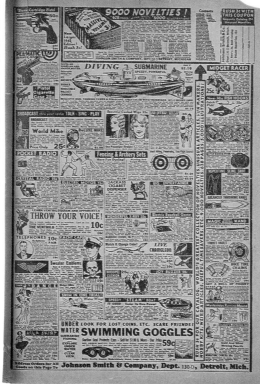

important. Comics are graded for sale on a scale which ranges from mint down through near mint, very fine, fine, very good, good, fair and poor to coverless.

Copies from very good down tend to be seen as reading copies only; fine comics, the minimum collectable grade, should be clean, flat, with no marks on the cover, and no writing anywhere. Slight wear is acceptable at the edges or around the spine. The pages should not be significantly yellowed.

Chipping (flaking at the outer edge of the cover seen on Marvel comics from the 1960s), creases and small tears, obtrusive price stamps on the cover, rolled spines, rust marks around the staples or loose centre pages all devalue a comic. Issues with missing pages, cut-out coupons and so on are virtually worthless.

Keep valuable comics in individual plastic bags, which should not be airtight. These can be bought from dealers. Ideally they should be stored upright, stiffened by acid-free backing boards, in a dark, cool, and not too dry place.

TOY TRAINS

*The romance of the railways and nostalgia for
innocent boyhood pleasures have made train sets
among the most collectable of toys*

*The appeal of toy
trains lies not only
in the fine detailing
and mechanical
ingenuity of the
engines and rolling
stock themselves, but
in the proliferation
of scaled accessories
– stations, signal-
boxes and other
buildings, trees,
trackside furniture,
staff and passengers,
bridges, level
crossings and
vehicles – that allow
the hobbyist to
create whole
landscapes and
communities through
which to run them.*

Railways, and particularly steam railways, have from the very first attracted the enthusiasm of boys and their fathers, and toy makers in England, France and Germany were quick to see the possible appeal of toy trains. Mid-Victorian toy makers produced thousands of 'penny' trains and later 'carpet toy' models in wood and tinplate. These did not run on a track, but were pushed across the floor by hand or pulled along by a piece of string. They proved very popular, with a variety of passenger carriages and goods wagons contributing to their appeal.

Some later 'floor-runners' were powered by clockwork or steam. The first toy trains to be provided with tracks were almost certainly what are known to enthusiasts as 'dribblers'. These ran on tiny steam engines that needed constant paternal vigilance to make sure the oil and water levels were topped up and that the spirit lamp regulated the steam properly.

The first great name in the field was the German firm, Märklin, who produced a figure-of-eight track in the 1890s. They are still in business today. Their locomotives, carriages, stations and accessories have always been treasured; old ones fetch fantastic prices.

Once manufacturers started selling lengths of track, they had to decide on standard gauges. Gauge 1 had a scale of 30 to 1, and gauge 0, 43 to 1. Smaller gauges, such as H0, 00 and, in the 1950s and 60s, the tiny 000, were introduced later for families with less space for layouts.

Continued adult interest in model trains led to an emphasis on attention to detail and good craftsmanship. Märklin, and their slightly down-market German rivals, Bing, always had high standards, but the most accurate scale models were produced by an Englishman, W J Bassett-Lowke.

The accuracy of model trains was sometimes hampered by the need to include a clockwork or steam engine to power them. This problem was solved with the introduction of electric train sets in 1898. Early electric models were powered by mains electricity at a dangerous 120 volts. By the 1920s, though, transformers had been developed that reduced the power to a more acceptable 20 volts.

Ray Duns

MODEL TRAINS

Colourful rolling stock is very desirable, especially coaches and wagons with inscriptions such as 'Pullman' or 'Fyffes Bananas' but it is the locomotives and tenders that fetch the highest prices. The livery of the set is also important. Southern Railway green, for instance, is seen less often than many of the pre-nationalization colours.

The nationality of a model train does not necessarily give a clue to the place it was made; all the major manufacturers produced export models of other railway systems.

Before World War 1, locos were generally made of printed tinplate, though later ones, especially those in HO and 00 gauges, tended to be made of die-cast metal.

METTOY SET 453, *made in 1937, is typical of the clockwork sets put out by lesser British companies. It had six curved tracks to form a circle. Price is reduced by the set's poor condition.*

LIONEL LINE'S *reproductions of American locomotives included some sleek, streamlined transcontinental models that had great appeal outside the USA.*

THIS 0-4-0 TANK ENGINE *is a Bassett-Lowke 20-volt locomotive made around 1940 in the livery of the Southern Railway. As a tank engine, it had no separate tender.*

Ray Duns Michael Michaels Peter Greenhalf

LIONEL LINES, THE USA's TOP MAKER, produced more than 3,000 locomotives. This 4-4-0 loco, complete with cowcatcher and tender, is typical. — ⑤

GOODS WAGONS provide colour and interest to a layout. Here, the same double bogie chassis is fitted with a petrol tank and with a lithographed tinplate boxcar. — ③

HORNBY DUBLO's MODELS, in the 00 gauge, are often masterly pieces of miniaturization. This GWR loco and first-class carriage are modern. — ⑤

THE DUCHESS OF MONTROSE in spanking new LMS livery is one of Bassett-Lowke's finest models. It is electric, running on a current of just 12 volts. — ⑦

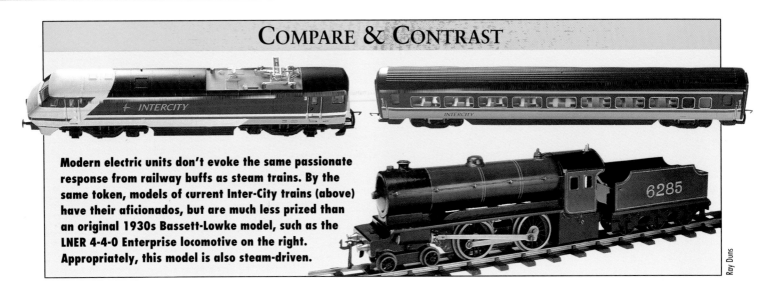

COMPARE & CONTRAST

Modern electric units don't evoke the same passionate response from railway buffs as steam trains. By the same token, models of current Inter-City trains (above) have their aficionados, but are much less prized than an original 1930s Bassett-Lowke model, such as the LNER 4-4-0 Enterprise locomotive on the right. Appropriately, this model is also steam-driven.

Ray Duns

COLLECTOR'S NOTES

Train sets were often seen as special. Even the most humble sets were treated with care, even reverence, by their owners, who were always careful to return them to their boxes. This means that a remarkable number of them have survived in good condition.

There was a time when no collector worth his or her salt would have bothered with anything other than sets made by Märklin, Bing or Bassett-Lowke. However, these can be fantastically expensive, and sets made by Hornby, the British firm that produced the much-loved Meccano, are now also very collectable and more reasonably priced. Other British companies, such as Chad Valley, Mettoy or Brimtoy, are less collectable.

Condition is paramount in setting the price of an old model train. Missing bits and battered boxes can have a dramatic effect on price. Sets that have been tampered with by small boys with paint brushes are best avoided. They can be restored to their

original livery, but the value is greatly reduced.

Pieces of rolling stock, locomotives and accessories can still be found in a variety of places, from jumble sales to auctions, and individual pieces of line-side equipment can be picked up relatively cheaply if you are prepared to shop around. Rolling stock is often sold in lots. It is still possible to pick up lengths of track in junk shops, but do check first that it's not too badly dented.

Boxed sets and locomotives by the more sought-after makers are more usually found in specialist shops and auctions and through advertisements in specialist magazines. Serious collectors must be prepared to travel and learn about their subject. As with all potentially expensive collectables, knowledge of the subject is your greatest protection against disappointment. Try to make contact with other enthusiasts. They are not only the best source of valuable information, but also, potentially, of items for your collection.

Although boxed sets, early Märklin and Bassett-Lowke locomotives now fetch the highest prices, items bought individually or in lots at auction can soon be made up into an interesting collection, providing that you concentrate on one format – electric, steam or clockwork – and one gauge. Wagons or carriages with print on them tend to attract higher prices, too, even when, as here, the writing is in French.

Micheal Micheals

POST-WAR TOY CARS

Toy cars capture the magic of childhood for everyone,
young or old, and the Dinkys once bought for shillings
are selling today for pounds

Lyndon Parker

Toy cars, whether diecast (by injecting alloy into a mould under pressure) or made in tin plate, date back to the turn of the century, and boomed in the post-war era. Frank Hornby (who founded Meccano in 1901) introduced tiny diecast cars in 1934. He sold them first as accessories to his model railways, but the Dinky cars, as they were called, were an instant hit in their own right.

Lesney launched their Matchbox cars in 1953, closely followed by Mettoy's Playcraft Toys with their Corgi range in 1956. 1965 saw Lesney's Models of Yesteryear series.

Tin-plate clockwork cars were produced by companies such as Tipp, Gunthermann and Paya. In the 1950s, the Japanese share of the battery-operated tin-plate toy market gradually overtook that of the Germans and, by the 1960s, Japan had become the world's largest manufacturer of battery-operated toys. Many of these were copies of American vehicles.

In the late 1960s, the American company Mattel produced their Hot Wheels cars. These had low-friction axles which allowed them to be pushed along the floor at high speeds or to whizz along a flexible plastic track. Other manufacturers copied the idea, but their products were often inferior to the original.

Your beloved old toy cars could be astonishingly valuable. These cars are selling at prices ranging from £25 for the Matchbox Hillman Minx (blue-grey with a white roof and bonnet) to £280 for the big tin-plate Japanese Cadillac.

CARS, CARS, CARS

Collectors generally agree that the 1970s should be the terminal date for collecting. Apart from the Matchbox Yesteryear models, the heyday of diecasts is over.

Meccano's Dinky series held a monopoly until the 1950s, when many new companies threatened their hold on the market. European manufacturers also began producing quality cars during this decade.

The 1960s is reckoned to be a great decade for diecast cars. Manufacturers, realizing the potential market for adult collectors, began paying greater attention to detail. Doors and other opening parts of the car had previously been cut into the mould, showing in relief on the finished item. This method was now improved although, as early as 1956, Corgi cars had been advertised on television as being 'the ones with the windows'.

Prices for toy cars can be be astronomical. A boxed tin-plate friction-driven 1959 Cadillac four-door sedan by Bandai will command around £1500. Even more expensive is the boxed Japanese tin-plate, friction-driven ALPS Chrysler New Yorker. In pristine condition, one of only 50 produced and the only known example in yellow with a red top, the car was valued in 1989 at just under £10,000.

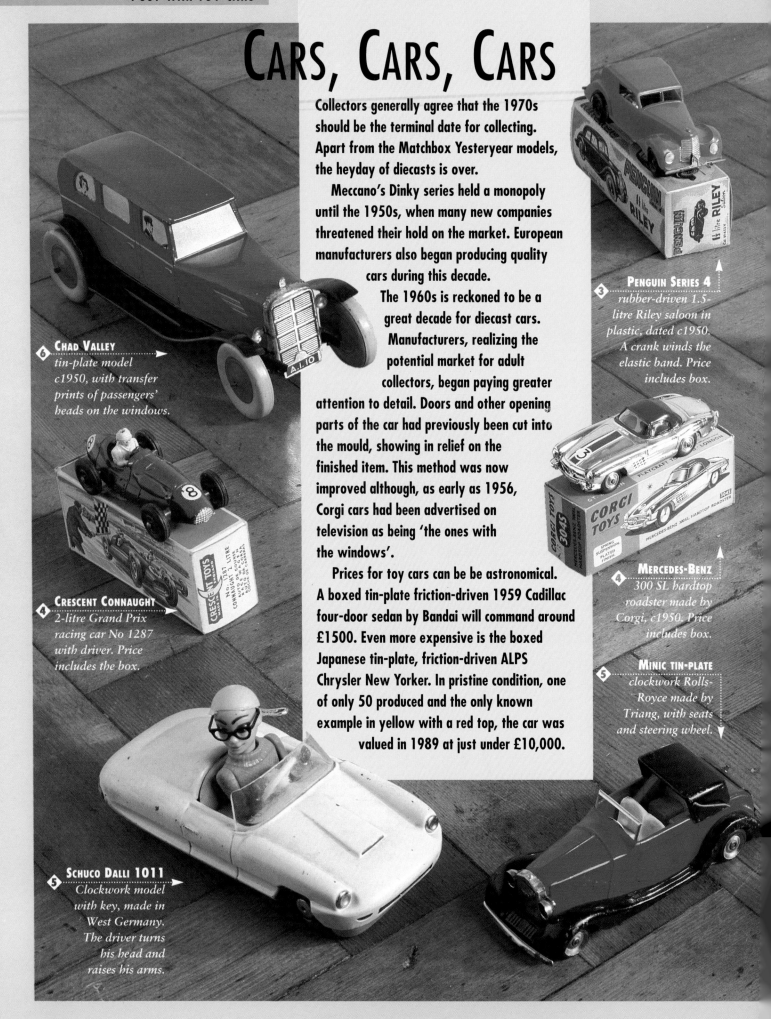

CHAD VALLEY
tin-plate model c1950, with transfer prints of passengers' heads on the windows.

CRESCENT CONNAUGHT
2-litre Grand Prix racing car No 1287 with driver. Price includes the box.

SCHUCO DALLI 1011
Clockwork model with key, made in West Germany. The driver turns his head and raises his arms.

PENGUIN SERIES 4
rubber-driven 1.5-litre Riley saloon in plastic, dated c1950. A crank winds the elastic band. Price includes box.

MERCEDES-BENZ
300 SL hardtop roadster made by Corgi, c1950. Price includes box.

MINIC tin-plate
clockwork Rolls-Royce made by Triang, with seats and steering wheel.

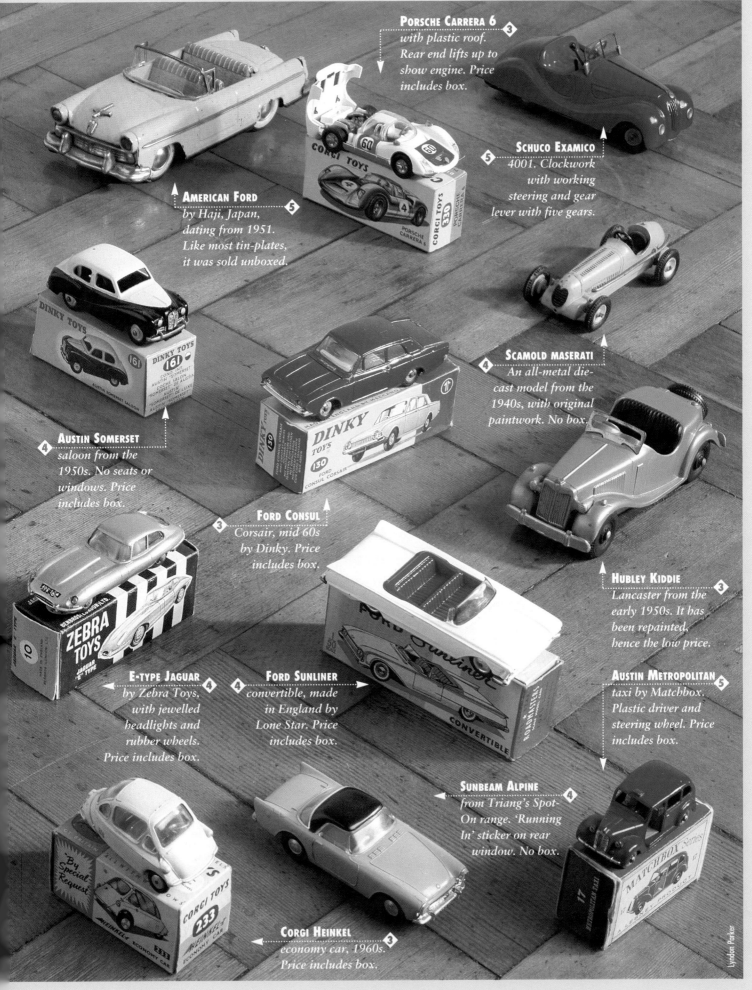

PORSCHE CARRERA 6 3
with plastic roof.
Rear end lifts up to
show engine. Price
includes box.

SCHUCO EXAMICO 5
4001. Clockwork
with working
steering and gear
lever with five gears.

AMERICAN FORD 5
by Haji, Japan,
dating from 1951.
Like most tin-plates,
it was sold unboxed.

SCAMOLD MASERATI 4
An all-metal die-
cast model from the
1940s, with original
paintwork. No box.

AUSTIN SOMERSET 4
saloon from the
1950s. No seats or
windows. Price
includes box.

FORD CONSUL 3
Corsair, mid 60s
by Dinky. Price
includes box.

HUBLEY KIDDIE 3
Lancaster from the
early 1950s. It has
been repainted,
hence the low price.

E-TYPE JAGUAR 4
by Zebra Toys,
with jewelled
headlights and
rubber wheels.
Price includes box.

FORD SUNLINER 4
convertible, made
in England by
Lone Star. Price
includes box.

AUSTIN METROPOLITAN 5
taxi by Matchbox.
Plastic driver and
steering wheel. Price
includes box.

SUNBEAM ALPINE 4
from Triang's Spot-
On range. 'Running
In' sticker on rear
window. No box.

CORGI HEINKEL 3
economy car, 1960s.
Price includes box.

Lyndon Parker

201

CLOSE UP   BASE PLATES

Lyndon Parker

As competition increased, manufacturers began to include details of patents on the stamped base plates.

Corgi, with their more modern models and realistic features like windows and treaded tyres, were Dinky's major rival.

This post-war car from the German maker Schuco includes a piece of history in its country of origin stamp.

Names to look out for include Triang's Spot-On series, Corgi, Britains, Timpo, Solido, Dinky and Matchbox. These are all British makes. It is worth remembering that early Dinky cars bore the name 'Meccano', sometimes placed in an obscure position. The most collectable foreign diecast cars are Märklin and Siku, both from Germany. Plastic cars include Triang's Minic, Airfix, and Marx.

TIN-PLATE CARS

The Japanese dominated the tin-plate car market, so look out for models by Bandai, Ichiko, Linemarus, Yonezawa and Aoshin.

With tin-plate cars, the maxim is the bigger the car, the better – and more expensive. Check for soundness of the clockwork and/or battery-operated mechanism. In order of desirability, go for Japanese tin-plate cars first, then the German makes, followed by British (Wells or Mettoy, for example) and, finally, cars made by the Spanish company Paya.

COLLECTOR'S NOTES

The first criterion in collecting toy cars is good condition. Wear and tear from their young owners has drastically reduced the value of many vehicles. Restoration and repainting also lowers the value enormously. Some collectors, however, will buy rare examples and repaint them for their own pleasure.

The box in which the car was sold is also of extreme importance and greatly increases the value if in pristine condition. It is worth remembering, though, that pre-war cars were never boxed, and Dinky cars manufactured before 1950 were also sold without boxes.

REPLACEMENT PARTS

Tyres frequently went missing when the car was played with, and these can often be bought from specialist shops. However, check for replacement parts on cars (other than tyres) as they will reduce the value of the car. These parts are usually brighter than the original, and the white metal used is soft and can be bent easily under pressure.

Many of the same models were issued both before and after the war. Post-war cars can be recognized by the differences in casting. For example, pre-1946 hubs on Dinky cars were plain; those produced after this date have a raised circle to represent a hub cap. Windscreens and working parts first appeared in the 1950s, and 1959 saw wheels made of aluminium.

IN FOCUS   FORD CONSUL CORSAIR

Most diecast cars, especially those made in the 1960s, were produced as accurate scale models with all the details authentically reproduced. Dinky produced cars to a constant scale of $\frac{1}{42}$ while Corgi cars were scaled at between $\frac{1}{44}$ and $\frac{1}{48}$. Different types of suspension became popular, in particular the 'Prestomatic' type which allowed the car to be steered by pressure with a finger on one side or other of the roof. Bonnets were opened, by pressing a lever under the car, to reveal a detailed engine. Windows slid up and down, steering wheels and seats were separately moulded in plastic and some models even had opening doors. This example is worth £35-40.

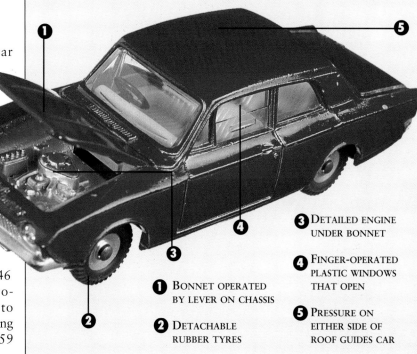

1 BONNET OPERATED BY LEVER ON CHASSIS

2 DETACHABLE RUBBER TYRES

3 DETAILED ENGINE UNDER BONNET

4 FINGER-OPERATED PLASTIC WINDOWS THAT OPEN

5 PRESSURE ON EITHER SIDE OF ROOF GUIDES CAR

Lyndon Parker

BARBIE DOLLS

One of the more recent arrivals on the collectables scene, Barbie, with her fabulous fashions, is here to stay

Lyndon Parker

Barbie – probably the most famous doll ever made – was the brainchild of Mr and Mrs Elliott Handler of the American company, Mattel. First sold in 1959, Barbie, who was named after the Handlers' daughter, was one of the first teenaged dolls to appear on the market. She had – to begin with – 22 beautifully made outfits which were, to many people, the most appealing thing about her. By the following year she had become a great success in the States, and Mattel introduced more outfits for her, as well as a boyfriend – named Ken after the Handlers' son.

Soon Barbie had become a multi-million-dollar industry: Mattel produced a huge family of friends and relations; pet animals; hundreds of outfits; houses, theatres and shops; aeroplanes and sailing boats; a swimming pool and an 'Olympic Gymnast' set, not to mention a board game and a 'Barbie Sings!' record.

THE FASHION MODEL

Barbie was created as a young fashion model with a voluptuous figure. Her rooted hair (either blonde or brunette) was pulled up into a long ponytail with a short, curly fringe. She was sold wearing gold hoop earrings, a black and white striped strapless swimsuit and black plastic high-heeled sandals, and carried a pair of white sunglasses with blue lenses.

Her poodle (Dog & Duds) has just won first prize, so Barbie (wearing Poodle Parade) is showing him off to the girls. Dolls, outfits and dog range in value from £60 to £250 (for the pink Jackie Kennedy-inspired Fashion Luncheon outfit); the room setting and furniture from £25 to £50.

FASHION PARADE

Barbie had annual makeovers in order to keep up with the times. The pointed eyebrows and white irises of the first models – Numbers 1 and 2 – changed to curved eyebrows and blue irises by 1960. Her bright red lipstick and nail polish became soft pink on some dolls in 1962, and in the same year she got a new red, round-necked swimsuit.

1964 welcomed 'Miss Barbie' with bendable legs and eyes that shut. Barbie 'Color Magic', introduced in 1966, had treated hair and clothes that could change colour with the application of a special solution. In 1967 Barbie got a new, more girlish face, real eyelashes and a 'twist 'n turn' waist, and in 1968 she learned to talk. In '69 she got a new 'flip' hairstyle with a long, side-swept fringe, but she soon tired of setting her hair every night, and by the following year it was straight, with an eyebrow-length fringe. In 1971 Barbie's eyes were painted looking straight ahead – on earlier dolls, they had looked to the right. By the next year she had hair that grew and hands that could hold things. The changes went on and on...

NUMBER 3
This doll dates from 1960 and has brown eyeliner instead of the more usual blue. As she's just about to go in the water, she's not wearing her earrings or sunglasses.

'BUSY GAL'
The Number 4 Barbies of 1960 were made of a different sort of vinyl and have retained their tan, while earlier models have now become much paler. Her portfolio contains several sketches.

'FASHION QUEEN'
This Barbie, dating from 1963, has brown-painted moulded hair. She came with three wigs and a wig stand.

NUMBER 5
Few early Barbies had titian-red hair; the price is also increased by the tag and box. She wears the spectacular 'Evening Splendor'.

BUBBLE-CUT HAIR
was new in 1961. Here's Barbie in one of her most famous outfits, 'Solo in the Spotlight'. Her microphone and pink scarf are not shown.

'TWIST 'N TURN' BARBIE 5
from 1966 wearing the
mod-style 'Sunflower'
outfit dating from 1967.

DRAMATIC NEW LIVING Barbie

NOW AS POSEABLE AS YOU ARE!

MATTEL

'COLOR MAGIC' BARBIE 6
wearing 'Fraternity Dance'
of 1965. Her hair can be
changed to bright orange.

'MISS BARBIE' 6
From 1964,
this doll, with
rolling eyes and
bendable legs,
was rapidly
discontinued.

Barbie

TEEN-AGE FASHION MODEL BY MATTEL

'LIVING BARBIE' 4
in 'Pretty Power',
1971. Head, neck,
waist, arms, hands
and legs turned,
and her elbows
and knees bent.

TALKING BARBIE, 4
1968, wearing
'Rare Pair'. Some
Barbies could
speak Spanish.

1972 STANDARD 5
Barbie. This
doll was sold
only in Europe.
The outfit is
called 'Made for
Each Other'.

1971 BARBIE 6
The doll has
never been removed
from its box, which
greatly increases the
value.

Lyndon Parker

205

COLLECTOR'S NOTES

The most valuable Barbie is undoubtedly Number 1 – in unopened packaging she could fetch £1000 or more. She can be identified by the holes in the balls of her feet (and in her sandals) which enable her to pose on a two-pronged black stand. Number 2 is worth almost as much and is exactly the same, except that she no longer has holes in her feet, and her posing stand has a wire to hold her up instead of prongs. (A few of these dolls have pearl earrings instead of hoops.) Look out for the following characteristics to identify 1 and 2: pointed eyebrows; eyes with white irises; pale skin; stock number 850; torso marked 'Barbie TM Pats Pend © MCMLVIII by Mattel Inc'.

CONDITION

Though millions of Barbies have been manufactured since 1959, most have been treated as the much-loved play-things that they were intended to be, and you would be lucky indeed to find one of the first models in mint condition. If you do manage to find an early doll in unopened packaging, its value will be greatly increased; such a doll could be worth more than ten times what a nude doll, even in good condition, would fetch. Similarly, outfits in sealed packets are the most desirable.

Various defects will reduce a doll's value. Look out for marks or stains; worn paint on face or nails; missing fingers, eyelashes or earrings, and hair that's been cut or rearranged. Check that the doll's head and body are of the same shade and type of plastic – a difference indicates that the parts have been assembled from different models.

STORING

Store your Barbie dolls without their shoes, earrings and wigs: the open-toed sandals can stain her feet if they're left on for a long time and plastic boots can cause swelling; her earrings have been known to turn Barbie's face green, and the wigs can react with the vinyl of her face to cause distortions. Sometimes the vinyl that the doll is made from can stain the outfit she's wearing, so keep a close check.

Barbie's Suburban Shopper outfit was manufactured from 1959-64 and is worth about £50, even without packaging. The phone had a metal dial in the earliest versions.

This carrying case, from the early 60s, is worth about £40.

Barbie was such a moneymaker that Mattel created a vast social network for her. Front row: Chris, Tutti (Barbie's tiny sister and Chris's friend). Second row: Tutti's sister Skipper, Skipper's pal Ricky. Third row: Skipper's friend Skooter, Barbie's 'mod' cousin Francie, 'Colored' Francie, Francie's chum Casey. Back row: Barbie's friend PJ, Stacey (who spoke with a British accent), Ken, Ken's buddy Allan, Barbie's best friend Midge.

Lyndon Parker

ACTION MAN FIGURES

Before the 1960s, it was thought impossible to sell dolls to boys, but Action Man, undeniably macho and virtually indestructible, changed all that

Dolls have long been a popular subject for collectors, but today it's not only gorgeously gowned Victorian china dolls which command good prices. As the children of the 1960s and 1970s grow into adulthood, the vinyl fashion dolls or dress-up dolls of their youth, such as Sindy, Tressy, Tina and their American cousin, Barbie, are increasingly sought after.

To toy manufacturers, the dress-up doll was a marketing godsend. Once they had sold the basic doll, they had a captive market for the various outfits and accessories – even furniture – they produced for them. The only problem was that they were only reaching half the children – just the girls. Then, in 1964, the American firm, Hasbro, produced G I Joe, a soldier doll that boys could play with without being taunted by their peers.

Two years later, Palitoy, the British firm that created Tressy, launched Action Man, voted Toy of the Year in 1966. The secret of his success was his flexibility; jointed at the neck, shoulders, waist, elbows, hips, knees, wrists and ankles, he could be posed in many different action situations. By regularly introducing new, finely detailed uniforms, equipment and weaponry Palitoy ensured Action Man's continued popularity.

Rival British firms tried to capture a share of the new market with their own versions, but dolls such as Pedigree's Tommy Gunn had very short runs before failing and are now collectable only for their scarcity value.

TAKEN OVER

In 1968, Palitoy was taken over by General Mills of America, but production of Action Man continued until rising costs priced him out of the market in 1983. During this time, the doll was produced in over 36 body variations, and with an enormous range of clothes and accessories, which were sold separately.

Military gear, including dress uniforms and battledress, were the most popular costumes, but Action Man could be dressed as a police motorcyclist, a frogman, a polar explorer complete with skis and a first aider. He also wore uniforms of other countries, including Germany and Canada, while the Space Ranger series came with space helmets and cloth or rubber suits as well as a ferocious alien doll.

Action Man is most widely remembered as a soldier in battledress, but one of the range of international costumes you could buy was that of an Indian Brave or, as here, an Indian Chief. The American Indian canoe and its paddle were part of the ever-expanding transport range of Action Man accessories.

Ray Duns

MILITARY SUPPLIES

Palitoy added an extra play feature every three years, including 'realistic' hair (a soft, flocked crew-cut) in 1970, gripping hands with moveable fingers in 1973, which enabled him to cling to rocks and window-ledges as well as weaponry, and moveable 'eagle' eyes in 1976. It's the early models with unblinking gazes, fixed hands and painted hair that attract the most attention from present-day collectors, though the later styles are bound to become more popular as the generations that grew up with them get nostalgic for their youth.

The most valuable accessories are the larger ones, especially vehicles – Action Man could travel by jeep, racing car, armoured car, go-kart, space capsule or helicopter, although the small print on the box warns, disappointingly, that the 'Helicopter does not fly'. These vehicles sold in relatively small quantities and are therefore scarce and more valuable today.

A SOLDIER ③
from Palitoy's Action Man 'Combat Division' range. He wears a beret, army pullover, camouflage trousers, army boots and carries an automatic gun fitted with a telescopic sight. On the box were the sales lines: 'Go into action with the modern army. They're the stuff heroes are made of!'

A SAILOR ④
from the earliest Action Man range, which was marketed in the UK in 1964. He has stiff hands rather than gripping ones. Like all Action Men, he has a scar on his right cheek.

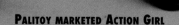

PALITOY MARKETED ACTION GIRL ②
but she never attained the success of Action Man. She stood 29cm/11½in tall, with attractive long silky hair in a range of colours, and large, painted, pale blue eyes. Like Action Man, she was jointed at the neck, waist, shoulders, hips, knees, elbows, wrists and ankles, but the joints looked ugly beneath skirts and sleeveless blouses – one reason, perhaps, for her lesser appeal.

3 ▸ ACTION MAN IN HIS INDIAN CHIEF UNIFORM.
The Red Indian accessories available included a shirt, trousers, moccasins, a belt, a headband (for the Indian Brave) or a feathered head-dress (for the Indian Chief), a black wig, a rifle, a tomahawk and a knife. This example is in 'played' condition – the hair, for instance, is a bit wild.

3 ▸ AN ACTION MAN
soldier ready for combat. He wears a hard helmet and has an army belt over his pullover. His tough cotton trousers have pockets. In his hand he carries a knife in readiness for hand-to-hand fighting.

◂ THE POLAR EXPEDITION OUTFIT 4
was very popular since it was a fantasy that boys readily identified with. Very similar was the 'Mountain and Arctic Outfit', which came with a snowsuit, cap, skis, ski sticks, boots, rifle, belt, bayonet and scabbard, two pouches, gloves and goggles. This figure is bearded.

Roy Duns

209

Military uniforms and kit, such as the frogman's outfit (near right), were avidly collected. Palitoy found that sports kit, like this cricket gear (far right), was much less successful. They tried football strips and tie-ins for the 1968 Olympics and 1970 World Cup.

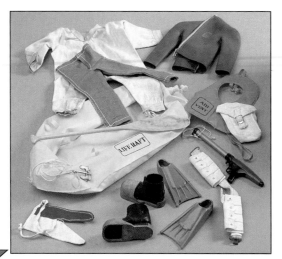

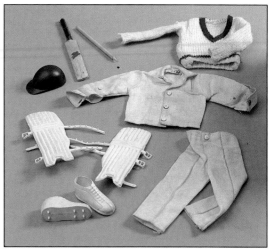

DESIGN
IN FOCUS
UNIFORMS AND EQUIPMENT

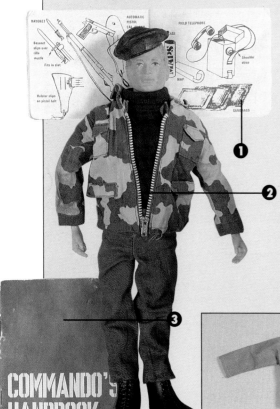

First issued in 1964, the Action Man Commando (left) wears a camouflage jacket. He could be kitted out with a range of weapons and came equipped with the *Commando's Handbook.* Below are items from the Special Operations Kit. Other equipment in this pack (catalogue no. 34286) included binoculars, grenades and a lightweight machine gun. Uniforms and equipment were often sold together.

❶ BOOKLET OF ACTION MAN ACCESSORIES, SHOWING HOW THEY WORK

❷ CAMOUFLAGE JACKET HAS A WORKING ZIP

❸ THE *COMMANDO'S HANDBOOK* GIVES DETAILS OF THE REGIMENT'S SPECIAL FIGHTING SKILLS

Ray Duns

COLLECTOR'S NOTES

It's still possible to find Action Man dolls and outfits, particularly ones from the late 1970s and early 1980s, at jumble and car boot sales, as well as in old toyboxes that have been relegated to attics. Toy fairs have the best selection. There are still bargains to be had, although dealers specializing in modern dolls and other toys are on the increase. The recent introduction of a modern version of Action Man by Hasbro may boost interest in the original dolls, pushing the price up further, so now is the time to start a collection.

Dolls are always more valuable if they are in mint condition, in their original box and original outfit. Better still if the box is still sealed, although it seems rather sad to see a toy that has never been played with.

Sets will be more valuable if they still contain all the accessories as listed on the box. This is unusual as the small plastic items, such as grenades, guns and so on, were easily lost once the box was opened. Outfits and accessories were usually sold mounted on card and bubble wrapped, which makes it easy to tell if a set has never been used.

Vinyl is more or less unbreakable, but it can be damaged by heat, and body parts could, if the action got a little too rough, be separated from the rest at the flexible joints. Evidence of this, or of the effect of fireworks, say, will render an Action Man valueless.

Although the loss of an odd rifle from a rack will not be too serious, missing wheels or other vital moving parts will seriously downgrade the price of a vehicle. Some of the toys included battery-operated moving parts. Before buying any of these, look in the battery compartment to check there has been no leakage and that the connections are clear and bright. If there's a battery in there, take it out and examine the compartment closely.

BEATLEMANIA

The Beatles horrified parents, delighted teenagers and summed up a decade. Thirty years later, memorabilia from four pop stars is selling for thousands

Beatlemania offers a wide range for the collector; this selection varies in price from £5 for a badge to £500 for the dartboard.

While John, Paul, George and Ringo were busy conquering the world with their unique Mersey Beat sound, fans of the musicians were equally occupied in hoarding any Beatles-related material they could lay their hands on. It is these wide-ranging items – anything from a toy Yellow Submarine to a scribble from John Lennon on a piece of hotel notepaper – which have become the substance of an international market running into thousands of pounds.

But don't be put off from starting your own collection by the astronomical prices you might read or hear about. Beatles records were pressed in huge numbers during the 1960s, and while they will cost considerably more than the current rate for LPs, prices are still within range of the average collector's pocket.

ORIGINAL RECORDINGS

A 1962 mint copy of their first-ever single, 'Love Me Do', can be bought for an affordable £20. Beatles records can be found at boot sales as well as second-hand record shops, where an original pressing will cost £15-£30, depending on its condition and which recording it is. And take a look at any records you bought at the time – there could be a rarity lurking in your collection.

The market for souvenirs began in the early days of the Beatles' success. Opportunists quickly produced gimmicks such as Beatles toothpaste, Beatles dolls, Beatles lampshades and Beatles wigs. All of these are now highly collectable.

In fact, anything with any Beatles connection at all can be of interest to Beatles fanatics – from promotional posters and programmes for concerts to the front covers of foreign magazines. Items hitting the top of the price range are mostly those with a direct and authenticated personal connection with the Fab Four themselves, especially the murdered Beatle, John Lennon.

A 1963-64 tray by Metal Box would be worth £40-50; however, this mid-1980s re-issue is worth about £5.

Lyndon Parker/All memorabilia supplied by Peter Nash

BEATLEMANIA

Beatles enthusiasts need not spend a fortune in order to pick up some highly collectable items. For instance, an original mint copy of 'Sgt Pepper's Lonely Hearts Club Band' from 1967, with cut-out inserts and coloured inner bag, can be bought from most record specialists for around £20. An 'Abbey Road' picture disc, released during the picture disc boom of the early 1980s, sells for £20. A little more expensive are the Beatles Christmas flexi-discs; good quality copies of any of these, released exclusively to fan club members between 1963 and 1969, are currently on the market at around £40.

Mass-produced items such as albums, singles, and promotional posters usually come a poor second when compared with the more personal items usually found in the possession of Beatles fans. For example, a scrapbook, compiled by a Beatles fan and containing a playlist for a concert, written in John Lennon's hand, three autographed letters from John, Paul and George, publicity postcards and other related material, was recently priced at £4500-£5000. Concert programmes, containing one or more of the group's signatures, range in value from £100 to over £3000.

CLOTHES HANGERS ❷
with black and white photos, used in Carnaby Street boutiques and other fashionable shops.

TALCUM POWDER ❹
dating from 1963. This tin is in good condition; in mint condition it would be worth up to £150.

CHRISTMAS ❸
flexi-discs sent out to fan club members. The first is worth £80; price refers to the others.

DISK-GO-CASE ❹
record holder, made by Charter Industries Inc (USA) in 1966, for holding singles.

BEATLES BADGES ❶
were made in a vast range of designs.

NEW BEAT GUITAR ❻
of plastic, made by Selcol in 1963-64. Price includes the box.

Limited Edition

BEATLES ABBEY ROAD

4 CHINA MUG AND SAUCER
made by Washington Pottery Ltd in 1963, as part of a larger set.

FOUR PLASTIC DOLLS 5
by Remco (USA) 1964. John's guitar is missing and Ringo's hair is damaged.

BEATLE WIG 3
by the Lowell Toy Manufacturing Corp (USA), 1964, in its original packaging.

3 PICTURE DISCS
released by EMI to mark the tenth anniversary of the original 'Sgt Pepper' in 1977 and of 'Abbey Road' in 1979. Price refers to each disc.

WOW! the BEATLES ARE HERE!

the only **AUTHENTIC BEATLE WIG**

YELLOW SUBMARINE 5
made by Corgi containing Beatles figures, in mint condition and with original box.

LUNCH BOX 5
and thermos flask with Yellow Submarine motif, by King-Seely Thermos Co.

APPLE RECORDS 7
dartboard, made 1969-70. It was sold with a set of plain darts with green flights.

CORGI TOYS THE BEATLES YELLOW SUBMARINE

3 TOBY JUGS
modelled by Stanley James Taylor and produced by Royal Doulton, 1984. No longer in production.

4 1960s APPLE WATCH
made by Old England, with no hands. In mint condition it would be worth around £400.

Lyndon Parker

213

COLLECTOR'S NOTES

There is a huge range of collectable memorabilia associated with the Beatles. As well as the group's recordings, there are the Fab Four's autographs, clothing, letters and musical instruments – and of course the vast array of souvenirs which were produced at the time.

China from the 1960s depicting the Beatles is often a good starting point for collectors. Look out for egg cups, mugs and plates. Other memorabilia to look out for include 'Star Club' flight bags and items bearing the Apple logo. Fan club magazines, especially those that are signed, are very collectable.

AUTHENTIC SIGNATURES

As a general rule, if you have a piece of Beatles memorabilia that has evidence, usually in the form of a signature, that it has in any way been in direct physical contact with a Beatle, it is well worth having the article priced by an expert.

Any ephemera (as short-lived articles such as programmes, photographs, magazines and so on are called) should ideally be in mint condition and not creased, torn or bent. However, any Beatles item is highly collectable, so even damaged ephemera will still be of value, though reduced in price.

The top five collectable Beatles records are: the first 'Please Please Me' LP in stereo with a

DEALER'S TIPS

● **Anything which wasn't on general sale – for example, Apple items such as headed notepaper, address labels and banknotes, which were for promotional purposes only – is rarer and therefore more valuable.**

● **A signature on any item will raise the value considerably. However, you should always have any signatures authenticated by an expert or a reputable auction house – 'roadies' and secretaries often did the autographs on behalf of the group. If the inscription is personalized – that is, if it mentions a particular name, this will raise the value again.**

● **Illegally produced bootleg recordings of alternative versions of songs are also collectable.**

One-night tour programmes (top) are worth around £100 each. The photo with all four signatures, dedication and a doodle (bottom) is worth £500-600.

THE 'BUTCHER' COVER

The album 'The Beatles...Yesterday and Today' was first released with the legendary 'butcher' cover, which depicted the group dressed in white surgical smocks, holding lumps of meat and decapitated dolls. Lennon thought the cover 'as relevant as Vietnam', but EMI thought otherwise. A photo known as the 'trunk' cover, showing the Beatles sitting around a packing case, was quickly glued over.

Most owners tore off the trunk cover to reveal the original photo.

An undamaged cover, complete with Paul McCartney's autograph.

gold on black Parlophone label (worth about £1000); the original 60s demo record of 'Love Me Do'/'PS I Love You'; 'Our First Four', a presentation record by Apple including 'Hey Jude' and tracks by three other artists in a presentation box; the export issue of 'The Beatles' double LP (also known as 'The White Album') with a yellow and black label and inserts, and the 'Yellow Submarine' export LP with a yellow and black label. Also of particular interest to collectors is 'Bangladesh', the 1971 release from George complete with picture sleeve, and John and Yoko's 1968 album, 'Two Virgins', banned at the time because the cover depicted the singer and his wife naked.

If you're interested in starting a collection but are working on a limited budget, there are quite a few items closely related to the group and their work which you can look out for. Beatles collectables at under £100 include John Lennon's 1965 book of nonsense poetry, *In His Own Write*; acetates and drawings from the 1968 film, *Yellow Submarine*; signed photographs of the group, and even unsigned photographs – especially if they were taken in unusual settings or poses.

SINGLES POP RECORDS

*Few things are more of their time than pop records,
but their ephemeral nature has made them the subject
of a lively collectors' market*

In the 1950s, the 7-inch, 45rpm vinyl single replaced the 10-inch, 78rpm shellac single as the basic currency of popular music. This didn't happen overnight. For a few years, new recordings were issued on both formats, but no more 78rpm singles were released in Britain after 1960.

The new vinyl records were much less fragile than their predecessors, but were still seen as essentially throwaway items by most people who bought them, while the companies that produced them were quick to delete from their lists any record that did not sell.

The change in the format of records coincided with other changes in the popular music business. Teenagers, a group that as far as most people were concerned did not exist before World War 2, were suddenly the major buyers of records, and the new generation embraced rock 'n' roll, the rebellious new music from the USA, as their voice.

BEAT BOOM

The sale of singles reached its peak in the 1960s, with the British beat groups and the American rhythm & blues and soul artists who inspired them all selling well. At the same times, a small collectors' market began to appear, as late-comers and nostalgics tried to obtain hard-to-get, deleted classics.

By the mid-1970s, 33rpm LPs had taken over as the main form of recorded music. A few major acts, such as Led Zeppelin, never released singles, while most people saw them only as trailers for LPs. Then, in Britain, a new teen-led movement, punk, brought excitement back to a moribund market.

Though the prime movers of the scene, the Sex Pistols and The Clash, signed to major labels, others signed short-term deals with new, independent companies such as Stiff and Chiswick, which was set up by the owner of a record shop. Many bands took advantage of the excess capacity at record-pressing plants to release and distribute their own singles, most of them in picture sleeves, and many of these products of what was essentially a cottage industry are widely collected today.

In the 1970s, new forms of packaging (left) gave a fillip to the sale of singles and brought colour as well sound to the hobby of record collecting.

Roy Duns

215

THIS OBSCURE B-SIDE BY TIMI YURO **6**
*became a huge Northern soul hit
some 20 years after its release.*

ROCK & SOUL

Four companies dominated the British record market in the 1950s and the 1960s. EMI, Decca, Pye and Philips, known collectively as the majors, issued the vast majority of British singles on one of several labels. The most important source of rock 'n' roll was Decca's London. It is still the most collectable label, with rare rockabilly and doo-wop of the mid to late 1950s fetching huge prices.

Soul fans covet early releases from the Tamla and Motown labels in the USA. They appeared first on London, then, in the early 1960s, on the independent, Oriole. After this, they appeared on EMI, first on the Stateside label and then on Tamla Motown.

Demonstration records – demos – were sent out to DJs. The labels were marked Not for Sale, with a large letter A on the play side, Soul demos sell for two to three times the price of the standard issue. All-night dances in Wigan and elsewhere in the 1970s and 1980s created the Northern soul scene. Dance-hall DJs competed to find obscure, danceable tracks, and the most popular ones became instant collectables.

Prices are for records in mint condition.

4 DEMO VERSIONS
*of soul records, particularly
on the Tamla Motown and
Stateside labels, attract
premium prices.*

3 THE INDEPENDENT SUE LABEL
*specialized in soul reissues.
Every release was collectable,
even in the 1960s.*

Ray Granger

THE PUNK LEGACY

The independent spirit and do-it-yourself ethic of punk rock in 1976 and 1977 radically altered the British record industry. Hundreds of new, independent labels were set up, many of them releasing just one or two records. Some of them, like Factory, Rough Trade, Postcard, Stiff and Chiswick, are now widely collected.

The independents' bright new marketing ideas were copied by the major labels: within a year or so, every single was issued in a custom-made sleeve. Independents and majors set out to create instant collector's items with limited editions using special sleeves, different

versions of the same song, inserts and coloured vinyl. Picture discs, where an image was printed directly onto the vinyl, and shaped singles, that were no longer discs at all, were issued as promotional items. Independent labels also provided the impetus for the introduction of the 12-inch single, which provided more playing time and better sound.

FAC-2

A FACTORY SAMPLE

HEAVY METAL BANDS ◀ *also put out independent releases. This single, Def Leppard's first, also appears in other versions.*

A FACTORY COMPILATION, ◀ *the label's first release, featured cult act Joy Division and three others on a double single.*

FIRST ISSUED IN 1957, Tutti Frutti *and* Long Tall Sally *were Little Richard's second British release. The label style shows this to be a later pressing.*

A NUMBER 1 HIT, *High School Confidential sold in great numbers, but it's increasingly hard to find in mint condition.*

FOUR TAMLA STARS FEATURE *on this Stateside EP. The format was used either to repackage single releases by one artist, or to introduce new talent, as here.*

ORIOLE RELEASES *of Tamla-Motown records are much prized. Value is added because the Beatles later recorded the song.*

Being Boiled,
the first Human League
single, was released on
Edinburgh's Fast label by an
early version of the group.

The well-named Notsensibles ②
from Burnley, Lancashire,
were typical of the bands that
were nurtured by provincial
labels in the wake of punk.

Never commerically issued, ③
this limited edition Elvis
Costello recording was
given away free to those
attending one of a series
of concerts.

God Save the Queen ①
on Virgin is easy to find.
The same Sex Pistols' single
on EMI, withdrawn before
release, is worth a fortune.

The 'O' Level single, released in 1977, ③
captures the spirit of punk in its brash,
irreverent songs and endearingly 'home-
made' photocopied cover.

Roy Granger

219

CLOSE UP *on* LONDON AMERICAN

Every London single has the date it was first issued printed on the label, but popular records were re-pressed several times. Collectors prefer early issues, and details of label styling give a clue to this. All records had push-out centres so they could be used on jukeboxes. If these are miising, value plummets. London first had triangular centres, phased out in favour of circular ones by February 1960. Some purists only collect 'London triangles'.

Any release with 'London' written in gold script on a black ground was produced before April 1957.

Subsequent releases had silver lettering. This label design was discontinued in April 1959.

The new 'silvertop' design with 'London American' in black first appeared with triangle centres.

London's standard label through the 1960s carried the name of the US label of origin in small capitals.

American companies with a high profile got their own customized labels from the early 1960s.

COMPARE & CONTRAST

Coloured vinyl and picture sleeves (below) were rarely seen before the mid-1970s. Previously, picture sleeves were seen in Britain only on four-track 'EP' releases (right).

COLLECTOR'S NOTES

Some record collectors specialize in one or two artists, while others follow interests in different labels or styles of music. Almost all of them, though, start with an interest in music. Let your ears be your guide.

If you're looking for rarities, arm yourself with one of the published price guides to rare records before beginning the hunt. Bargains can still be had by sifting through the record boxes in junk shops, charity shops and jumble sales, while there are usually one or two record stalls in every flea market. Specialist dealers won't provide you with a bargain, but will save you ploughing through stacks of rubbish looking for the occasional gem.

Record fairs are advertised in local newspapers and the monthly magazine *Record Collector*. The latter also lists hundreds of postal sales and auctions, which are the best way to get a good price for any records you want to sell; dealers will give you only around half of the listed price for a rarity.

The condition of a record is all-important. It is traditionally graded as mint, excellent, very good, good, fairly good, poor or bad. Most collectors insist on at least very good condition. Records in poor or bad condition ones are worth little and should be avoided.

If you can't listen to a record before you buy, at least examine it under a good light, looking for scratches, scuff marks and general signs of wear and tear. Make sure that any picture sleeves or inserts are present.

Records should be stored upright. Plastic outer sleeves help protect their covers and seal the records from dust. Always keep records away from heat and damp, and never handle them except by the edges. Old record players with auto-changers have a period charm about them, as have jukeboxes, but you should *never* play valuable records on them.

TELEPHONE CARDS

With thousands of attractive, colourful, informative
and potentially valuable cards available, fusilately
has a lot to offer the dedicated collector

Collecting phone cards, or 'fusilately', is one of the fastest-growing hobbies to emerge in recent years. There are thought to be well over two million collectors worldwide, with half a million in Germany alone. Telephone companies now issue prepayment cards in almost all countries of the world, and thousands of new card designs appear each year, many for advertising or private promotional purposes.

The first phone cards appeared in Italy in the late 1970s. Issued in values of 2,000, 5,000 and 9,000 lire, these cards were printed in a vertical format and had one corner which had to be detached before use. These cards are rare and valuable now, particularly as all the fully-used cards were retained by the payphones and destroyed.

Most phone cards are made of plastic, although some early examples were of laminated card. They are of a standard credit card size. The basic cards are manufactured by a relatively small number of companies and supplied to telephone companies who print their own designs.

There are three types of card technology. 'Optical' cards such as British Telecom (BT) cards are manufactured by Landis & Gyr in Switzerland; the payphone 'reads' information on the number of units from a visible horizontal strip. Some cards, including Mercury's in the UK, operate using a magnetic strip within the card, and are manufactured by such companies as GPT and Autelco. The third type, an electronic phonecard popular in France and other countries, works by an embedded silicon chip and is made by German companies such as Schlumbeger.

Phone cards are standard in size, but they come in an amazing variety of designs. Usually the design is printed in horizontal format and often it includes an arrow to indicate the direction for insertion into the phone. The value is given in currency or in the number of 'units'. Production data often occurs on the back of the card.

Ray Duns

In most countries, the card normally on sale is the 'definitive', produced in a range of values for use by the general public for everyday use in ordinary payphones.

Apart from definitives, cards are issued for a variety of other, secondary purposes. Some advertise the major retail outlet (eg the Post Office) that sells them. Others are issued to mark a special event. These are often very colourful and attractive and are generally issued for a limited period, making them highly collectable.

Many phone cards sold nationally carry advertising for big companies like Coca-Cola. Private firms or individuals sometimes commission their own cards, perhaps to give away free with a product or as a novel form of business card. These types of cards are extremely collectable because they tend to be produced in quantities as low as 500, or sometimes less, and are not always available to the general public.

Some cards can be used only by a particular group at a specific location. Prisons, for example, have special cards for the use of the inmates to prevent ordinary cards being smuggled in and used as 'black market' currency. Hotels, ships and hospitals may also have their own cards not usable elsewhere.

Sometimes cards are sold to raise money for charity. In 1989, the British Virgin Islands issued a card after 'Hurricane Hugo', with one dollar donated to the relief fund for every card sold. Phone cards may also incorporate competitions. For example, a set of BT cards to raise money for the RNIB depicted the eyes of mystery celebrities and buyers were invited to guess who they were.

PHONE CARDS

The value of phone cards is determined by rarity and condition. Some early Japanese cards have been sold for thousands of times their face value, and also highly desirable are the set of three commemorative cards produced by BT in 1987 for the Open Golf Championship at Muirfield. Mint cards usually fetch high prices, especially if they are still in their protective wrappers, but there is also a good market for used cards, particularly of rarities. Some collectors are also interested in 'peripherals' — things such as the envelopes in which the cards are issued or the small instructional booklets that come with some of them.

CARTOON ANIMALS
are among the virtually limitless range of subjects that have been included on phone cards. Many of them are extremely skilful pieces of miniature design.

AUSTRALIA
began issuing phone cards in December 1989, the first trials taking place around the town of Geelong in Victoria. This example features two of the most famous sights.

SYDNEY OPERA HOUSE
SYDNEY HARBOUR BRIDGE

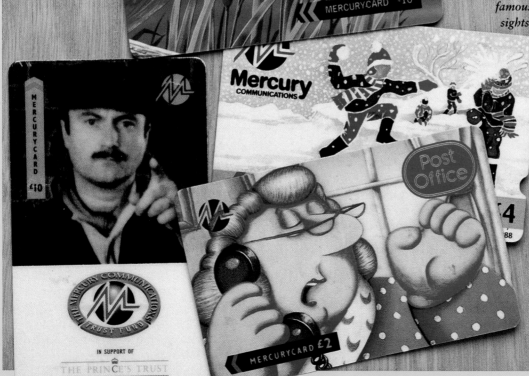

MERCURY COMMUNICATIONS
introduced payphones in London in 1988 and since then has expanded to cover other major cities in the United Kingdom. Like BT, Mercury has now issued a large range of cards, including commemorative and advertising issues and others that feature designs that are specific to the particular areas in which they are sold.

FRENCH PHONE CARDS are often notable for their bold and highly stylish designs. Blue is a much favoured colour.

BRITISH TELECOM has issued cards in hundreds of different designs. Advertising cards first appeared in late 1986 and special or commemorative cards were first issued in 1987.

THE ISLANDS of Antigua and Barbuda first issued phone cards in the early 1990s. This one suggests the romance of the Caribbean islands.

THIS STRIKING FLORAL DESIGN is from the Netherlands. The Dutch first issued advertising cards in 1989.

THIS CAR is on a Swiss card, though the setting looks tropical. Switzerland manufactures cards for many countries.

TWO CARDS FROM JAPAN, where more than 25,000 different phone cards have already been issued. The main Japanese company is NTT, which has also issued cards in Geneva, London and New York, intended for the use of Japanese tourists abroad.

Roy Duns

223

CL*O*SE UP *on* CARD DETAILS

To the true enthusiast, no detail of a phone card is too small to notice. Some experts even note minute differences in the pattern of contacts on the microchips of certain French cards. Manufacturers are often unaware of the subtleties that fascinate collectors.

£4

TMAS 1988

The contact patterns on French phone cards are of four main types. The one shown here (above left) is Type IV.

A feature seen on many cards is a small notch on the edge – a useful aid for blind users.

Some phone cards now have a strip indicating how many units have been used up and how many are still left.

The 'control number' on the back of a card gives information about production data.

20MERE169593

COLLECTOR'S NOTES

Most phone card collectors specialize in a country or a type – for example, definitives. Others choose a theme such as sport. Enthusiasts can obtain cards through collectors' clubs and fairs or swop shops and there are now a few dealers specializing in phone cards. Private promotional cards not on sale to the public are sometimes available through collectors' clubs or direct from the telephone company. The catalogues produced by phonecard expert Dr Steve Hiscocks are an excellent reference and a guide to prices. They cover all countries known to have issued cards, except Japan. But for the keen collector of Japanese cards a 12-volume catalogue exists!

Cards may be stored in special albums with transparent pockets to hold eight cards on a page. These cards may be displayed, but some early cards have been known to discolour with exposure to the light, so care is needed. The cards are fairly resilient but can be scratched or bent by clumsy handling. Special care should be taken with mint cards, particularly if they are in a sealed wrapper, which increases their value.

Phone cards are printed in sheets and sometimes minor flaws and variations go undetected before they are issued. Control numbers are sometimes missing or inverted. Occasionally small runs of cards with a spelling mistake or colour fault may slip through. All such cards can be very valuable.

Up until now the phone card scene has not been disturbed by serious forgery, but as phone cards increase in value it is well to be aware of the risk of offers of apparently rare cards in suspicious circumstances. As the risk increases, telephone companies may switch to less forgeable technologies such as optical or electronic cards rather than magnetic ones.

Various categories of card are recognized. 'Definitives' are everyday cards (left); advertising cards aim to sell products (above); closed location cards are for specific places (below).

Cards that are still sealed in the wallets in which they were issued are highly desirable for card collectors. Some special issues appeared in leather wallets.

British Telecom/Ray Duns